The Weekend Millionaire's Secrets to Investing in REAL ESTATE

MIKE SUMMEY
ROGER DAWSON

McGraw-Hill

New York Chicago San Francisco Lisbon London
Madrid Mexico City Milan New Delhi San Juan
Seoul Singapore Sydney Toronto

7 8 9 10 DOC/DOC 0 9 8 7 6 5 4

ISBN 0-07-141291-3

McGraw-Hill books are available at special quantity discounts to use as premiums and sales promotions, or for use in corporate training programs. For more information, please write to the Director of Special Sales, Professional Publishing, McGraw-Hill, Two Penn Plaza, New York, NY 10121-2298. Or contact your local bookstore.

This book is printed on recycled, acid-free paper containing a minimum of 50% recycled, de-inked fiber.

Library of Congress Cataloging-in-Publication Data

Summey, Mike.
   The weekend millionaires secrets to investing in real estate : how to
build wealth in your spare time / by Mike Summey and Roger Dawson.
      p. cm.
Includes index.
   ISBN 0-07-141291-3 (alk. paper)
   1. Real estate investment—United States. 2. Rental housing—United
States—Management. 3. Real estate management—United States. I.
Dawson, Roger, 1940- II. Title.
   HD255.S85 2004
   332.63'24—dc21
                              2003009940

 **Dedications**

- To my mother who instilled in me the drive and determination to succeed in whatever endeavor I attempted.
- To my family and friends who have worked with me to ensure that the information throughout this book is understandable, honest, practical, and easy to follow. Thanks for all your help.
- To Albert Sneed Jr. Esq., my general attorney for over 30 years, who has played devil's advocate as I tested new ideas and methods.
- To Sheryl Williams Esq., my real estate attorney, who has met every deadline, been available to answer every question, and never made a mistake on a closing document.
- To Gary Mathes, my CPA, who has been available day and night to take my calls, answer my questions, and provide me with tax advice.
- To Fred Carpenter, Gary Collins, Randy Davis, Gerald Deaver, Walt Gladding, Alex Gourlay, David Hammett, Latrella Higgins, John Isgrig, Hayes Martin, Bob Roberts, Mark Stone, and Mike Willett, all professional and knowledgeable bankers from whom I have learned much over the years.
- To the many people from whom I have purchased real estate, with the hope that the purchases turned out to be as good for you as they have been for me. Many of you will recognize your stories in this book.
- To my best friend Roger Dawson, from whom I have learned negotiating skills that have made millions for me over the 18 years of our friendship. And, whose persistent encouragement finally persuaded me to join him in writing this book.

Mike Summey

- To my darling wife, Gisela, who enriches my life more than fortunes ever could.
- To my delightful grandchildren, Astrid and Thomas.
- To Bruce Mulhearn, an icon in California real estate, who taught me a great deal about real estate, speaking, and life.
- To the memory of my dear friend, Jack Harvey, who affected my life in so many ways.
- To all the real estate investors who willingly share their knowledge and expertise at real estate investment clubs around the country.
- To my long-time friend and now coauthor Mike Summey. You certainly didn't have to do this, but you did it right.

Roger Dawson

- To our agent, Jeff Herman, who suggested this project to us.
- To our editor, Mary Glenn, who shared our enthusiasm.
- To our special friend and golfing buddy, Carleton H. Sheets, who is as genuine a person as we have ever met (… and very damned lucky at golf too).

Mike Summey and Roger Dawson

 **Contents**

Foreword by Carleton H. Sheets — ix

Preface: Why Read This Book? — xi

Section 1. Principles of Real Estate Investing — 1

1. Get Rich Slowly — 3
   Leverage — 4
   Tax Benefits — 6
   Other Advantages — 7

2. Wealth Is an Income Stream — 10

3. Income to Value Ratios — 14

4. Small Rent Increases Snowball Your Net Worth — 18

5. What Makes a Property a Good Buy? — 23

Section 2. Learning Your Real Estate Market — 29

6. Finding a Property Manager — 31

7. The Threshold Theory — 35

8. Stick with Bread and Butter Properties — 37

9. Learn Your Market — 40

10. Don't Be Discouraged by Asking Prices — 44

Section 3. How to Find the Ideal Seller — 49

11. The Seller Has Moved — 51

Contents

12. Sellers Have Divorced   58

13. Seller Has High Equity in the Property   66

14. Converting Home Equity to Retirement Income   71

15. Sellers in Financial Trouble   76

16. Real Estate Owned by Banks   81

Section 4. How to Power Negotiate   91

17. Profit Is Made When You Buy   93

18. Negotiating Pressure Points   96
    Time Pressure   96
    Information Power   99
    Projecting That You're Prepared to Walk Away   100

19. Win-Win Negotiating   102

20. Beginning Negotiating Gambits   107
    Ask for More Than You Expect to Get   107
    Expand the Negotiating Range with Strangers   108
    Other Reasons for Asking for More   109
    Bracket the Seller's Asking Price   110
    Think of *No* as an Opening Negotiating Position   111
    Never Say Yes to the First Proposal   111
    Flinch When the Seller First Tells You the Price   112
    Always Play the Reluctant Buyer Role   114
    The Vise Technique   115

21. Middle Negotiating Gambits   118
    Use the Power of a Higher Authority   118
    The Counter-Gambits to Higher Authority   121
    Never Offer to Split the Difference   124
    Always Ask for a Trade-Off   126

22. Ending Negotiating Gambits   128
    Good Guy/Bad Guy   128
    Nibbling   133
    The Walk-Away Gambit   135
    The Positioning for Easy Acceptance Gambit   136

23. You're Negotiating All the Time   138

Contents

Section 5: How to Structure the Offer   141

24. Valuing Single-Family Properties   144
    Calculating the Net Operating Income (NOI)   144
    Calculating Return on Investment   147

25. Structuring Your First Deal   154

26. How to Write the Offer   163
    What All Offers Should Include   163
    Optional Items That You May Want to Consider   167
    Miscellaneous Considerations   169

27. Nothing-Down Deals That Work   170
    How the Due-on-Sale Clause Changed No-Money Down Deals   172
    Sellers Who Own the Property Free and Clear   172
    Structure the Purchase So That the NOI Covers
         Your Acquisition Costs   173
    A Typical No-Money-Down Purchase of a House   174
    The Value of Owning a Property Free and Clear   175
    Using Your Home Equity to Finance Purchases   176
    Anatomy of a Commercial No-Money-Down Purchase   176

28. Tax Benefits of Owning Real Estate   181

Section 6. Moving into Larger Properties   187

29. Valuing Multifamily Properties   189
    Expenses for Apartment Buildings   191
    Advantages of Buying Apartment Houses   192
    Disadvantages of Buying Apartment Houses   193
    Our Recommendation   193

30. Valuing Commercial Properties   194

31. Building Your Support Team   199

Section 7. Getting Started   207

32. What to Do Your First Weekend   209

33. What to Do Your Second Weekend   212

34. What to Do Your Third Weekend   216

Contents

35. What to Do Your Fourth Weekend   219

36. What to Do Your Fifth Weekend   222

37. What to Do Your Sixth Weekend   226

38. What to Do Your Seventh Weekend   228

39. What to Do Your Eighth Weekend   232

    Your First Eight Weeks in Review   235

40. The 14 Biggest Mistakes New Investors Make
    (Bonus Chapter)   237

Appendix A: Inspection Form   247

Appendix B: Net Operating Income Calculation Form   255

Real Estate Investment Glossary   257

Index   279

 # Foreword

When Mike and Roger asked me to write a foreword for this book, I was flattered. But, when I read the manuscript, I became truly excited. It is an excellent how-to book, with nuances running the gamut from creative ways to buy and manage property to the psychological mindset of individual and institutional sellers.

I am so pleased to make this small contribution, because Mike and Roger's investment philosophies are so much like mine: Buy real estate; hold on to real estate; have your real estate professionally managed; let the cash flow from your real estate, and the passage of time makes you rich.

Sound simple? You're right. It is. However, you would be amazed at the people I run into that try to "brain" their way through investing. They buy the right property but in the wrong neighborhood. They buy the wrong property in the right neighborhood. They pay too much for a property. They run into severe management problems. They experience any one of a myriad of problems that never would have happened if they could have taken advantage of the advice and directives available in this book. *The Weekend Millionaire's Secrets to Investing in Real Estate*, written by two professional and successful investors, is going to create many self-made millionaires.

If you're trying to change your life financially, real estate has no peers. Armed with the right knowledge and a roadmap showing you what to do, you can create a substantial cash flow and build a large estate as well. Early in my adult life, I remember someone telling me that you could become a millionaire investing in the stock market. I later learned that's true—all you need to do is start with two million. Marshall Field said it best: "Real estate is not only the best and quickest way to make you wealthy, for the average person it truly is the only way."

This book will give you the knowledge you need and the roadmap to follow. It is well written, easy to follow, and exciting to read. Just remember, becoming wealthy in real estate is not a get-rich-quick program. It is a get-rich-over-time course of action. The nice thing about the "trip" though, is that getting from where you are now to where you want to be is not only fun, but you will start enjoying some of the cash flow, equity buildup, and tax benefits immediately.

As an investor for over 30 years, I can tell you that a trip of a thousand miles begins with a single step. Reading this book is that first step. The second is putting what you read to use. Very soon, you'll be thanking Mike and Roger (and in a small way, maybe even me) for getting you started.

Good Investing!

Carleton H. Sheets

Author of *How to Buy Your First Home or Investment Property with No Down Payment*

Preface

Why Read This Book

When you picked up this book, something must have caught your attention. We assume the idea of becoming a Weekend Millionaire intrigued you. Are you skeptical that you can become rich? Many people, when they first saw William Nickerson's book with the outrageous title *How I Turned $1000 into Five Million in my Spare Time*, probably thought, "If this guy is really worth $5 million, why is he bothering to write a book about it?" We can't speak for Mr. Nickerson, but we have written this book to share information that we feel will help you achieve the kind of success we have been fortunate enough to enjoy—in other words, to give back some of our good fortune.

There are thousands of books on how to get rich. Many of them promise a lot and deliver very little. The difference in this book is that the ideas and concepts we'll teach you are simple, realistic, and doable, and they work. They are not gimmicks, tricks, or attention-grabbing publicity stunts designed to mislead you into thinking you will get rich quick.

Real estate investing is not limited to wealthy tycoons. Many ordinary people own rental properties, and they are becoming rich doing so. You don't have to be a slave to a weekly paycheck.

All successful people have defining moments that change their lives forever. Moments when they have a flash of insight about their potential and ability to be successful that forever sticks in their mind as a moment that turned their life around. This book can produce one of those defining moments for you.

Colonel Sanders, of Kentucky Fried Chicken fame, had such a day when he went to the mailbox and found his first social security check. "I'm not going to do this," he thought. "I'm not going to spend the rest of my life living on a small government check." That's when he mixed up a batch of his "special herbs and spices," put a portable cook stove in the trunk of his car, and went around selling his fried chicken to local restaurants. Today you can buy his "secret recipe" fried chicken in virtually every city in the world.

For Mike Summey, it was a day in 1966 when at age 20 he was terminated, or as we would say today, "downsized," from his $80 per week factory job. He was flat broke, living in a small rented house, and making monthly payments on an old car. He couldn't come up with $50 cash the day before payday if his life depended on it.

The shock of suddenly being out of work was enough to create a defining moment in Mike's life. He vowed never to be caught in a situation like that again. He resolved to control his own destiny from that point forward. He wrote down a goal that he carried in his wallet for years. It read, "I will become a millionaire by age thirty and be able to retire by age fifty."

With no money and little education, he could hardly be considered millionaire material. His goal was not lengthy, but it was very specific. It was his goal, and it was a big goal! A goal against which he could measure all his future activities to determine if what he was doing was leading him toward the goal or away from it.

One of the first things his goal did was to help him figure out that he could not get there working at another $80 per week factory job. At $80 per week, it would take over 240 years just to earn a million dollars, let alone be worth that much. If he was going to become a millionaire by age 30, it meant he would have to build his net worth by an average of $100,000 a year for 10 years. Was this an impossible goal? Evidently not, because he made it by age 28 and went on to reach his goal of being able to retire by age 50 and accomplished this with no partners and no investors.

Was it easy? Absolutely not! In fact, the first few years were excruciatingly difficult. Mike thought the answer was to own his own business, so he used his artistic talents and started a small, one-man sign company. His first year, he earned less than he had at the factory job. Although he was technically "in business for himself," he quickly learned that making signs was not much different from working in a factory—he was simply selling his time, just in a different way. Having the big long-term goal helped him determine that he would have to find a way to invest each day's time in assets that could pay him dividends for years to come, dividends that would grow and compound over time.

He found that by renting rather than selling the signs, he could build a growing income stream. Gradually, one sign at a time, he built a billboard company with offices in two states. Although his company was successful, increasing pressure from environmentalists led his bankers, accountants, and attorneys to advise him to diversify his holdings.

Taking their advice, Mike started looking at real estate on the weekends and during his spare time. Once he made a few purchases, he set a goal to buy enough houses to generate an income of $10,000 per month. Within a few short years, he reached this goal and set another one—$100,000 per month in income. Unrealistic? Do you doubt that you could do the same thing? Don't answer that until you have finished reading this book.

Roger Dawson's defining moment came the day that he realized he had wasted 13 years of his life trying to climb a corporate ladder. Roger wasn't a top candidate for becoming a millionaire either. Born in England, his father drove a London taxicab and he quit school when he was 16. As a shipboard photographer, he visited California and fell in love with it. A year later, he moved to San Francisco with only $200 to his name. He went to work for Montgomery Ward department stores as a management trainee, the last management trainee they ever hired without a college education. Thirteen years later, after being transferred six times, he still wasn't making enough money to support his wife and three children. Inspired by William Nickerson's book, each time he was transferred he bought a home and then rented it out when he moved on to the next assignment. He suddenly realized that his income from the real estate was more than the salary he was drawing from full-time employment at Wards, so he quit his job and went into real estate. He not only built a portfolio of rental properties worth several million dollars, but went on to become president of one of California's largest real estate companies and acquired the negotiating skills that made him one of the country's top business negotiating experts.

If you are serious about wanting to turn your life around and become rich investing in real estate, this book can show you how to do it. Mike and Roger first met when Mike hired Roger to speak at an outdoor advertising convention in 1986. Since that time, they have become close friends who respect and admire each other's unique talents and skills.

With the stock market in disarray and investor confidence at a dismal low, Mike and Roger have come together in this book to bring you investment strategies that will allow you to build a strong financial future using your spare time. They will show you how to become a *Weekend Millionaire*.

Mike Summey

P. O. Box 16648
Asheville, NC 28816
Email: Mike@weekendmillionaire.com
Email: Wkendmillionaire@aol.com

Roger Dawson

P. O. Box 2040
La Habra, CA 90631
Email: Roger@weekendmillionaire.com

Mike and Roger, both members of National Speakers Association, are called upon to address audiences throughout the country on their areas of expertise. Mike speaks on real estate investing and motivation, while Roger addresses the topics of negotiation, persuasion, decision making and motivation. Either may be contacted at the above addresses.

Disclaimer

While we have tried to make everything is this book accurate, please be aware that all 50 states have different real estate laws and those laws are constantly changing. Even legal interpretations of those laws change constantly. We cannot guarantee the accuracy or completeness of the information in this book. For your own protection, you should consult with local real estate professionals, attorneys, and CPAs before making decisions based on the information in this book.

SECTION 1

Principles of Real Estate Investing

We don't say that real estate investing is the only way to get rich. If you have a law degree or a master of business administration (MBA) from an ivy-league college, there are plenty of ways to make a lot of money in this country. If you have exceptional talent in sports or music, you have a good chance of making some serious money. If you inherited capital or connections, you can leverage those into big bucks.

However, if you're like us, and don't have a college degree, don't have exceptional talent, and are not in line for a big inheritance, investing in real estate may well be the only way for you to get rich.

In this section, we'll help you understand why Andrew Carnegie said: "Ninety percent of all millionaires became so through owning real estate. More money has been made in real estate than in all industrial investments. The wise young man or wage earner of today invests his money in real estate."

You'll see why we advocate getting rich slowly in real estate. Even if you only buy one rental house a year, it will make you rich. Buying right is far more important than buying frequently.

We'll change your definition of riches by convincing you that true wealth is a passive income stream; that the income your properties generate is far more important than how many properties you own.

We'll show you a new way to value properties so that your investments generate an income stream. It may not seem right to you, but the price you pay for the property is not nearly as important as the cost of owning it.

You'll learn how to turn a trickle of income into a stream by raising rents just a small amount each year.

All these benefits make real estate a wonderful investment whether you have capital to invest or need to buy your first property with no money down. Understanding the principles of real estate investing is the foundation of your career as a real estate investor and your path to becoming a *Weekend Millionaire*.

1

Get Rich Slowly

The Weekend Millionaire is not an overnight get-rich-quick scheme. It's a get-rich-slowly program. You can become wealthy even if you only buy one rental property a year.

So, you've invested in a book that tells you that you can become a millionaire by working at it only on weekends. And you're skeptical. Can this be true? Or is it just an overblown scheme concocted to sell more books? If it's so easy, why are the authors writing about it instead of doing it?

Well, the authors have done it, and it's not a scheme. The *Weekend Millionaire* is an investment program based on very sound market principles. It is not speculation; it is investing. That's an important difference. Speculation requires that the value of your investments go up.

While there is a very good chance that the property you buy will go up in value, it's not the key ingredient of the Weekend Millionaire program. You can become a millionaire investing in real estate even if the value of the property never goes up.

What's so special about investing in real estate? There are some sound underlying principles that cause real estate to be a superb investment. Here are the two big ones: leverage and tax benefits.

Leverage

Leverage means that you can control a large investment with a small amount of money. You can leverage an investment in the stock market. If you have $10,000 to invest, your stockbroker will let you buy $20,000 of stock. That's a 50 percent margin, which is the most the government will allow.

When you invest in real estate, you can easily accomplish a 90 percent margin. You do this anytime you buy property with a 10 percent down payment and a 90 percent loan. Why can you borrow 90 percent to buy real estate and only 50 percent to buy stocks? Good question! It's because the risk of real estate going down in value is very low and the risk of stocks going down in value is very high.

Here's a key principle for you. It's simple to become a millionaire. All you have to do is start with a dollar and double it 20 times. Since you probably don't believe that, take a moment and figure it out.

$1-$2-$4-$8-$16-$32-$64-$128-$256-$512-$1024. That's 10 times. See how it starts out slow and begins to snowball? That's exactly the way your real estate portfolio grows. It starts out slow and gradually begins to snowball until one day you wake up and realize that you really are a millionaire! Let's keep going:

$2048-$4096-$8192-$16,384-$32,768-$65,536-$131,072-$262,144-$524,288-$1,048,576!

Simple isn't it? Just double a dollar 20 times and you'll have over a million dollars! Note that we said simple, not easy.

Here's where you have to change the way you think. The reason that it's not easy to make a million dollars is that very few people know how to double a dollar. We challenge you! Within the next 24 hours try to buy something for a dollar and sell it for $2. In all the years that we have thrown out that challenge in seminars, we have only had one person report back that he did it. He went into a store that sold postage stamps to collectors. He found a few loose ones lying in the bottom of a counter bin and asked the storeowner if he would take a dollar for them. He then sold them for $2 to a stamp collector that he knew.

Why is it so hard to double the dollar? Because our education system teaches us how to earn money, not make money. Teachers prepare you to graduate, get a job, and go to work five days a week just as they do. *Change the way you think about that, and you'll change your life!* From now on, view yourself as an investor, not a laborer! Laborers sell their time to generate income. Investors acquire assets that generate income. Big difference!

It is especially difficult if you can't use the principle of leverage. Let's take the example of the man who had enough initiative to buy stamps for a $1 and sell them for $2. Let's say that he decided to follow through, double his investment every week for 19 more weeks, and become a millionaire. By the fifth week, he needs to buy $32 worth of stamps and sell them for $64. No problem, he easily accomplishes this and with great drive and persistence, he presses on. By the tenth week, the task has become considerably more difficult, but still doable. He now needs to buy $512 worth of stamps and sell them for $1024. He spends his evenings on the Internet buying stamps, sets up a booth at a swap meet, and works hard all weekend. He asks everyone who passes by to invest in his stamps. Since he has great drive and determination, and is very charismatic, he succeeds and presses on. However, by the fifteenth week, his task is almost impossible. He needs to buy $32,768 worth of stamps and sell them for $65,536. That's virtually impossible for one person alone to do. First, he can't find that many stamps to buy. Secondly, even if he could, he couldn't serve that many customers, so he collapses in exhaustion and frustration. Although he made it 15 weeks, he is still $967,232 away from his goal of a million dollars. This is why so many people, with good intentions, give up without ever realizing the goal of becoming wealthy. They try to use their labor to get the money, and they just can't do it.

Compare that to the way leverage works. If our man selling stamps had recruited two other people to sell for him the first week and gotten each of them to recruit two others the second week, and so on and so on, within a few weeks he could have thousands of people selling stamps all over the world and become very wealthy. "But wait a minute," you say. "That's a multilevel scheme like network marketing companies use, isn't it?"

Yes, it is similar, but it uses the principle of leveraging people rather than assets. When you own rental properties you do have a down-line of people supporting you, but instead of going out and selling soap or cosmetics, they are tenants who go to work for someone else and earn money to pay off your mortgages.

Let's compare the difference. You buy a house for $100,000, pay $10,000 down and take out a loan for $90,000. You now control a $100,000 asset with only $10,000 invested. You rent the house out for enough to cover the mortgage payments and expenses. If the house appreciates 5 percent per year, in two years, it is worth over $110,000 and the mortgage has probably been paid down $1000 to $2000. If you could sell the house and net this amount, after you paid off the mortgage you would have between $21,000 and $22,000 instead of the $10,000 with which you started.

Question: What was your return on investment? You bought it for $100,000, sold it for $110,000. Many people would say your return was 5 percent per year or 10 percent total. But, that's all wrong. You originally invested $10,000, which represented the difference between what you owed and what the house was worth. When you sold it, you got back between $21,000 and $22,000. Your actual return on investment was between 55 and 60 percent per year, and you didn't have to go to any swap meets or sell any stamps! That is how the principle of leverage works.

The Weekend Millionaire program is even better. Note that in the above example, you invested $10,000 and turned it into $21,000 to $22,000 when you sold the house. Here's the beauty of the Weekend Millionaire program. You don't sell the house. Instead, you take $10,000 of the equity from this first house and use it to buy a second one and start the whole process over again. Only you now have two assets going up in value and two tenants paying down mortgages.

Tax Benefits

The government is smart enough to realize that private property owners make much better landlords than it would. Because of that, it gives some impressive tax benefits to encourage private investment in real estate. We're going to devote Chapter 28 to this, but here's a list of the tax benefits you may enjoy just so that you can get a feel for them:

- *Favorable income tax treatment.* The passive income you receive in the form of rent is not subject to social security or self-employment taxes like the money you earn working.
- *Passive loss deduction.* Within limits, you can deduct any losses you incur after deducting expenses, interest, and depreciation from the income you earn working.
- *Interest deduction.* You can use the interest you pay on your mortgages to reduce taxes on the income you receive from renting the property.
- *Depreciation deduction.* You can use a portion of the cost of buildings and personal property to reduce taxes on the income you receive from renting the property even though the buildings are probably going up in value.
- *Tax deferral on exchanges*. You can defer income tax on the sale of property by reinvesting the proceeds in another real estate investment within certain allowed periods.
- *Tax-free sale potential.* You can avoid taxes altogether on the sale of a property if you live in it for 2 of the 5 years prior to selling it.
- *Long-term capital gain.* If you sell a property you have owned for 12 months or more, your profit is taxed as a long-term capital gain and you will pay a rate of 20 percent or less on it. When compared with rates as high as 39 percent on ordinary income, this is a tremendous break.

Leverage is one of the two big reasons that real estate investing is a terrific way to build a fortune. Tax benefit is the other, although you should consult with your tax advisor prior to taking advantage of any tax breaks. While these are the big advantages, here are some others.

Other Advantages

Solid Value. Real estate is a great investment to hold, because it retains its value. As Will Rogers pointed out, "They ain't making any more of it."

Principles of Real Estate Investing

There is danger; however, when you speculate in real estate. Speculators often bid up prices on the bigger fool theory. They think, "It doesn't matter how much I pay because there'll always be a bigger fool coming along who will pay me even more." Eventually a correction takes place, and prices drop. As you'll see when we teach you how to evaluate property, the Weekend Millionaire method protects you from getting into an overheated market. Keep in mind that Weekend Millionaires are investors, not speculators.

Potential for Rapid Equity Buildup. You can dramatically increase the value of real estate by fixing it up. We'll teach you how to invest money wisely in improvements that will enable you to raise your rents, increase your cash flow, and quickly improve the value of your property. When prices are escalating and the market becomes overheated, your best investments are often in upgrades to the property you already own.

Hedge against Inflation. Inflation has been with us for the last 50 years and is probably here to stay. Granted, it's currently under control, but it's still with us. Real estate is a terrific hedge on inflation; in fact, it may well be the best hedge. That's because it increases in value at or above the inflation rate. Let's say you buy a property today for $100,000 cash. If it appreciates in value 5 percent a year for 10 years, it will be worth about $163,000. If inflation averaged 3 percent a year during this same period, and you invested your $100,000 cash in something that matched the inflation rate, this investment would only be worth approximately $135,000. The real estate investment would have beaten inflation by $28,000. On the other hand, if you had put the $100,000 under your mattress, you would be $35,000 behind where you are today in buying power.

But, let's assume that instead of paying cash, you paid 10 percent down, financed the balance, and your tenants covered all your expenses (the heart of the Weekend Millionaire program!). If we don't consider the amount of principle by which the tenants reduced your mortgage, you would benefit from the full $63,000 increase in value, even though your actual out-of-pocket investment was only $10,000. The higher the inflation rate, the greater your growth in value, but there's more. While the value of the property is going up, so is the monthly rent. Can you see how owning real estate is probably the best hedge against inflation that you'll ever find?

Debt Reduction. Every month, on every property, you will be slowly paying down the mortgages—or will you? Since you will make your payments from the rent you receive, your tenants will actually be paying off your mortgages. Perhaps, when you start, the mortgage reduction will be small, maybe only $25 to $50 per month per property. This doesn't seem like much, but considering that it's every month on every property you own, it adds up quickly. In addition, as you make each payment, the amount that goes toward reducing the mortgage goes up and the interest goes down. For every month you own the property, the amount of debt reduction keeps increasing until the mortgage is fully paid.

Cash Flow. Rental real estate is a great investment because it provides cash flow. Unlike gold or silver sitting in a vault or stock certificates in your stockbroker's safe, rental real estate starts generating cash flow as soon as you purchase it. With inflation growth pushing up rents, cash flow will grow from a trickle to a stream, then to a river of income in a few short years. Real estate is one of the few investments that can generate enough cash flow to purchase the asset without having to use any of your earned income.

Cash flow is such an integral part of the Weekend Millionaire program that we've devoted the entire next chapter to it. Read on to change your mind about the definition of wealth.

2

Wealth Is an Income Stream

It doesn't benefit you to own a lot of real estate if it doesn't generate income for you. We'll teach you how to develop a stream of income for the rest of your life.

"**W**ho wants to be a millionaire?" asks the popular television show host and the Cole Porter song from the MGM movie High Society. Your answer of course is, "I do!"

We want to change your thinking on that one. What you want is not a million dollars, but the income stream that a million dollars can generate for you. What you own is far less important than the stream of income it generates.

One investor we know built up a $5 million portfolio of rental properties. He owed about $3 million in mortgages, so he was a multi-millionaire, right? He thought so, but he hadn't bought the way that a Weekend Millionaire would buy. Many of his mortgages had adjustable interest rates that caused the payment amounts to fluctuate when the prime rate changed.

Wealth Is an Income Stream

When rates started to climb, the payments grew and started choking off cash flow. As they continued to climb, he became unable to maintain the properties in good condition and tenants started to move. His number of vacancies grew, which compounded the problem. He tried to sell some of the properties to raise cash, but the only buyers he could find were bargain hunters who didn't even want to pay what he owed for the properties. In the end, he lost everything and had to start over. "That's when I found out," he told us, "that how much property I owned didn't matter. Unless I had the cash flow to support it and didn't have to gamble on inflation to bail me out, I was sunk."

The Weekend Millionaire program doesn't focus on how much property you own but on how much cash flow it can generate. How much property you own may give you bragging rights down at the corner bar, but what really counts is how much money you have left each month after all the bills are paid.

Here, in a nutshell, is what you will learn from this book. We're going to teach you how to buy rental real estate in such a way that you will be able to cover all the expenses, maintain the properties well, and pay off the mortgages within 15 years. Once the mortgages are paid off, the rent coming in, minus the expenses you incur to maintain the property; will be all yours to keep.

When you buy that first house, you'll probably think, "Where does the getting rich part come in? I'm barely breaking even after I pay all my expenses!" Patience, patience, patience! That's the name of the game at this point. If you start out just breaking even, you will be paying down the mortgage, which is almost like making a deposit each month to a savings account. If this is the case, you will soon learn that rents rise with inflation and it won't be long before you start receiving an extra $25 a month, then $50 a month, and so on. It may not sound like much in the beginning, but as you watch both the extra income you receive and the amount you pay down on the mortgage grow each month, and you realize this trend will continue for the rest of your life, it becomes significant. What starts out as a trickle, becomes a stream in a few years, and the stream eventually becomes a torrent when the mortgages are paid off and you get to keep nearly all the income.

If you bought only one house a year like that, in 15 years you'd be able to retire very comfortably with the rental income from your 15 houses. If each house only rented for $1000 a month, you'd have an income stream of $15,000 a month, which is $180,000 per year. Remember that when your mortgages are paid off, the bulk of that income stream will be yours to live on or invest. By comparison, you would have to deposit $3.6 million dollars in certificates of deposit paying 5 percent per year to have an annual income of $180,000.

We think that you will do much better than buying one house a year once you get started and gain some experience. We only use this one house per year example to illustrate how the Weekend Millionaire program is a plan to help you get rich slowly, not an unrealistic get-rich-quick ploy.

How hard is it to buy one rental house a year? Not hard at all! You can do it on your weekends or in your spare time without breaking a sweat. There are five things you need to do, and we're going to teach you these by the time you get through with this book.

1. You need to learn and thoroughly understand the Weekend Millionaire investment program.
2. You need to spend time learning about your local real estate market. We'll show you how to do this.
3. You need to have the courage to make enough low offers to sellers until you feel comfortable doing it. We're going to take you through the process systematically until you feel confident that you can do it.
4. You need to understand and practice the negotiating techniques that we will teach you.
5. You need to study the chapters on how to structure offers until you thoroughly understand them.

When you start doing these things, and putting the ideas and principles to work, your confidence will grow, and this will transform your financial future and make you a Weekend Millionaire.

You will feel very good about what you're doing. You will realize that you can become a Weekend Millionaire without taking advantage of anyone. In fact, you will actually serve others:

- You will serve your tenants by providing them with housing.
- You will serve the sellers by solving their financial dilemmas.

Wealth Is an Income Stream

- You will serve your community by providing private-sector housing so the government doesn't have to do it.
- You will serve your city and county by paying property taxes.
- You will serve your state and country by paying income taxes.

You'll do all this good and get rich in the process! That's what we call a worthwhile endeavor!

3

Income to
Value Ratios

Many people think that real estate investing is buying property you can sell later at a big profit. The Weekend Millionaire program is not about buying property hoping you can sell it later for a profit. It is about teaching you how to buy property that will build you a large income stream. Because of that, you need to view the way you value real estate completely differently.

Buy/Sell Investors. Most investors want to make a killing on real estate. They look for bargains, try to beat sellers down on their price, and then hope to resell later at a big profit. The income that the property produces while they own it is secondary to this goal. They are usually happy if they can break even (meaning that the rental income covers mortgage payments and expenses) or only take a small loss. We're not knocking this approach, because many people have gotten rich doing it. The principle of leverage makes it possible to get rich this way. For example, if you put $10,000 down to buy a $100,000 property and the property goes up in value

Income to Value Ratios

5 percent per year, your investment will double in two years. Do you follow us on that one? (Five percent per year equals $5,000 per year.) At 5 percent inflation per year the property will be worth $110,000 (actually more than that because of the compounding effect), and your $10,000 equity has doubled to become $20,000.

We like to refer to this kind of investor as a Buy/Sell Speculator. These investors are primarily concerned with the price of the property. Because Weekend Millionaires buy property to develop income streams and not to re-sell, they are more concerned with the value of the property than the price. What's the difference between price and value? *Price* is simply the number of dollars that you pay to acquire the property. *Value* takes into account both the price that is paid and the manner in which it is paid. So it follows that Weekend Millionaires value property completely differently than Buy/Sell Speculators. We'll explain later how Weekend Millionaires can often pay a higher price than Buy/Sell Speculators and still be successful.

Annual Gross Multipliers. Buy/Sell Speculators make a lot of buying decisions based on annual gross multipliers. If you look through the Investment Property for Sale column in the classified section of your local newspaper, you'll see apartment buildings offered for sale at a gross multiplier. Here's a typical ad:

> *16 Units. 8 2s, 6 1s, 2 furn. studios. Well-maintained. Long-term tenants. Pool, laundry. 8.2x. $787,200.*

What does this tell you? There are 16 apartments in the building. In many states that means you must have a resident manager, which can be expensive. There are eight two-bedroom units and six one-bedroom units that are unfurnished, plus two furnished studio apartments. Unfurnished apartments tend to attract better-quality tenants who are likely to stay longer, while furnished apartments are easy to rent but tend to attract more transient tenants. "Well-maintained" and "long-term tenants" is puffery and means very little. A pool may make the property more attractive to tenants, but the maintenance costs can be high. Since the property includes eight two-bedroom apartments, you'll attract couples with children, and screaming kids at a pool will deter older tenants. There is a laundry, which can generate a little income and is attractive to tenants. 8.2x, (pronounced 8 point 2 times) means that the seller's asking price is 8.2 times the annual gross rents. Because we know that the asking price is $787,200, we can calculate that the annual rents are $96,000 or an average of about $500 per month per unit.

A Buy/Sell Speculator might find the gross multiplier a useful tool if he or she knows the market and knows that similar properties are selling at a much higher gross multiplier, or use it as a quick rule of thumb to eliminate the property if it is too high for the market.

It is not a good rule of thumb for a Weekend Millionaire because it does not take into consideration the expenses that come with ownership of property. The Weekend Millionaire wants to know how much money will be left over after all the expenses are paid.

Monthly Multipliers. William Nickerson, who wrote *How I Turned $1000 into $5 Million Investing in Real Estate in my Spare Time,* popularized the concept of monthly gross multipliers, saying that if you can buy a property for 100 times the monthly rent or less, you've got a good buy. According to his theory, if you can rent a house for $1,500 a month, you can afford to pay $150,000 to buy it. There is little difference between monthly gross multipliers and annual gross multipliers other than the mathematics. An 8.33 annual gross multiplier is about the same as a 100 times monthly gross multiplier, because 8.33 times annual gross rent is virtually the same as 100 times the monthly gross rent. A Buy/Sell Speculator could use either one and come to the same conclusion.

The Fallacy of Buying Using Gross Multipliers. Many Buy/Sell Speculators and would-be long-term investors have gone broke making buying decisions based on gross multipliers. So what's wrong with doing it that way? A lot, that's what! Let's look at some of the problems this can create:

- It doesn't tell you who pays for the utilities. Is each unit metered separately or does the landlord pay? You'd be amazed how much air conditioning a tenant can use on a hot summer's day when they don't have to pay for the electricity.
- It doesn't tell you how much you'll have to pay in property taxes.
- It doesn't factor in an allowance for vacancies.
- It doesn't allow for management costs. You may have to give a resident

manager a free apartment, pay a management company a percentage of the gross rents, or manage it yourself. In any event, management costs you money or time.

- It doesn't allow for the cost of fire, liability, or flood insurance.
- It doesn't allow for the cost of maintaining the property.
- And, most importantly, it doesn't consider the cost of purchasing the property, which is a major factor.

Net Return on Investment. Sophisticated commercial real estate brokers know that using gross multipliers is a crude rule of thumb that doesn't tell you very much. They usually calculate the net return on investment for potential buyers by dividing the net operating income (NOI) (you'll learn how to calculate this in Chapter 5) by the purchase price. An example of this is a property that cost $200,000 with an annual NOI of $20,000 will give you a 10 percent annual return on the purchase price. This works if you are paying cash for the property, but it does not consider the cash flow requirements if you have to make mortgage payments.

Net return on investment is a good way of comparing a prospective real estate investment to other types of investments. Using the above example, if you had $200,000 cash to invest, you could buy the property, which would give you a 10 percent return on your money; put it in certificates of deposit earning 3 to 4 percent; buy corporate bonds paying a higher rate but with more risk; put it in stocks and roll the dice; or simply put it under your mattress and get no return. Using this method to compare various investments is great if you have cash, but it is far too crude for the Weekend Millionaire who expects to use leverage to build a portfolio of income-producing properties.

Weekend Millionaires Buy Based on Value Rather Than Price. Because Weekend Millionaires are not buying for resale but buying to create an income stream, they need to factor in all the expenses of ownership, including the cost of purchasing and financing the property. As you'll learn, the way that you purchase the property is more important than the price that you pay. In Chapter 5, we'll give you an overview of how to figure net operating income, which you will use to determine whether to buy a particular property. In Section 5, How to Structure the Offer, we'll show you in detail how to determine the best way to buy and how to write the offer.

4

Small Rent Increases Snowball Your Net Worth

One of the big advantages to owning income-producing real estate is the effect small rent increases have on your net worth. Net worth is the difference between the value of what you own and the amount that you owe on it. Since property grows in value as income rises, it makes sense that the increased value resulting from small rent increases adds to your equity in the property and grows your net worth. What may not be so obvious is just how much impact small rent increases can have over a period of years.

A Case Study of a Long-Term Investment. In 1980 Mike bought a basic starter home in a subdivision of similar type homes. He put $620 down and assumed the seller's Veterans Administration (VA) loan. The payment on the loan was $225 per month, which included taxes and insurance. This property is a good example of what small rent increases can do to increase value and snowball your net worth.

    The first year Mike owned this property, he rented it for $250 per month.

Small Rent Increases Snowball Your Net Worth

He used the $25 that was left after paying the mortgage payment to pay someone else to manage the property. That's an important philosophy for the Weekend Millionaire. Most people would say, "Why pay someone 10 percent of your gross income when you could easily do it yourself? Chances are the property manager won't have to do anything except deposit the check." "Why pay an electrician $100 to replace a breaker switch when you could do it yourself for $20?" We want you to focus on the highest and best use of your time, which is locating and buying properties. If you also take on the chore of managing your properties, you'll soon find that you have taken on a second job as a maintenance person, and investing will become less and less fun for you. Mike hired a property manager to collect the rent because he wanted to be an investor, not have a second job.

Reducing the Mortgage Builds Your Net Worth. After spending that $25 a month for management, Mike only broke even the first year—or did he? Each month, when he made the payment, the amount he owed on the property decreased. In order to track this reduction, he ordered a loan amortization schedule that showed what portion of each payment went to pay interest and what portion went to reduce the outstanding loan balance. Each time he made a payment, he would circle the principal, interest, and balance amounts for the payment and put his check number out beside the balance. This enabled him to see that although he had no excess cash, the amount he owed was going down each month. At the end of the first year, he saw that he owed about $300 less than he did when he purchased the property.

The second year he owned the house, his property manager raised the rent to $275 per month, but the loan payment remained at $225. Mike now had an extra $25 per month over and above the loan payment, taxes, and insurance. This amounted to $300 in addition to the loan reduction he enjoyed during the second year. Let's compare this to investing his $620 down payment in a bank. How much money would you have to deposit in an interest-bearing account to have generated the same $300 in income? You would have to deposit $2,500 in an account earning 12 percent interest, or $3,333 in an account earning 9 percent interest, or $5,000 in an account earning 6 percent interest.

Principles of Real Estate Investing

The third year he owned the property, Mike's property manager raised the rent another $25 per month to $300, and this continued year after year for several years, with some increases of even more than $25. Eventually, after he had owned the property for six years, the county tax assessor's office revalued the property for tax purposes. In the county where Mike lives, properties are appraised for tax purposes at market value. When he received his new tax assessment, Mike was surprised to learn that the value of his property had increased by 58 percent. His rents had increased from $250 to $395 per month, or slightly over 63 percent.

During this six-year period, the balance of his loan had only decreased by $2,300, but the value of the property had increased over $22,000. This meant that his equity or net worth had grown 10 times as fast from the small rent increases as it had from debt reduction.

Over the next several years, Mike continued to own this house, keep it well maintained, raise the rent, and pay down the mortgage. Today he still owns the property, which rents for $950 per month. The tax assessor now values it at more than $120,000, which is all net worth because the mortgage has been paid off.

Granted, more than 20 years have passed since he first made this purchase, but let's look at his return on investment. When he first bought the property, he put $620 down and has not put any additional money into the property other than what it has earned. The value of the $620 investment has grown to more than $120,000 and during the same time, he has taken out thousands of dollars to invest in other properties. This is an example of how small rent increases can grow to become a snowballing increase in net worth.

Comparing Real Estate to Other Investments. Let's again compare this investment to any other investment. Had Mike invested his $620 at a 25 percent per year return, compounded for 20 years, he would still have less than $55,000 and not been able to take any funds out for other investments. Can you see how real estate can be a secure investment, unmatched by any other kind of secure investment? Imagine what could happen if you owned 10, 20, or 30 or more investments like that. Can you see how you could become a Weekend Millionaire in a relatively short time?

Small Rent Increases Snowball Your Net Worth

This property is representative of the hundreds of other properties Mike has acquired over the years. It is one of the reasons he realized his goal of becoming a millionaire by age 30 and retiring by age 50; a goal that he set at age 20 when he had no credit, no assets, and very little education. A goal that he shared with family and friends who laughed at him and thought he had lost his mind. A goal he never doubted and constantly sought ways to achieve. A goal that was achieved because he understood the tremendous effect that small rent increases could have on net worth if he could just acquire enough properties to take advantage of them.

The Story of a Reluctant Investor. A student of ours told us that he had thought about real estate investing for 10 years before he bought his first property. He was doing well in the insurance business and wasn't interested in diversifying into anything else. Finally, at age 60, he called us to say that he had an opportunity to purchase a house near his and asked if we thought it was a good idea. We ran the numbers and encouraged him to go ahead with the purchase. This was his first venture into real estate investing, but not his last. Once bitten by the bug, he continued to purchase good rental properties and expand his income and net worth. A short five years later, he called to say that he had passed a milestone—his income from rental properties was going to exceed $100,000 for the year, which was more than he had ever made in the insurance business. This wouldn't have been possible if he hadn't followed our advice of raising rents by a small amount regularly.

Raise Rents Frequently by a Small Amount. We strongly recommend that you raise rents by a small amount frequently rather than by a large amount occasionally. Your property manager will advise you on this, but our experience has been that tenants will pay a small increase without protest. If you skip a year and then try to double the increase, you will meet resistance. It doesn't make sense, but that's the way it works. If you were a tenant, would you rather have a 5 percent increase in 12 months and another 5 percent increase in 24 months, or would you prefer a 10 percent increase in 24 months? Obviously, you would be better off to take the 10 percent increase in 24 months. You delay half of the increase for a year, and you don't have the compounding effect of a 5 percent increase on top of a

5 percent increase, which amounts to a 10.25 percent increase. But that's not the way most tenants think. They will accept a 5 percent annual increase but balk at a 10 percent increase every two years.

Apartment Buildings Can Compound the Effect. In the prior examples we have shown you how small increases in rent increase the value of single-family residences. This effect is even more dramatic with apartment buildings. Appraisers use a different method to appraise single-family residences than they do to appraise apartment buildings. Appraisals of single-family homes use the comparison method. The appraisers find similar houses in the area that have sold recently. They add or subtract from those selling prices to allow for features that your property has or doesn't have. What the property rents for has little effect on how they value the property. Conversely, they appraise apartment houses based on the amount of income they generate. This multiplies the effect of rent increases on the value of the property. Let's say that you own a 20-unit apartment building that rents for $500 per unit and would sell for $1,200,000. If you increase the rents by 10 percent, it is likely that you will also increase the value of the building by 10 percent. That means that a $50 per month rent increase instantly raises your net worth by $120,000!

Small Increases Will Make You Rich. We can't emphasize enough the impact that small rent increases can have on net worth. Almost without fail, the increased property values you can achieve with small rent increases can be enough to allow you to refinance one property and pay off another of comparable value within five years. You can then use those properties as collateral for additional purchases. The Weekend Millionaire method is very simple: buy as many properties as you can find that will pay for themselves. The more you own, the more small rent increases you can implement and the more your net worth will snowball.

5

What Makes a Property a Good Buy?

Beginning real estate investors often tell us, "I can't figure out how to make money on rental property because purchase prices are so high these days. I can't get enough rent to make the numbers work."

If you're only looking at the seller's asking price and only considering conventional bank financing, that may well be true.

Real Estate Markets Vary. Real estate markets vary around the country. In a few cities, rental rates are very high when you compare them to purchase prices. In those markets, you could buy at retail prices, pay retail for the financing of the property, and still have cash flow. In most cities, however, rental rates are low when compared to purchase prices. In those markets, you cannot afford to buy at retail prices and get conventional financing because you will not be able to generate enough rent to cover expenses and make a profit.

We're going to teach you how to buy at wholesale and use creative financing to lower your mortgage expenses. That's what makes the Weekend

Principles of Real Estate Investing

Millionaire program viable in almost any market. In addition, it makes real estate investing much more profitable in those markets, which have high rent-to-purchase price ratios.

You can always do better when you learn how to buy at wholesale using a combination of price and creative financing to establish wholesale values.

It's Nearly Impossible to Be Successful if You Buy at Retail Prices and Finance at Retail Rates. Trying to be a successful real estate investor by paying market prices and bank rates for financing would be like saying, "I'm going to go into the car leasing business. I'm going to pay full sticker price for the cars and finance company interest rates when I buy them." If you did that, we can guarantee that you wouldn't get rich. To become a Weekend Millionaire, you will need to know how to buy houses at wholesale values and negotiate advantageous financing. That's what we're going to show you how to do. Each property is different, so you can't make blanket assumptions that the numbers won't work in your community. As a real estate investor, you must evaluate each property on its own merit and value it based upon whether or not it meets the criteria that we will teach you.

You Must Show a Profit in the First Year. The most important thing you must learn as a real estate investor is that when you buy a property you must structure the purchase so that the property will show a profit in the first year. If you invest in a property that doesn't show a profit from the time you purchase it, you probably paid too much. Here are a few simple suggestions to help you avoid this problem:

1. Don't buy properties without a positive cash flow, gambling that escalating market conditions will improve the picture.
2. Don't expect to be able to buy most houses at wholesale. For every offer that is accepted, you will have dozens rejected. Don't let this discourage you or cause you to become impatient.
3. The best deals often come with the most problems. A Weekend Millionaire knows enough about buying property that he or she can recognize a diamond in the rough. Also, some of the best buys we have

made have been from sellers who were in difficult financial situations, such as being in the middle of a sticky divorce or trying to dispose of inherited property. Properties other investors wouldn't bother with because they didn't know enough to help the sellers solve their financial problems.

4. View each real estate offer as an investment decision. Don't fall in love with a property and let your heart rule your head or you will pay too much. Emotion is the primary difference between wholesale and retail when buying real estate.

5. Have a plan and stick to it. We're going to teach you the techniques needed to develop your own investment plan. Use the information to establish goals and benchmarks that fit your personal situation. Once you create your plan, let it guide your investment decisions. Don't be tempted by the occasional property that looks good but doesn't mesh with your plan.

6. Be wary of the lure of a quick buck. The Weekend Millionaire program is a get-rich-slowly plan.

Calculating the Value of a Property. Now, let us show you how to evaluate a property so that you can avoid the pitfalls that we have just given you. First, you need a formula that you can use to analyze a property to determine its investment value.

Learn your market by making a habit of driving through potential neighborhoods where you may want to invest. Gather information about the communities and get information about houses that are for sale. Get a feel for what properties are worth and learn to evaluate their condition. Watch for open houses that listing brokers often hold and use these to start looking around inside some homes. Observe the neighbors to see if they take good care of their homes. Once you begin to feel comfortable, start identifying properties that seem to have potential as good rental properties. "Fine," you say, "I've done all that, but how do I know if they are good investments?" Here's how you make that determination.

Inspect the Property. First, you need to do a more thorough inspection of the exterior and interior of the house. Appendix A in the back of this book contains an excellent form that you can use when inspecting property. It contains a room-by-room listing of the items you need to check as well as a section on the exterior and the overall condition. Should you find items that need attention, you can use the column on the right to estimate the cost of bringing each item up to satisfactory condition. This is important, because you will need to total this column in order to arrive at the amount of money that you will need to spend to make the property attractive to potential renters. This dollar amount will play an important part in determining what you will offer as a purchase price and will also determine whether or not you even want to make an offer.

Either during your inspection or after you have completed it, you will want to meet with a property manager who knows the area where the property is located and ask how much the property could be rented for if it were in good condition. Eventually, as you gain knowledge and experience you may be able to make this determination on your own, but until then, we recommend that you seek the advice of a professional.

Calculate the Net Operating Income (NOI). Here's where most real estate investors get into trouble. They don't make their purchase based on the net operating income of the property. We're going to call that the NOI and refer to it frequently throughout the book. The NOI is the net income that the property will generate after you have paid all the operating expenses. The NOI tells you, more than any other thing, what you can afford to pay for the property.

Most beginning investors don't take the time to calculate the NOI. They see a potential investment and find out what the payments on the mortgage would be. If the income from renting it exceeds the mortgage payments, they go ahead and buy it. Big mistake! People who buy like this are only able to survive if the price of real estate is going up rapidly, or if they have very deep pockets. We don't recommend this method of investing.

In Chapter 24 we're going to show you in detail how to use the form in Appendix B to calculate the NOI, but for now we'll just give you an overview of how it works. Here's what a completed NOI calculation form for a typical property might look like.

What Makes a Property a Good Buy?

Net Operating Income Calculation Form		
Property Address:	**114 Elm Street**	
Income	Monthly	Annually
Gross rent	$ 1,100.00	$ 13,200.00
Vacancy factor	($ 55.00)	($ 660.00)
Net rent	$ 1,045.00	$ 12,540.00
Expenses		
Management fee	($ 104.50)	($ 1,254.00)
Maintenance reserve	($ 104.50)	($ 1,254.00)
Utilities	($ 0.00)	($ 0.00)
Taxes	($ 50.00)	($ 600.00)
Insurance	($ 25.00)	($ 300.00)
Other expenses	($ 11.00)	($ 132.00)
Net operating income	$ 750.00	$ 9,000.00

As you can see from this NOI calculation, we have not deducted the biggest cost of owning the property, which is the mortgage payment. The bottom line is that 114 Elm Street is a good buy only if you can keep the mortgage payments, plus a return on any cash you have to put into the property, at or below $750 a month.

Notice that our calculation of NOI makes an allowance for taxes and insurance, which are the standard expenses that most property owners pay, but where we differ from other investors is that we also include an allowance for management and a maintenance reserve.

We included management because we want you to spend your weekends looking for properties to buy and leave the collecting of rents and doing minor repairs to management professionals.

We show maintenance reserve because we want you to be able to keep your properties in good condition, which will maximize the rents you can get and improve the overall property values.

We'll go into all this in detail in Chapter 24, but for now, we just want to give you an overview of how we value properties. We decide whether properties can work for us, based on the NOI, not what the owners are asking, what the real estate agents say they're worth, or the sales price of other nearby properties.

Warning! You must finish reading this book before starting to look for properties, in order to avoid becoming discouraged. If you start after only reading this far, you will probably check out a few properties and think to yourself, "This won't work in my town. Rental incomes here won't even cover the mortgage payments, let alone all these other expenses." Or, you may ask a real estate agent to help you find properties only to be told, "If I could find properties that would show a positive cash flow after all those expenses are deducted, I'd buy them all myself."

Stay with us until the end of the book. We know that you can't pay retail for properties and make this work. We're going to show you how to find buyers who will sell well below retail. We're going to show you how to negotiate with the sellers to get better deals than you can imagine. But, most importantly we're going to show you how to structure financing to create wholesale values even at retail prices.

SECTION 2

Learning Your Real Estate Market

Knowledge is power, goes the old slogan. Nowhere is that more true than in real estate investing. In this section, we're going to show you how to learn your marketplace thoroughly. Later we'll show you how to develop a farm. That's an area of homes in which you invest, where you know the properties and the people who live there. You'll cultivate this farm just as a farmer prepares the land, plants the seeds, and reaps harvests.

In this section, we'll show you how to develop relationships with property managers who will teach you about real estate in your area. Property managers can give you excellent information on how much rent houses in your farm will bring and the kind of tenants you can expect them to attract.

In Chapter 7, we'll teach you the threshold theory, which says that the more properties you inspect, and the more offers you make, the better your purchases will be.

Then we'll teach you the importance of sticking with what we call "bread and butter" properties. The rental properties you'll acquire may not be the kind of houses in which you want to live, so they probably aren't going to be in your neighborhood. However, within 10 miles of where you live you'll find many neighborhoods of homes where good people live who will probably always be renters. We'll show you that there's a gold mine waiting for you and teach you the importance of focusing your efforts in these bread and butter neighborhoods.

In Chapter 9, we'll show you how to select the area for your farm and give you techniques you'll need to get to know the properties and the people who live there. We'll teach you that good buys don't always have to come from desperate people. A great buy for you may also be a perfect solution for the sellers. The better you know your farm, the better you know the people who live there and the better they know you, the greater advantage you will have over other investors.

Then in Chapter 10, we'll teach you not to let asking prices discourage you. We know it's practically impossible to generate cash flow when you pay full price and use conventional financing. Before we're through, we're going to show you how to get the best buys, how to negotiate with sellers for even better deals, and how to structure purchases that will meet the Weekend Millionaire's goal of generating cash flow in the first year.

6

Finding a Property Manager

As we have stressed all along, the best way to start your real estate investing career is by building a portfolio of single-family properties that you plan to keep long term. Many other investors would give you that advice too.

A big difference in the Weekend Millionaire program is that from your first property, we want you to get established with a good property manager whom you can trust to handle the day-to-day activities involved with renting and managing properties. In addition to managing your properties, this person (or persons) will become a valuable resource you can use when evaluating new properties for purchase.

Don't Let Other Investors Talk You out of This. Let us explain that this will be controversial. When you talk to other real estate investors, they'll tell you that you're crazy to hire someone to manage one or two properties when you can do it yourself. Remember, we're assuming that you have a "real job" and are only spending a few hours each weekend building your real estate portfolio. We want you to spend those hours on what is the highest and best use of your time, and that is looking for properties that you can buy wholesale. If you're spending your time mowing lawns, showing property, and painting bathrooms, you will very quickly decide that the effort is more than you can handle. And more importantly, if you're spending all your spare time on real estate management, you're going to lose the enthusiastic support of your family, which is critical to your success.

Find a Firm That Specializes in Property Management. When selecting a property manager, you will want to make every possible effort to find a firm that specializes in managing residential properties. A good place to start your search is with your local telephone directory. Turn to the yellow pages and look under Real Estate. You will find a subsection for Management, under which you will find listings for the firms in your area that manage property. Although many companies will be listed in this section, not all of them specialize exclusively in residential property management. Some will be real estate brokers whose primary interest is in sales, but who might manage a few properties on the side. Others will deal only with commercial property. A few simple questions can help you narrow the list to those you will want to interview.

The first question you will want to ask is, "Are you, or do you have a division, exclusively engaged in property management or do you primarily list and sell properties?" If the firm is not exclusively engaged in management, or if it does not have a division that specializes in property management, place it on a list to call back later if you can't find a full-time management firm.

Find a Firm That Specializes in Local Residential Properties. If the firm does have full-time management capability, the next question you will want to ask is, "Do you deal primarily with residential or commercial properties?" If its primary focus is on commercial properties, and you are planning to invest in single-family homes, the firm probably won't be any more interested in you than you are in it. As you narrow down the list to the full-time residential management firms, you will want to ask, "In what geographic area(s) of the market are most of the properties you manage located?" This information will be helpful in further narrowing the list down to those firms that handle properties in the area(s) where you want to start investing. The more your management company knows about the market where you will be investing, the more important a resource it will become.

Meet to Confirm Compatibility. Once you have narrowed the list through telephone contacts, you will want to set up appointments to meet face to face with the people on your short list. The first thing you will want to learn from these meetings is whether you are compatible with them. If you don't like their attitude or personality or if you simply don't get a good feeling from the meeting, you probably aren't going to be happy working with them. If you are comfortable after your initial discussions, find out what services they offer. Determine how they advertise vacancies, how they show properties, how they screen tenants, what procedures they follow in collecting past-due rents, how they supervise evictions when required, how they control maintenance costs, how they deal with after-hours emergencies, what type of accounting they provide owners, and what their fee structure is. You can usually find management companies that provide all these services for a fee of 6 to 12 percent of the rents collected. This varies depending on the area in which you are located, the number of properties being managed, and maybe how well you negotiate.

Read the Agreement Carefully. One important item you will want to discuss is the type of agreement the management company wants you to sign. Be cautious about this, because many management agreements are very one-sided—and it's not your side. You should always ask to insert a clause that gives you the right to cancel the agreement with a 30- to 60-day written notice for any reason and to cancel it immediately, without advance notice, if any of the representations in the agreement are breached. This protects you in the event the management company does not perform up to expectations. A clause like this should not be a problem if you are dealing with a reputable firm.

Is the Property Manager Company Licensed? You should also find out if the firm is licensed. Many states require property managers to be licensed. You will want to know if the owner's funds are handled through an escrow account or whether they are commingled with those of the management firm. It's never good business, and in some states it's illegal, to commingle funds. Also, find out the type and amount of liability insurance the firm carries to protect you from lawsuits arising out of their actions or inactions.

Will They Work with You on New Purchases? Finally, you will want to find out if the property managers will be willing to look at potential new purchases with you. Have the understanding that you will allow them to manage the properties if you buy them. This is helpful because it allows you to obtain professional advice, from people who know the market. They can give you an estimate of what rent a property can generate, and you can usually rely on this figure being realistic or maybe even conservative. Managers don't like to tell you they can get a certain rent for a property and then look foolish if they can't. This input will be very useful as you formulate offers for properties. Professional property managers are excellent resources, both when you are learning the market and even later when you become a seasoned investor.

Building a solid relationship with one or more property managers is one of the best things you can do when you start investing in real estate. Unfortunately, many markets do not have a large number of choices when it comes to property management companies. In smaller markets, there may not even be one full-time management firm. In these situations, you will probably have no choice but to work with a full-service real estate firm where management is not its primary function. If this is the case, you will still want to discuss the items previously mentioned and attempt to reach an agreement about what each party expects of the other. Who knows, you may acquire enough rental properties that it will cause the firm to develop full-time management capability.

You may think the concerns discussed in this chapter will make it impossible or at least difficult to find a good management firm, but we assure you that reputable firms expect this kind of scrutiny. Just remember, it's always better to deal with these issues before they become a problem rather than afterward. We recommend that you use professional management because it takes the worry of day-to-day problems off your shoulders. Moreover, it allows you to concentrate on acquiring properties, a much more profitable activity. However, possibly the biggest advantage is that it places a buffer between you and your tenants—a buffer that can eliminate many of the problems that turn people off to real estate investing.

7

The Threshold Theory

The threshold theory is very simple, but understanding it can make a huge difference to your success as a real estate investor.

When Roger was a young human resources director at a department store, he studied the theory, which his company used to improve the quality of the people it hired. The theory states: The more people who walk across your threshold to apply for a job, the better quality the hires will be. Therefore, instead of advertising for applicants only when there were vacancies, the human resources director was always recruiting. He maintained a large pool of qualified applicants to choose from when an opening occurred.

Roger's daughter Julia graduated from the University of Southern California (USC) in Los Angeles. You can get into USC with only a 3.4 grade point average in high school. Across town at its archrival, the University of California, Los Angeles (UCLA), it takes a 4.0 grade point average to be considered for admission. Why is UCLA able to attract better students than USC? It's simple! Far more students apply at UCLA. USC is a private university. Four years there costs over $100,000. That high price severely limits the number of students who can afford to apply. UCLA is a state university with much lower tuition costs. As a result, far more students apply, and it has more people crossing its threshold.

How Does This Apply to Real Estate Investing? The more front doors you walk through, the more thresholds you cross, the better your chances of making quality real estate buys. If you look at 100 properties before making your first purchase, we can almost guarantee that it will be a good buy. If you only inspect 30 properties, your chances of getting a good buy are considerably smaller. It's a numbers game.

We would much rather you took six months to buy your first property than have you settle for a lesser deal just because you got impatient. That means you may wear out a pair of shoes and put a lot of gas in your tank before you buy your first property. Becoming a Weekend Millionaire takes patience and a great deal of perseverance. Don't forget, we told you in the beginning, this is not a get-rich-quick scheme.

As you'll see when we get into specifics about what to do each weekend, we will want you to look at a lot of properties just to get a feel for your market and for what's available. Then we will ask you to make many offers that may not be accepted. We want you to learn to handle rejected offers. When you take it slowly, you cross many thresholds, make many offers, and find a few excellent buys. It only takes one per year to make you a Weekend Millionaire!

8

Stick with Bread and Butter Properties

As you begin your real estate investing career, we urge you to stick with bread and butter properties. By that, we mean single-family homes that fall in the middle range of rents for your market. They are typically two to four bedrooms, with one to two baths and vary in size from 800 to 1400 square feet in size. They are often located in subdivisions containing a number of similar homes. These attract first-time homebuyers and are by far the best rental properties for new investors to purchase.

Most Rentable of Investment Properties. Bread and butter properties are by far the most rentable of all the properties you will consider. The market for multifamily and commercial properties is primarily with investors. Single-family, starter homes are attractive to everyone from the first-time homebuyer to sophisticated investors. The marketability of these homes gives them appeal to beginning investors, so this also makes finding wholesale deals on them more difficult. That's why we stressed the importance of the threshold theory in Chapter 7. The percentage of wholesale purchases you make compared to the number of offers you make will be very small. You may feel that you expend a lot of effort with minimal results, but when you buy properties, the way we teach you, what you purchase will make good, safe investments.

Beware of Good Deals on Expensive Properties. You will find that properties in the very high and very low ends of the market are easier to buy, but are much riskier investments. Homes priced in the upper 30 percent of your market price range are not as marketable because there simply aren't that many people who can afford them. Deals are always available in the upper end of the market from people who bought thinking they could afford it, only to find out they couldn't. When maintenance and utility bills start rolling in on these larger properties, people who didn't plan properly and who acquired a larger mortgage payment, find themselves in financial trouble. Often these people are willing to sacrifice their equity in order to salvage their credit.

To a new investor, a bargain price on an expensive home seems too good to be true. That's because they are only thinking about the discounted price. The problem is that the rental market for these homes is extremely small. If the midrange of rents in a market is between $500 and $900 per month, a house that you would need to rent for $1,500 to $3,000 per month may sit vacant for months before you can find a new tenant. Although management, maintenance, taxes, insurance, and other expenses may increase in somewhat the same proportion as the cost to purchase, the vacancy factor you need to consider when computing NOI may be several times what it is for bread and butter properties. Be very cautious as you approach the upper end of your market.

Beware of Good Deals on Inexpensive Properties. Like expensive properties, ones in the lower price range of a market can also be risky investments. We're not talking about bread and butter properties that you can buy cheaply due to lack of maintenance by previous owners. These make excellent properties to fix up and turn into mid-priced rentals. What we're talking about are properties that rent in the bottom 30 percent of the market price range. Even after you've spent money to improve them, they will still only rent in the low end of the market. Some people refer to these as "slumlord properties." They tend to be located where surrounding conditions make it difficult, if not impossible, to attract higher rents and better-quality tenants. It may be in a neighborhood where surrounding properties have deteriorated; or road, railroad, or industrial noise is a problem; or in a high crime area. These factors make the property undesirable regardless of condition. Our advice: If you don't feel comfortable walking in the neighborhood and talking to the people who live there, don't invest.

Because of these conditions, rents are low, which often attracts tenants who are struggling financially. It is difficult to raise rents, collections are often a problem, and maintenance costs tend to be high. As with expensive homes, there are what appear to be great deals on these low-end properties. The deals are often good because no one wants the properties, including the person who currently owns them. Our advice: Avoid properties with undesirable surroundings. Instead, buy undesirable properties with superior surroundings.

Value and Liquidity. Two things that make an investment attractive are solid value and liquidity. Everyone understands the value of single-family homes. Out of all types of real estate, these are unquestionably best understood and the easiest to finance. No one questions their value as investments. What some investors do question about real estate is its liquidity, or ability to convert the investment to cash. Granted, real estate is not like a savings account, but if an emergency did arise and you had to sell something, single-family homes have the biggest potential market and sell the most quickly.

By sticking to bread and butter properties, and keeping them well maintained, you will appeal to the midrange of the rental market. These are primarily working-class people, many with families, who for one reason or another have not been able to buy a home or are saving to buy one. They make excellent tenants and tend to take good care of the properties. For beginning investors, properties with fewer problems are the way to start, even though they are harder to find. Wait until you gain experience and build some equity before branching out into riskier areas.

9

Learn Your Market

earning your market is one of the most important things you will have
to do to become a Weekend Millionaire. In Section 7, Getting Started,
you will find that your assignment for the first weekend is to start learning
your market. You may want to equate this to the early pioneers sending out
a scout to survey what lies ahead. We suggest that you begin by scouting the
area within a 10-mile radius of where you live. Before branching out from
this target area, you should locate every neighborhood of bread and butter
homes in the area and get to know the people living in them. These people
will become your eyes and ears in the communities. You're probably thinking, "How do I do that?" Well, that's what we plan to teach you in this chapter.

Ride. That's right: You start by riding. Just get in your car and ride. The
area within 10 miles of where you live encompasses over 300 square
miles—more than 200,000 acres. Hard to believe, isn't it? Unless you live
in the middle of a wilderness, there could be dozens of bread and butter

neighborhoods within this area. If you live in or near a metropolitan area, there could be hundreds of these neighborhoods. Your task is to get out and find them. The more you pursue this ongoing process, the more successful you will become as a real estate investor.

Map Your Area. Find a map that covers the territory you plan to ride. This could be a city map, a county map, or any other map that covers the area. The more detailed the map, the better. When you locate neighborhoods with bread and butter properties, mark them on the map. Continue this process until you have successfully marked all these type of neighborhoods that lie within your area. Now, find a place where you can display the map. Hang it on a wall, put it under a glass on your desktop, or place it wherever you can easily refer to it. You will use it to help you schedule regular and efficient visits to your target neighborhoods. By referring to this map, you can set up concise rides that maximize the area you visit with a minimum of wasted travel time.

View Your Target Area as a Big Farm. You should treat the area on your map as a big farm and see yourself as a farmer. Each neighborhood of bread and butter properties is like a field to harvest; only you aren't the only one harvesting it. Other investors are looking for deals as well. Every week, new houses go on the market, other houses sell, and somewhere on the farm a deal ripens and becomes ready to pick. The better you know the area and the better people in the area know you, the greater your chances of harvesting deals when they ripen.

How Does a Deal Ripen? As unfortunate as it may be, people are constantly losing jobs, being involved in accidents, suffering illnesses, getting divorced, dying, or suffering a myriad of other events that put them in a position where they need to sell their home or rental properties quickly. Often, these events occur suddenly and without warning creating crises that only quick action can resolve. When people throughout the area know you and know what you do, you will start receiving calls about these deals rather than having to stumble upon them.

Please don't think that we advocate preying on helpless, down-and-out people. Yes, some of the best deals come from other people's misfortunes, but you need to view it from a different perspective. When people are in trouble, they are very vulnerable. Sometimes they are so desperate that you could literally steal their property, but we urge you to be fair. Let them know that as an investor, you intend to hold the property for rental if you can reach an agreement with them. Don't be ashamed of what you do. Empathize with their problems, and let them know that you understand if they had time to find a buyer that wanted to live in their house, they could probably get more for it than you can pay. Then make them a fair wholesale offer. Don't be greedy! Don't make them feel even worse by trying to squeeze them for their last dollar. If you can find a combination of price and terms that allows you to buy the property with its current NOI and solve the seller's problem, you have a win-win situation that will make you money.

Deals Don't Always Have to Be with Desperate People. Mike once helped a young couple dispose of their first investment property even before the first payment came due. Within days of closing on the purchase, the husband's company offered him a big promotion requiring a transfer to a city 500 miles away. They wanted to sell the investment property before leaving the area so they wouldn't have to worry about it. The promotion was worth so much that they were willing to take a loss, if necessary, to get rid of the property. They were discussing their problem with a nearby neighbor who knew Mike and knew that he bought investment properties. The neighbor gave the couple Mike's phone number, and the rest is history. He purchased the property and got a great deal. The couple lost very little money, which made them happy; and this all happened because Mike had farmed the neighborhood, met people, and made them aware of his interest in investing in their neighborhood.

Talk with People. When you are riding your neighborhood, try to meet as many people as possible. Whenever the opportunity presents itself, stop and talk with them when they are working in their yards, walking their dogs, getting their newspaper, or doing any other activity that makes them accessible for a few minutes of conversation. Simply letting them know you are interested in buying in their neighborhood is usually all that is necessary to open a very informative dialogue. They will want to learn more about you and in the process may reveal valuable information on their community during the discussion. There may be water, sewer, drainage, or other problems in the area that are not readily apparent. Oftentimes, neighbors learn about developing situations that produce flexible sellers long before the properties go on the market for sale. This is worthwhile information that may help you avoid problems or discover great deals.

Pass out Your Business Cards. Business cards are very important to real estate investors. They are "leave behinds" that many people will put in their wallet or purse or store away in their home, just in case they ever have a need. The cards don't need to be elaborate or expensive, but they do need to let people know what you do. Mike's business cards identify him as a "real estate investor" with a line underneath that reads, "I buy houses, apartments, other income properties." This information together with his address, telephone, and fax numbers give all the information needed to identify who he is, what he does, and how to get in touch with him. You can purchase professionally printed business cards for just a few dollars per thousand or make your own using a computer and blank business card paper available from any office supply store.

You should have business cards printed as soon as possible. Pass them out to everyone you meet. Don't be bashful! You are a real estate investor from the time you decide to be, even if you have yet to purchase your first investment property. Many investors look for a long time before they make their first purchase. What's important is getting your cards in the hands of as many people as possible. You can't predict when a situation will arise that causes a seller to become flexible. You can't predict who may know a flexible seller and might recommend you. In the introduction to Section 3 and in Chapter 11, you will learn how a business card that changed hands at a casual meeting made Mike over $42,000. By getting cards in the hands of people living in the neighborhoods you are farming, you dramatically improve your chances of making purchases there.

Summary. The suggestions in this chapter will get you started learning your market. By using your imagination, you will discover numerous other ways to uncover unique characteristics of neighborhoods within your target area and get to know the people who live in them. You will continue this ongoing process throughout your real estate investing career. The better you know your neighborhoods and the better the people within them know you, the more successful you will become.

10

Don't Be Discouraged by Asking Prices

Don't equate *asking prices* with *selling prices*. Smart sellers will always ask for more than they expect to get in order to give themselves room to negotiate. In all markets, there is a difference between average asking prices and average selling prices. This difference is small in some markets and quite significant in others. Local boards of Realtors maintain statistics on selling prices as a percentage of listing prices. This difference may range anywhere from 2 to 20 percent. You can spend a lot of time researching statistics, or you can take our word for the fact that this difference means very little to the investor.

Don't Be Swayed by Appraised Values. Appraisals are calculated estimates of market values assuming that sufficient marketing is conducted and reasonable time is allowed to find a buyer. Appraisals, especially ones involving single-family homes, establish retail values and are necessary when obtaining conventional financing from banks, but they have little to do with the investment value of properties. Appraised values often give new investors a false sense of accomplishment. We once had a very excited buyer approach us with the closing papers and appraisal of a house he had just purchased. He was so excited because the house appraised for $87,600 and he had purchased it for $85,000—$2,700 less that the appraised value. Upon further questioning, we learned that he put $20,000 cash down and financed $65,000 for 15 years at 7.5 percent interest. He was excited because the house was renting for $795 per month and his payment was only $602.56 per month. In his mind, he had a positive cash flow of nearly $200 per month and attributed this to having bought the property below the appraised value.

His enthusiasm waned when we pointed out that he would have to pay taxes and insurance from this $200, plus maintenance and management, and the amount left after paying these items, if any, would be his return on the $20,000 he paid down at closing. He made the mistake many new investors make by focusing on appraised value rather than cash flow. Fortunately, he had the cash reserves to support the property, because it was several years before it showed a positive cash flow.

Stick to Your Determination of Property Values. In Chapter 5, you learned the Weekend Millionaire method of valuing single-family properties. By using this method, you arrive at wholesale values instead of market values. Real estate investing is a business, and to be successful, you have to make a profit. If you pay market value for properties and then rent them for market value, there is rarely any profit. As you will learn in Chapter 17, you make your profit when you buy, which means buying wholesale. This takes patience, because as we keep stressing, it takes many wholesale offers to make a few wholesale purchases. You must stick with your determination of value and not be influenced by market value appraisals. It's not how many properties you own, its how many you own that make money that turns you into a Weekend Millionaire.

Don't Let Seller Dissatisfaction Deter You from Making Offers. Wholesale offers offend some sellers! This is understandable, because most sellers base their asking prices on appraisals or optimistic estimates of value by real estate agents. In addition, if you're talking about their home, they will attach sentimental values that mean something to them, but have no value to an investor. They are much less flexible immediately after listing their properties than after months of little or no activity, but that's no reason to avoid making offers early on. We have had offers summarily rejected, without so much as a counter; only to receive a call months later to see if an offer is still open. An example of this is an offer that Mike once made for a group of properties in the month of May. The seller rejected his offer of $525,000 in favor of another one that was $60,000 higher. In September of that same year, he received a call asking if his offer was still good. The people making the higher offer had been unable to obtain financing. Since he had lost the summer months, which he planned to use refurbishing the properties, Mike reduced his offer to $510,000. Although it was $15,000 less, this offer was accepted, and the transaction closed in October. The most telling part of this transaction was not the fact that he got a lower price by waiting four months; it was the fact that the listing or asking price for the properties at the time of his first offer was $750,000.

Big Gaps Often Exist between Asking Price and Selling Price. As the example above illustrates, the gap between what sellers ask and what they may accept can be quite large. The difference of $240,000 between asking and selling price represents a 32 percent reduction from the asking price. The sellers based the asking price on a recommendation from the real estate broker who listed the properties. Mike based his offer by using NOI to calculate the value. When marketing and time produced no activity near the asking price and the one buyer with an offer higher than his was unable to obtain financing, the sellers decided to accept Mike's offer.

Because he calculated his value using the Weekend Millionaire method and ignored the asking price, Mike bought the group of properties at wholesale. If he had been too intimidated to make the original offer that was substantially below the asking price or had been influenced by the higher price offered by the other investors, he would have either missed the deal altogether or paid a much higher price. Because of his original offer, he put himself in the running to buy the properties. As for the higher offer, we can't say for sure, but we suspect that lenders felt the NOI from the properties would not support the financing request made by the other investors; thereby allowing Mike to actually negotiate a lower price.

New investors need to develop this kind of discipline as quickly as possible. The itch to make that first purchase often produces impulsive decisions similar to the one described in the beginning of this chapter. Patience and persistence are the rule. Forget about asking prices, forget about appraised values, calculate the value of properties using the Weekend Millionaire method and keep making offers. Mike was only interested in buying the above group of properties if the numbers worked. If he had missed this deal, he would simply have gone on making offers and purchasing only the properties that met his criteria.

SECTION 3

How to Find the Ideal Seller

So, you want to be a Weekend Millionaire, but you don't have a clue how to start? You've read and studied every book and tape you can get your hands on, but you still don't know how to move from exploring the potential of real estate investing to becoming a real estate investor.

Don't feel alone. The first investment property you buy is always the most challenging. It gets a whole lot easier after you have the first one under your belt. We've heard that from so many of our investors that we want to give you something simple you can do to get started.

Buy some business cards. The simple act of putting your name on a business card that says you are a real estate investor can give you the encouragement you need to begin. You have to see yourself as a real estate investor before you can become one. When you begin passing out cards that identify you as such, you will gradually feel more and more like an investor.

As other people begin thinking of you as an investor, opportunities start coming your way. We didn't realize this when we first started. If we had, we would own much more property than we do today. Mike didn't realize just how important it was until he finally had some cards printed. At the time, he was already an investor, not just thinking about becoming one. The problem was that no one else knew about it.

So, get yourself some business cards. It's a great way to start. Business cards are cheap. You can find several printing companies on the Internet that do a nice job and only cost around $50 for 1,000 cards. That's nothing when you consider what they can be worth. Many local print shops can do the job as well. Business cards are to a Weekend Millionaire what seed is to a farmer. The more you scatter, the more opportunities that sprout. Mike had a situation in which one of his business cards resulted in him making a $42,000 profit. Sound impossible? Well, it's not, as you'll learn from the story in Chapter 11, where we talk about people selling because they have moved out of town. We can't guarantee that you'll make $42,000 from a single card like Mike did, but we strongly believe that by handing them out regularly, at least some will result in you buying properties. The problem is, we don't know which ones, and neither will you. What you have to do is get some cards and keep handing them out.

In this section, we're going to tell you a few stories about some of the reasons why people sell at prices and terms that make good wholesale purchases. There's no way to cover them all, because there are as many different situations as there are people and properties. We want these stories to stimulate your creative juices and get you thinking about new and innovative ways to buy rather than making excuses why you can't.

These chapters describe problems involving real estate that are typical of situations you will encounter as an investor. From them you will learn techniques used to make wholesale purchases and solve other people's problems. Some of these stories involve situations that are painful and may appear to be taking advantage of people. Keep in mind as you read them that one person's loss is another person's gain only when measured financially. If taking a loss results in emotional stability or peace of mind, is it really a loss?

The chapters in this section will show you some ways to enjoy financial gain by helping sellers with unique needs solve their dilemmas.

11

The Seller
Has Moved

In the preface to this section, we stressed the importance of printing business cards that identify you as a real estate investor. It's a great way of letting people know that you buy houses. The following story will help you understand why Mike refers to his card as a "$42,000 business card."

One election night several years ago, he was sitting in the lounge of a local restaurant watching the voting returns come in. He was at a table with several people discussing politics and speculating on who would win the election, when a young woman sitting next to him asked where he worked. He told her he was a real estate investor.

"Oh! I have a house I may want to sell. Do you have a card?" she asked.

This was an interesting coincidence, because just the week before he had gotten cards printed that identified him as a real estate investor. He reached into his pocket, took out several cards, and gave one to each person at the table. The cards contained his address and phone number, as business cards usually do, but his card was unique in its overall appearance. The background was a bright green with all the lettering in white. It had a color picture of him on the left side, and it read, "Mike Summey, Real Estate Investor." Under his name was the statement, "I buy houses, apartments, other income properties."

When he passed out the cards, everyone commented on how different they looked. Most of the people at the table said they didn't realize he was involved in real estate, but most importantly, they all put the card in their wallets or purses. The conversation returned to politics, and Mike didn't think any more about it.

Nearly two years later, he received a phone call. "This is Kathy," the voice on the other end began. "Do you remember me? I met you at the election night party a couple of years ago, and you gave me one of your cards. You told me to call if I ever decided to sell my house."

Before he could say anything, she added, "I got married last spring and moved to Florida, but I still own the house in North Carolina. My best friend wanted to rent the house, so I agreed to let her stay in it if she would make the payments and look after the place."

Mike could hear the disappointment in her voice. He asked, "What happened, did she not make the payments?"

With that, Kathy started to sob. "No, she didn't make them. She didn't even make the first one. My husband and I thought they were being made until today when we received a registered letter from the mortgage company, giving us until the end of the month to pay over $2,000 in back payments or they are going to foreclose on the house." She continued, "We don't have the money, and we don't know what to do. While we were discussing how we could come up with the money, I remembered putting your card in my wallet. I found it, and that's why I'm calling. If you're still interested, we'd like to talk about selling you the house."

It was obvious that she was upset, so Mike gently asked her to describe the situation.

"I inherited the house from my mother when she died," she began. "I lived there for six years until I got married and moved to Florida," She continued. "I wanted to keep the place since it had been my mom's, but after this has happened, my husband and I agree it would be in our best interest to sell it."

"Is there any way you can arrange for me to look at the house?" Mike asked. "If I can get in and inspect it, I'll be happy to make you an offer."

"My girlfriend is still living in the house," Kathy responded. "I'll call her and arrange for her to let you look at it. It may take me a little while to reach her, so I'll have to call you back."

"That's fine, just let me know when you get it set up."

About an hour later, the phone rang.

"Hi! It's Kathy, I just got hold of Mary, and she said you could come by tomorrow afternoon at two and inspect the house."

Mike got the property address and directions from Kathy and made plans to be at the house at the appointed time the next day, which was Friday. When he arrived, there was a car parked in the driveway and music and voices were coming from inside the house. He walked up to the front door and rang the doorbell. No one answered the door, so he rang again. After ringing the bell several more times, continuing to hear music and voices from inside, no one responded.

Mike returned to his office and called Kathy.

She answered on the second ring.

"Hello!"

"Hi, Kathy, this is Mike."

"Oh! Hi! How'd you like the house?" she interrupted.

"Well, I didn't exactly get to look at it."

"What? Was Mary not there like she was supposed to be?"

"I don't know," Mike responded. "Someone was there because I could hear them talking inside, but they wouldn't answer the door. I never got to see the inside."

"I'm so sorry," Kathy said. "I can't believe this. Let me see if I can get ahold of her and call you back."

It wasn't 30 minutes before she called back.

"I'm so mad I could just scream," she sobbed. "I'm really sorry you had to make a trip to the house for nothing, but I've got a bigger problem than I thought. I'll explain later. My husband and I are leaving within an hour to drive up there. It will take us all night, but if we call you when we arrive, do you think you can meet us sometime in the morning?"

Mike didn't press her for details, but it was clear the problem was more serious than she had first thought.

"That'll be fine," he said. "I'll be here all day, so just give me a call when you get in. Oh, by the way, I liked the looks of the house from the outside; if it's as nice inside, I'd like to try to buy it from you," he added.

"Thanks," she said. "We'll give you a call when we get there."

It was just before 10:00 Saturday morning when she called.

"Hi! We just got into town and are on our way to the house," Kathy said. "When would be convenient for you to meet us there?"

"I've been waiting for your call," he responded. "I can leave within 30 minutes and be there within an hour. Will that work?"

"That will be great," she replied. "We'll be at the house waiting."

When he pulled into the drive, Kathy was at the door. Her eyes were red and her face was puffy. She had obviously been crying. When he stepped through the door, Mike could understand why. The place looked like a pigsty. The stove and refrigerator were filthy. Dirty dishes were all over the kitchen and dining area. The floors looked as if they hadn't been swept in months. Trash was everywhere. Mary, who wasn't there at the time, had not only failed to make the payments, but had done nothing to take care of the property either.

"I'm so sorry," she cried. "I'm an excellent housekeeper, and I can't believe my house is such a mess."

"Don't worry," Mike said, trying to comfort her. "I've looked at houses in much worse shape than this one."

"It's just such a mess," she continued. "I'll understand if you don't want to look at it."

"Quite the contrary, aside from the mess, it seems to be a very nice house. Would you like to show me around and let me make a few notes?"

Kathy led him through the house. It had three bedrooms, two baths, a large den, and a fireplace. It was air conditioned and situated on a nice corner lot. The carpet needed replacing, the interior was in need of paint, and the place was filthy, but other than that, the house was in remarkably good structural condition.

After his inspection of the house, Mike, Kathy, and her husband John sat down at the kitchen table to talk. She began the discussion by telling about the situation Mary had placed her in and the terrible predicament it had caused. Mike just listened as Kathy described her marriage, her move to Florida, and the chain of events that led to her leaving Mary to care for the house. It took quite a while for her to calm down and dry her eyes, but once she did, she wanted to talk about the house. She explained that the mortgage was several months past due. She said the late notices had been coming to the house address and had not been forwarded to her, which was the reason she did not know about the past-due situation until it became critical. Apparently, someone from the mortgage company had stopped by the house and gotten her new address from Mary, which is how the registered letter found her. She explained that the mortgage company was going to start foreclosure proceedings by the end of the month if they didn't bring the mortgage current and that they didn't have the money.

"Mike, John and I talked about the situation all the way from Florida," Kathy said. "As much as I hate to get rid of the house, we both agreed that it would be better to sell it and not have to worry about things like this."

"Well, do you have a price in mind you want for the house?" Mike asked.

"We talked about that too," she said. "We owe about $22,000, including the past-due payments. We decided if we can get $20,000 for our equity and close by the end of the month we would be happy."

"You realize the house is worth more than that, don't you?" Mike asked.

"Yes, we know, but we don't have time to fix it up and wait to find a buyer. We know its worth more, but we felt like if we offered you a good deal, and you took it, it would also be good for us because it would get us out of this jam."

Mike knew it was a great deal. Just using rough mental calculations, he figured the wholesale value would be at least $60,000. Kathy's offer, including paying off the mortgage was about $42,000. He didn't even need to think about it, yet he still went through the exercise of doing his calculations and appearing to agonize over the decision. *(We'll explain the importance of this later.)*

While he was pondering the decision, Kathy said, "We'll even pay the closing costs if we can make a deal right now."

At that point, Mike let her talk him into buying the house. They sat there at the kitchen table and wrote an offer to purchase for $42,000 cash, contingent upon closing by the end of the month.

Once everyone had signed the contract, Kathy came over, put her arms around Mike's neck, and said, "You don't know how much we appreciate this.

John and I know we can get more money if we put the house on the market, but we just want to get it sold, go back to Florida, and get on with our lives. Thank you! Thank you! Thank you!"

The following Monday, Mike visited one of his banks to arrange a loan. The loan officer said the property would have to be appraised and the bank would be willing to loan 80 percent of the appraisal or 80 percent of the purchase price, whichever was less. The bank engaged a state-certified appraiser, who valued the house at $84,000, exactly double the amount of his contract.

The loan officer looked at the appraisal, then at the contract, and with a big smile said, "This looks great, we can loan you $33,600, which is 80 percent of your contract price."

"Wait a minute." Mike responded, "I want to borrow the entire $42,000. Even that would be only 50 percent of the appraisal."

With a somewhat dejected look, the loan officer said, "I'm sorry, but it's the bank's policy to only loan 80 percent of your cost when it's less than the appraised value."

Mike looked him directly in the eye and said, "Do you mean to tell me, if I had paid $84,000 for the property you would loan me $67,200, but because I made a good deal, you only want to loan half that?"

The bank officer sat there a minute with a puzzled look on his face, and then replied, "It doesn't make much sense, does it? Let me see what I can do."

He took the contract and the appraisal and disappeared down the hall. Within 10 minutes, he was back with a big smile on his face. "I've talked with our underwriter, and he agreed we could loan you up to $50,400 if you would like, which is 60 percent of the appraisal."

"That's great," Mike said, "but all I need is the $42,000 plus a couple more thousand to get it ready to rent."

Mike closed the deal by the end of the month without having to put any cash into the transaction. The bank loan was for 15 years with payments of $450 per month. Within two weeks, he had replaced the carpet, painted the inside, and rented the property for $750 per month.

He had purchased an $84,000 property for half its appraised value and financed the entire amount with a conventional bank loan. However, the point of this story is that it all happened because of a business card he handed to a stranger that election night nearly two years before. Now do you understand why he calls his business card a "$42,000 business card?"

What would have happened if he had not had a card to give Kathy that night? Would she have remembered him the next day, let alone a year later? Would someone else have gotten this super deal? Would the house have gone into foreclosure and been sold on the courthouse steps, which would have ruined Kathy and her husband's credit? The bottom line is that none of these things happened, because Mike gave her that business card.

Now go order your business cards before you read another page of this book!

12

Sellers Have Divorced

The most motivated sellers are often couples that are going through a divorce. Divorce situations are great opportunities for you to solve sellers' financial and emotional problems and still get great deals for yourself.

Mike's purchase of a house several years ago exemplifies the difficulties that can arise out of divorces. This single-family house was on the market because of a bitter divorce settlement. In the settlement, the court ordered the house sold and specified the allocation of the sale proceeds between the parties. Because they couldn't reach an acceptable agreement, the judge apparently got tired of hearing the attorneys wrangle and told them how the matter was going to be resolved.

The settlement stipulated that the wife was to receive half of the sale proceeds. The judge ordered the husband, who got their business, to pay off the small mortgage from his half of the proceeds and to make the monthly payments until the house sold. He also directed them to list the property for sale at $69,000 and ordered them to accept any offer in excess of $66,000 cash. He did give them the option of accepting less than $66,000, but only if they mutually agreed on the offer.

The couple's divorce followed a long and hostile separation that left both of them so bitter that they refused to even speak to each other. Shortly after the divorce was finalized, the woman remarried and moved in with her new husband, who was financially secure. A few months after her marriage, the business the ex-husband received from the settlement, failed. This forced him to accept employment that paid substantially less than what he had been accustomed to and created a situation that made a sale of the property nearly impossible because of the hostilities between him and his ex-wife. The ex-wife would not agree to any reasonable offer becasue she wanted to punish him by forcing him to make the payments on a much reduced income.

The man was suffering financially and was willing to accept almost any offer that would relieve him of the burden of making the payments. He was at the point where he felt like the mouse who said, "To heck with the cheese, just let me out of this trap."

The woman, on the other hand, was comfortable in her new marriage and financially secure. She was still angry with her ex-husband and was happy to see him struggling. She viewed each month the property remained unsold as another month of punishment. She adamantly refused to consider any offer less than the $66,000 cash that the judge had ordered them to accept.

It was two and a half years after the divorce when Mike learned of the situation. By that time, there had been over 20 offers made to purchase the house, but none of them had met the $66,000 cash requirement that would have mandated a sale. When Mike analyzed the property, he estimated its wholesale value at no more than $51,000.

When he learned of the situation, Mike assumed the man might be having financial problems and would be negotiable on the price. He also assumed that the woman, who had since remarried, needed to bring closure to the bitterness of her former marriage, but may want to feel as if she had won in the process. Finding a solution to meet the needs of both would not be easy and would definitely require creative thinking to solve.

Mike began by researching the public records at the county courthouse.

He obtained a copy of the divorce settlement, which confirmed the information he had been given. He also found that within the prior three months, creditors had recorded four judgments against the man and there were two additional cases pending against him in small-claims court. The only thing that he found involving the woman was the divorce proceedings.

He continued his research by going back to the subdivision where the house was located and visiting some of the nearby neighbors. He got an earful of the problems the couple had experienced when they lived there. One elderly neighbor, who turned out to be like a second mother to the woman, told Mike that they talked on a regular basis. When he mentioned that he was interested in purchasing the house and was trying to find out more about the neighborhood, she said she hoped he would buy it because it represented too many bad memories for her friend. She told him that her friend's new husband was also concerned because he was afraid the house would eventually become a source of friction in their marriage if it didn't sell soon.

When he asked why the house had not sold, the neighbor said that she felt that the price set by the court in the divorce settlement was too high. She also volunteered that due to the many hostilities still existing between her friend and the ex-husband, she didn't know if they would ever agree to a lower price. Mike asked if she thought there was a possibility of any owner financing if he could offer them the full asking price. She said she didn't think so, because although her friend would have no problem with it, she knew the ex-husband had already turned down several offers involving owner financing because he needed cash to pay off the existing mortgage.

Mike spent over an hour talking with this woman, discussing everything from gardening to property values in the neighborhood. He mainly just listened, but when he did talk, he managed to ask questions that kept her talking. He learned about events that led up to the divorce and discovered why there was such bitterness between them. The neighbor even joked that if he ever got them together he should wear a bulletproof vest. Most importantly though, he confirmed his assumption that the woman needed to sell the property to rid herself of the hatred and resentment it triggered. The house was the last thing tying her to her former husband and the deep negative feelings she still harbored about their relationship.

Sellers Have Divorced

Armed with the information he garnered from this research, Mike now knew that his task was to figure out how to meet the vastly differing needs of the two parties, and do so in a way that would let him buy the property wholesale. He concluded that he would have to deal with each one of them separately if he expected to solve the dilemma. He would have to treat it as two separate transactions, each for a one-half interest in the property, and each containing clauses making a closing contingent upon being able to purchase the other party's half of the property.

Mike arranged a meeting with the woman and her new husband first. He knew, from his discussion with her former neighbor and friend that she would have little interest in negotiating a price lower than the $66,000 mandated by the judge. He opened the discussion by expressing his interest in the house and letting her know that he was aware it had been on the market for over two and a half years. He said he had inspected the house and it seemed to be in reasonably good condition. He asked if there was something wrong with it that had kept it from selling.

He immediately found out what was wrong. She launched into a tirade about her ex-husband, and for the next half-hour, he got an earful of the things the ex-husband had done to destroy their marriage. He could see the bitterness oozing from her as she spoke. Her new husband just sat there with his hand on her shoulder trying to comfort her.

After allowing her to vent her anger, Mike brought the discussion back to his interest in purchasing the house. He asked her new husband how he felt about the situation. He said he would support whatever decision his wife made, but added that he would like to see the house sold so his wife could start focusing on the future and put the past behind her. Mike then turned to the wife, and the following discussion ensued.

"How would you feel about selling me just your half interest in the house and letting me deal with your ex-husband?" he asked.

"Can I do that?" she replied.

"I think so; do you have a figure in mind as to what your half is worth?"

"Well," she began, "The judge ordered us to list the house for $69,000 and said we would have to accept an offer of $66,000 cash. I guess that would make my half worth $33,000."

"I think you know that price is a little high, because no one has offered that much in over two and a half years," Mike responded. "But, if I agreed to pay you that much, would you be willing to let me pay you over time?"

"I don't know," she replied as she looked at her new husband. "What do you think honey?"

"I really don't want to get involved," he said. "But I would like to see you sell the property. If you want to let him pay you over time, I don't see anything wrong with it because we don't need money now."

"How would you want to pay me?" she asked Mike.

He took out his calculator and began to figure. After a few minutes of calculating, he looked up.

"I could pay you the full $33,000 if you would let me pay it at $227.90 per month for 180 months." Mike said. "That's just 3 percent interest, but as an investor that's as much as I can afford and still give you your full asking price."

"If I agreed to do that, what would you do about my ex?" She asked. "I know he can't sell his half that way because he has to pay off the mortgage, which is over $20,000, and he doesn't have that kind of money."

"Well, I considered that in my calculations. Since I'll probably have to pay him cash, I doubt if I can pay him much more than what he owes for his half."

It was obvious that she liked that!

"What I'd like to do is draw up a contract with you for your half and make it contingent upon being able to make a deal with your ex for his half," Mike continued.

"Does that mean I'll have to see him at the closing?" She asked.

"Not at all! If I can make a deal with him, you will not have to be involved in any way. We could close with one of you in the morning; hold that closing in escrow, then close with the other later in the day. You won't have to see him, talk to him, or have anything to do with him."

That seemed to be the decisive factor. She looked at her husband; he looked back and nodded. "Why don't we go ahead and see if he can work something out on the other half," he said.

She agreed.

Mike put the offer in writing, agreeing to secure the purchase money note with a first lien on the property and made the offer contingent upon being able to purchase the other half of the house. With signed contract in hand, he was off to meet with the ex-husband.

That meeting started much the same as the meeting with the ex-wife. He talked about how unreasonable his ex-wife was and how he guessed he would have to continue making payments until he paid the house off because it didn't look like anyone was going to offer the full $66,000. As with the ex-wife, Mike allowed him plenty of time to vent his anger and frustration before leading him into a discussion about the house. He didn't mention that he had already met the ex-wife and signed a contract with her. The discussion went as follows.

"A friend of mine told me about the house," Mike began. "He said it had been on the market for a long time and he couldn't understand why it hadn't sold. I guess what you are telling me now explains it."

"Damned right it does, that '#$*%' is having a field day," he said. "She knows I lost my business and had to go to work for someone else, and she's willing to keep her money tied up just so she can watch me sweat."

"That's too bad. It's a shame the two of you can't come to some agreement and sell the house."

"The problem is she doesn't have to sell! She married a rich guy and doesn't need the money. I'm back living with my parents, because with the house payment, I can't afford to even rent a place."

"Would it help you out if I bought your half interest?" Mike asked. "Maybe I could deal with her better than you have been able to."

"Right now, I'd almost give someone my half to get out from under the mortgage," he replied.

"By the way, how much is the mortgage?"

"It's somewhere between $21,000 and $22,000."

"What if I offered you $24,000 for your half interest and agreed to pay the closing cost?" Mike asked. "That would give you a couple of thousand dollars and get the mortgage off your back."

"Hallelujah! When can we close?" He shouted.

"Well, it's not quite that simple," Mike, responded. "I'm willing to sign a contract to that effect, but I'll have to make it contingent upon being able to reach an agreement to buy her half."

"Go ahead and write it up, but I won't hold my breath," he said.

After they drew up the contract and signed it, Mike headed to his bank to see about getting a loan for the cash he would need to close the deal. He had another property, which had no mortgage that he offered as collateral for the loan. The bank gladly agreed to make him a $25,000 loan on this other property. With his financing secured and both contracts signed, Mike called both parties to let them know they had a deal and scheduled a convenient closing date.

He closed with the woman at 10:00 that morning and with the man at 2:00 that afternoon. The real estate attorney held both closings in escrow until later in the day when Mike closed the bank loan and got the funds needed to complete the transactions. Both deeds were simultaneously recorded along with the deeds of trust securing the purchase money note and the bank loan. Because he was able to successfully identify and creatively fill the needs of both parties, he not only got a wholesale purchase, but also made a nothing-down purchase. It doesn't get any better than that.

"But wait," you say. "You told us that Mike had determined that the wholesale value was $51,000. By paying $33,000 for the ex-wife's half and $24,000 for the ex-husband's half, he actually paid $57,000 instead of $51,000. How could that be a wholesale deal?"

Well, here's how! Remember, how we told you earlier that the combination of price and terms is what determines the value of investment real estate? The going rate of interest at the time was 8.5 percent, which is what Mike had to pay the bank for the money he borrowed. The rate he paid the ex-wife on her $33,000 was 3 percent. (If you compute the present value of her income stream at the going rate of 8.5 percent, it comes to slightly over $23,000, which makes the present value of the total deal just over $47,000.) What he got was a wholesale price for the ex-husband's half and wholesale terms for the ex-wife's half. However, the most important part of this transaction was that the ex-wife was happy, the ex-husband was happy, and Mike was happy. It was truly a win-win-win situation.

By learning about the needs and concerns of the sellers and creatively coming up with solutions, Mike separated himself from the 20 or so other investors who had tried to buy the house. His approach obviously made a positive impact on the sellers, because both of them recommended him to other people. These recommendations resulted in additional wholesale purchases.

Learning the true needs and concerns of sellers enables you to structure wholesale offers where seemingly impossible situations exist. Wholesale purchases frequently arise from unique situations. Properties that have a waiting list of willing and able buyers ready to pay market values are not usually candidates for wholesale purchases.

Learning how to identify and solve problems makes you a more effective and successful investor than those people who rely on what we call the "stumbling technique" used by investors who believe that the only way to make a wholesale purchase is to stumble onto a deal. Weekend Millionaires know that creative problem solving comes from genuinely trying to solve sellers' problems. They also know that by doing this they can find some incredibly good buys.

13

Seller Has High Equity in the Property

Not all wholesale deals involve sellers who are down-and-out, going through divorces, or having other financial problems. Some come from simply using good negotiating skills, which is why we have devoted an entire section to negotiating. The purchase described in this chapter is one such transaction. It involved a nice mountain home owned by sellers who also owned a small farm in a valley not far away. They stayed at the mountain house during the summer and moved down to their valley home for the winter. The sellers owned the house free and clear and were definitely in no financial trouble. They had decided to sell because they were both in their mid-sixties and it was becoming increasingly difficult to navigate steps in the three-level home.

The couple listed the property with a real estate agent who offered it for sale in the Multiple Listing Service at $129,500. The price included a one-year home warranty and a $5,000 allowance to replace the carpet. Not exactly, the kind of situation most investors would consider having wholesale purchase potential. Tucked away in a heavily wooded area, with homes several times its value within a few hundred yards, this property was also not the type that would attract most investors as rental property.

Three things intrigued Mike about the property when a real estate agent friend brought it to his attention. The first was its location in a very desirable area with several more expensive homes nearby; the second was that there was no mortgage on the property; and the third was the fact that it had been on the market for several months and had not sold. He felt that this combination of factors made it worth pursuing.

Although it was a higher-priced rental for the general area, Mike felt that its location and unique features would make it easy to rent. His calculation of projected NOI produced a range between $950 and $970 per month.

He prepared an offer to purchase the house, following the first and most basic negotiating principle, which is, "Ask for more than you expect to get." He offered the asking price of $129,500, with $27,500 cash at closing, but he asked the sellers to carry the balance of $102,000 payable in 120 direct principal reduction payments of $850 per month—no interest. In addition, he asked for all personal property that was in the house including furniture, linens, dishes, and other accessories, and he asked the sellers to pay all closing costs including survey, termite inspection, home inspection, appraisal fee, and title insurance.

Did he expect the offer to be accepted? Of course not! What he did was make an offer that gave him plenty of room to negotiate. When he presented the offer, the real estate agent studied it for a few minutes and then began to chuckle.

"This is the screwiest offer I've ever seen," he said.

"What's wrong with it?" Mike asked.

"Well, to start with, you're asking them to finance the purchase over 10 years with no interest. Plus you're asking for all their furniture and expecting them to pay the closing costs."

"I realize all that," Mike replied. "But, I am offering the listing price and not asking them to replace the carpet. In addition, there's plenty of cash in the deal to pay your commission, all other expenses, and still have cash left over for them. Why don't you just present the offer as written and let them decide what they want to do? If there are parts of it they can't accept, they can always make a counterproposal."

An offer like this will sometimes insult the sellers enough that they won't respond at all. That happens occasionally. Some sellers take it personally and simply refuse to make a counteroffer. You take that chance. However, if the sellers do make a counteroffer, you establish a negotiating range. That's what Mike was trying to do.

In this case, the sellers did counter Mike's offer. They agreed to everything he asked except the no-interest provision of the loan. They wanted 6 percent interest on the purchase money note, which would raise the payment from $850 to $1,132 per month if financed over the 10 years Mike proposed. With NOI calculated at $950 to $970 per month, this would not work. It wouldn't even cover the payment, much less give any return on his $27,500 cash down payment. Not a good deal!

In an effort to determine if it was price or interest rate that most concerned the sellers, Mike presented three counterproposals at the same time. All three offers contained the original $27,500 cash down payment; however, the note amount differed in each one. The first was a $90,000 note bearing interest at 6 percent, the second was a $95,000 note bearing interest at 5 percent, and the third was the original amount of $102,000 bearing interest at 4 percent. The significant change between these counters and his first offer was that these notes were all 15-year notes. The payments ranged from $751 to $759 per month, which was nearly $100 per month less than the $850 payment in the original offer.

The sellers did not respond immediately to these offers. Several days passed before they finally countered with an acceptance of the $102,000 note option, but they changed the interest from 4 to 5 percent. This would raise the monthly payment from $754 to $806, which would still work based on the projected NOI of the property.

Mike decided to make one more counter. He rewrote the offer containing the $102,000 note, but changed the interest rate from 5 to 4.5 percent. A seemingly small change, but it lowered the payment from $806 per month to $780. Doesn't sound like much does it? However, $26 per month for 180 months is $4,680.

This offer was accepted, and Mike bought the house. But let's examine the transaction a little closer. Did he expect to get all the closing costs paid by the sellers? Did he expect to get all the furnishings and other personal property? Did he expect the sellers to finance the purchase over 10 years with no interest? The answer to all these questions is, "Probably not!" Was it a wholesale purchase according to Weekend Millionaire standards? Definitely yes! By subtracting the mortgage payment of $780 from the projected monthly NOI of $950 to $970, it left him with a return of $170 to $190 per month or 7.4 to 8.3 percent per year on his $27,500 down payment."

The closing costs and personal property were what we call throwaway items. Mike had no idea what value the sellers placed on these items, but whether he got them or not weren't deal breakers for him. He asked for them in order to have items he could give up in exchange for more important things in the negotiation. The 10-year loan with no interest was not a deal breaker either. Mike was comfortable with buying property he could finance over 15 years at the current bank financing rate of 8.5 percent. By making the first offer the way he did, Mike gave himself a negotiating range of 5 years and several interest rate percentage points.

Had the sellers placed a high value on the throwaway items in the offer, Mike could have traded all or part of these for a shorter loan or a better interest rate, or maybe both. These items never came up; therefore, the negotiations centered on the purchase money note. As a result, Mike got every one of the extras he asked for in addition to a financing package that produced a wholesale purchase.

This was a successful transaction between unrelated parties, neither of which was experiencing financial or other difficulties. It closed because each side used professional negotiating skills to reach an acceptable agreement. On the day of closing, Mike and the couple selling the house were sitting at the closing table, when a discussion took place that illustrates just how successful the negotiations were.

"I almost hate to see us close this deal," the husband offered.

"Why is that?" Mike responded.

"We knew what you were doing with those offers, and we don't blame you for trying to get a better deal," he said. "We would probably have done the same thing if we were buying."

"Well, you know I'm an investor, and unless I can find a way to make the numbers work, I can't buy a property."

"We realized that," the wife added. "We just enjoyed watching how you adjusted each offer to keep your monthly cash outlay at or below your original offer."

"That's why we decided to sell to you and finance the property," the husband said. "We got a feeling that as much attention as you paid to cash flow, we wouldn't have to worry about getting our money each month."

"We had some other offers asking for owner financing," she added, "but, they didn't seem to care about anything other than us financing the purchase. It almost seemed like they couldn't get a bank to loan them money, so we were a little leery."

"I appreciate the vote of confidence." Mike replied. "But, why didn't you try to get me to pay the closing costs or let you keep your furniture?"

"We didn't care that much about the furniture. We didn't have a place to store it anyway," the husband said. "And furthermore, since you didn't try to beat us down on our asking price, we decided to go ahead and pay the closing costs and not make an issue of it."

"We're just glad to get rid of the house, and we look forward to receiving your check each month for the next 15 years," the wife added.

The transaction closed, and everyone shook hands as they were leaving. As of the writing of this chapter, several years have passed since that day and Mike has never missed or been late with a payment. The note is half its original amount, and everyone is still happy. This proves you don't always have to deal with down-and-out sellers and people with problems to buy properties wholesale.

14

Converting Home Equity to Retirement Income

As the population ages we predict excellent opportunities for you to buy from aging homeowners. Many elderly sellers who are moving in with relatives or into retirement communities will want to convert home equities into retirement incomes. For the past 30 to 35 years, the baby boom generation has driven economic trends in this country, and this movement will continue. As this generation ages, it will precipitate a huge growth in retirees and place a strain on the social security system.

Many aging boomers have little for retirement other than their social security checks and the equity in their homes. Unfortunately, hundreds of thousands of them have had their retirement nest eggs wiped out or severely reduced by the tumble in the stock market and bankruptcies of major companies like Enron and Kmart. As these people retire, many of them will need to convert the equity in their homes into supplemental income.

Of course, they could sell their properties and invest the cash in dividend-paying stocks, bonds, or certificates of deposit. The problem is that fluctuating interest rates produce an income stream that is like a roller-coaster ride. Currently, CD rates are so low that a quarter of a million dollars barely produces $500 per month in income.

Since the Weekend Millionaire method teaches you to buy and hold properties for long-term income and appreciation growth, the concept of direct principal reduction, or zero-interest loans, can be very attractive to people who need to convert real estate equities into income streams.

Mike has made several purchases using direct principal reduction loans. We feel that one in particular illustrates well how this concept provides a steady income stream regardless of rate fluctuations and is useful in making deals with people who are steadfast in their resolve to get a predetermined price for their property.

This transaction involved a house owned by a woman in her early eighties. She was in reasonably good health, but at her age, she decided it was time to sell her home and move in with relatives who could be there to care for her.

She listed the house with a real estate agent for $89,500. Mike learned about it from another broker who had represented him as a buyer's agent in several transactions. The broker explained that the house had been on the market for more than a year and had received only two offers, both of which were less than $78,000. The woman had rejected both of these offers. He felt the problem was that both the floor plan of the house and its location made it more attractive as a rental than for homeownership. If it were located in a different neighborhood, it may have attracted a buyer wanting to live in it and sold for $89,500.

Mike went with the broker to inspect the house. The floor plan was perfect for two people; there was a large bedroom suite with a bath and walk-in closet at each end of the house. Each bedroom had its own outside entrance. The front entrance was in the center of the house and opened into a large living room. There was a wall containing a brick fireplace down the center of the house, with an opening at each end that led to the dining room and kitchen, respectively.

Fire had destroyed the woman's original home, and she had used the insurance proceeds to build this house on the same lot, and designed it to share with her older sister. After the sister passed away, she decided she should not be living alone any longer.

Mike's agent talked with the listing broker and learned that the woman's brother-in-law had advised her to list the property for $89,500 and said she was determined to get this price. Both brokers agreed that the price was too high, but no one had been able to convince the seller of that. When Mike calculated the value using NOI, he figured that he could not pay more than $68,000 for the house if he had to buy it for cash or use conventional financing. He asked his agent to check with the listing broker to see if the woman would consider financing the purchase.

Her broker told Mike's broker that the seller would need about $19,000 in cash to pay the real estate commission and take care of several small bills she wanted to pay prior to moving in with her relatives. Beyond that, she would prefer to have a monthly income instead of all cash.

Mike and his agent structured an offer to purchase the house for the listing price of $89,500. His offer was $19,300 cash at closing and the remaining balance of $70,200 payable in 120 direct principal reduction payments of $585 per month.

The listing broker immediately questioned the zero-interest loan.

"I realize you are offering the asking price, but how can I convince my client to accept a loan with no interest?" he said.

"I think we all agree that the house is overpriced," Mike replied. "Let me explain how I arrived at the numbers I put in the offer. When I calculated the value of the house based on the amount it would rent for, I found that I couldn't pay over $68,000 for it, unless she would be willing to consider some unconventional financing. You told us that she needed $19,000 to pay some bills and cover the commission, so I subtracted that amount from the $89,500, which left $70,500. I then divided that amount by $585, which was the amount of NOI remaining after I deducted enough to give me a 10 percent return on my $19,000 down payment. This came out to 120.51 months. In order to make the numbers work out evenly, I multiplied $585 by 120 months, which came to $70,200. This was $300 less than $70,500, so I simply added the difference to the down payment, which is how I arrived at the amount of $19,300.

"Then I calculated the present value of the income stream, which is the amount I could borrow at today's interest rate and pay it back with 120 payments of $585 per month. I arrived at a figure slightly under $47,200. This amount added to the $19,300 down payment comes to $67,500, which is within what I could pay using conventional financing."

"That all sounds fine, well, and good," the seller's broker responded. "But how does that benefit my client? Wouldn't that be the same as her selling the house for $67,500 and financing $47,200 at 8.5 percent for 10 years?"

"Yes it would, except for two things. First, my way lets the contract reflect the full asking price, which we all know is too high. Secondly, she will have the security of knowing the loan will be paid over the 120 months at a steady $585 per month," Mike added.

"How is that?" her broker asked.

"Simple," Mike replied. "Since the loan has no interest, only a fool would pay it off early. Unlike a $47,200 loan at 8.5 percent interest, she doesn't have to worry about rates dropping a couple of points and the loan being refinanced at a lower rate. If that happened, she would receive all the money in one tax year and then have to find a secure investment that would pay her a reasonable rate. My way is like having a loan with a 100 percent prepayment penalty secured with a first mortgage on the property."

"I never thought about it that way," he responded. "Let me talk with her and see what she says."

Two days later, the listing broker called to see if Mike would agree to deposit the payments directly to his client's bank account if she accepted the offer. This was no problem, and the next day she signed the contract.

We use this example, because it addresses two fundamental issues that frequently arise when dealing with elderly people. The first is price. Often, older people attach sentimental values to properties where they have lived their lives and raised their children, values that mean nothing to a buyer. Also, they may seek the advice of family members with similar sentiments or, as was the case with this woman, relatives with good intentions, but no knowledge of property values. This can cause properties to be priced too high to be purchased with conventional financing or cash. Since price is so important to many sellers, the use of unconventional financing is a way to negotiate without leaving them feeling "beaten down" on their price.

Converting Home Equity to Retirement Income

The second issue is the importance of providing a steady income stream for retirement. Since Mike purchased this property, interest rates have fallen to the lowest levels in 40 years. No doubt, he would have already refinanced the property and paid off the loan, if it had included interest. That would have put the woman in the predicament of having cash to invest at a time when the stock market was in disarray and CDs were paying less than 3 percent. The income from this note became even more important as her health declined. She now lives in a nursing home, but the equity from her home continues to provide her with a steady income that will carry on well into her nineties.

While zero, or very low, interest rate financing can enable you to pay higher prices for properties, there are some cautions to consider. Whenever you use this type of financing, don't use a standard bank-type note that contains a due-on-sale clause. The financing is so favorable, that if you ever did decide to sell or trade the property, having an assumable no-interest mortgage would be a big advantage. Also, you should include a clause giving you the right to substitute collateral. This is important, because even if you sell the property, you may want to keep the loan and secure it with another property.

We are now seeing furniture, vehicles, and other large-ticket items financed at 0 percent interest. We expect this type of financing will become more accepted in real estate financing, as large numbers of aging people need to convert their real estate equities into long-term income streams.

15

Sellers in Financial Trouble

There's no doubt that people with financial difficulties make flexible sellers. Failed business ventures, loss of employment, protracted illnesses, accidents, and downturns in the economy are just some of the mishaps that can lead to financial problems. You might view buying property from financially strapped sellers as preying on their misfortune. This may be true to a slight degree; however, preventing a misfortune from becoming a disaster can be a godsend. This chapter describes two of the many purchases Mike has made from people in financial trouble and explains how, by buying their property, he helped these people reestablish themselves and restore their finances.

Buying from a Couple after Their Business Failed. One September, Mike purchased a house in a large subdivision not far from his home. A real estate agent who knew that he invested in rental housing had brought the property to his attention. The owners, who lived in the house, were involved in a business venture that had failed and left them with significant debts. Selling their home was a last resort. Their children attended a nearby high school, and they wanted to protect them from the embarrassment that would come if their friends found out about the family's financial problems. The real estate agent took Mike to inspect the house and meet the sellers.

The couple discussed their predicament and explained that they were selling the house to raise the money to pay off debts from a failed business. Their asking price was about $5,000 more than Mike felt he could pay, but he understood their desire to get as much as possible from the property. They explained that they needed enough to pay off their debts and still have money left over to pay for a move and make the deposits necessary to rent a new home. It soon became apparent that they didn't want to move their children to another school and leave their friends behind.

Mike showed them how he valued rental properties and explained why he couldn't meet their asking price. He asked them whether they would consider lowering the price if he let them continue to live there and rent from him. This proved to be the decisive factor because it solved the seller's immediate problems. They agreed to lower the price because they wouldn't have to incur moving costs. Their children were able to continue attending the same school, and there was no need to tell them their home had sold. Mike got the price he needed plus a built-in renter.

This proved to be a win-win solution for everyone. The couple cleared their debts and made a fresh start. They remained in the house for three and a half years, during which time they acquired three new investment properties. Once the children graduated from high school, they moved across town to one of their investment houses. Today the husband has a successful business and is financially secure.

Many years have passed since that transaction. Mike and his family regularly patronize the husband's business, and they have become good friends.

Buying from a Builder Who Was Overextended. Mike was involved in a larger transaction that took place during the recession of the early 1990s. This one also demonstrates how financial distress can be relieved by a sale of real estate and free the seller to move on to greater success. The purchase involved a builder friend named Mack. In addition to doing building for Mike, Mack had built several small apartments, mobile home parks, and storage units that he kept as rentals himself. He maintained $100,000 to $150,000 cash that he used as working capital, and his relationships with local banks were good. He was doing quite well financially.

In early 1991, he approached one of the banks about obtaining a loan to build a commercial building that he would rent out. The proposed building appraised for $120,000, and his bank agreed to finance $80,000 once he had a signed lease for at least $1,000 per month. Based on that promise from his bank, Mack went ahead with construction using his working capital to construct the building. As it neared completion, he signed a long-term lease with a tenant who agreed to pay $1,000 per month rent.

At the same time he was building the commercial building, he invested $20,000 in some additional storage units and bought a parcel of land for $50,000, upon which to build a mobile home park. Although these projects depleted his working capital, he wasn't worried because he planned to get back $80,000 when he financed the commercial building.

That was where his financial difficulties began. When he returned to the bank, things had changed. The economy was in recession, and several of the bank's real estate loans were in default. The bank refused to make the loan it had promised the year before. Mack had plenty of equity, but no liquidity, and without working capital, he couldn't take on outside building contracts to generate income. He tried several additional lending institutions with no success. They all told him he needed some cash reserves. Although he explained that he needed the loan because his cash was tied up in the properties, it made no difference.

The situation continued to deteriorate until the fall of 1992. Mack's income from his rentals gave him money on which to live, but until he could free up some cash for working capital, he was effectively out of the building business. This was when he called Mike. They met, and he told Mike what had happened. He said he was going to have to sell something to get back on his feet.

"Why won't the banks loan you the money?" Mike asked. "Have you had any problems with them in the past?"

"No," Mack replied. "I've always been able to get whatever I needed, up until now."

Sellers in Financial Trouble

"What are they telling you?"

"Well, they've told me they would let me have the money if I would put my home up as additional collateral."

"So, why don't you do it?" Mike asked.

"Because that's my home," Mack said. "I don't owe any money on it, and I'm not going to get it tied up with my business properties."

"But it would only be for a short while until you could get back to work and restructure your loans."

"No, I'm not going to do it. I've decided to sell some of my rentals instead," he replied.

"So how can I help?" asked Mike.

"I have a tract of land with a house, a duplex, three triplexes, and an 18-space mobile home park on it. I owe about $330,000, and I am willing to sell it to you for $405,000. That will give me $75,000 cash with which to get back to work."

"How did you arrive at that figure?"

"Well," he began. "I've worked around you and listened to you long enough to know how you buy properties. I took the income they generated last year and subtracted the expenses, and then I deducted 10 percent more to allow for management and used that figure to determine what it should be worth."

"Do you mind if I verify your numbers?" Mike asked.

Mack reached into the folder he was holding and took out several sheets.

"I thought you would want to do that, so here are the Schedule E's from my tax return," he said.

"You really are serious, aren't you?" Mike said.

"Just look it over, and tell me if you're interested," Mack replied. "Don't try to beat me down any further because I know I'm offering you a good deal. I just want to get it closed quickly and get myself out of the hole."

"I'll let you know tomorrow," Mike responded.

That night Mike went through the Schedule E's, calculated the values himself, and discovered that Mack was right on the money. It was a good deal; so the next morning, he called Mack back. "I reviewed your numbers, and they looked good to me," Mike said. "Let me come out and inspect the property, and if there are no major problems, you've got a deal."

How to Find the Ideal Seller

The inspection confirmed Mack's representation of the property's condition. The only thing left to do was allocate the purchase price between the various buildings, land, and personal property and draw up a contract. There were no offers and counteroffers. There were no negotiations. The transaction was one of the simplest and easiest ones with which Mike has been involved.

Mack had a problem, and he knew it. He also knew that if he gave Mike a fair price, he wouldn't try to take advantage of the situation. Mike had dealt with Mack enough to know he could rely on what he said about the property. The transaction turned out to be good for both parties. Mack got the working capital he needed and freed himself of $330,000 in debts. Mike got a deal that was almost a nothing-down purchase. Based on an appraisal ordered by the bank; he was able to borrow $400,000 of the $405,000 purchase price.

Although this transaction was difficult for Mack to swallow and resulted from his financial problems, it never came between their friendship or business relationship. Mack got back on his feet, restored his credit, and began building again. The next year in 1993, Mike bought two city blocks of blighted properties and put Mack and his crews to work for the next two years renovating and rebuilding 43 rental properties.

We called Mack to see if he would mind us telling you the story.

"Not at all," said Mack. "But if you decide to put it in your book, can I give your readers a little advice?"

"What's that?" Mike asked.

"Tell them not to let their pride and ego get in the way of their better judgment. That's what happened to me," he said.

"What do you mean?"

"If I hadn't been so stubborn, I would have gone ahead and mortgaged my house. Then I would still own the property I sold you."

"I'll pass that on," Mike said.

"Thanks!" Mack replied. "Oh, by the way, I have another mobile home park I'm planning to sell, are you interested?"

How to Find the Ideal Seller

In 1990, following the acquisition of a bank in Texas, one of the nation's largest banks found itself awash in REOs and bad real estate loans. During the process of cleaning up its portfolio, it offered hundreds of these for sale. The bank offered Mike one of them in North Carolina. An officer of the bank contacted him and informed him that they had a small condominium they had taken in foreclosure. He said it would make a good rental, and since he knew Mike was an investor, he thought it might be worth pursuing. They arranged to meet at the property. Mike conducted a thorough inspection, and the following day, he delivered a written offer to purchase it for $36,000.

"We can't even consider this," the bank officer exclaimed. "The outstanding balance on the loan we foreclosed was $47,000. We're out that plus the foreclosure expenses. I have copies of public records showing that after eight comparable units in the same complex have sold for between $56,000 and $59,000 in the last two years."

"I don't doubt your figures," Mike said. "All I know is that based on the rent these units are bringing and the amount of the monthly association dues, that's all I can pay and make it work for me."

"We'll take it to auction before we'll sell it for $36,000," the bank officer replied.

"That's fine," said Mike. "If you change your mind, give me a call."

This exchange took place in August of 1990. Mike didn't hear back from the bank officer, but he did get a call in early October from an auction firm advising him that they were going to sell the property at auction on the twenty-third of the month.

More out of curiosity, than anything else, Mike decided to attend the auction. There were several people in attendance, but they were mostly neighbors wanting to see who bought the property. A representative of the auction company took those interested in bidding on a tour of the unit, ending up in the living room, which was the largest open space available. He explained that the bank was offering the property at absolute auction, which meant there was no minimum bid and it would be sold to the highest bidder.

The bidding opened at $24,000. Three individuals appeared to show interest in the property. One of them raised the bid to $24,500. The third

16

Real Estate Owned by Banks

When banks make loans secured by real estate, occasionally some loans go bad and end up in foreclosure. Quite often, at foreclosure sales, the lending institutions bid the amount of their outstanding loan and no one else tops the bid. As a result, they end up owning the properties. Known as real estate owned (REO), these properties are liabilities rather than assets. The quicker banks can dispose of them, the better. For this reason, these properties offer excellent opportunities for investors.

As we will discuss in Chapter 31, banks are businesses just like other companies. They make mistakes too! If they make too many mistakes and end up with an excessive number of nonperforming loans and foreclosed properties, it causes them to come under intense scrutiny from federal regulators. When this happens, banks become flexible sellers too. Like other businesses, when banks make mistakes, they try to cut their losses as much as possible. Occasionally, an attempt to cut their loss backfires and becomes another mistake.

upped it to $25,000. The original bidder offered $26,000. The person making the $25,000 bid upped it to $26,500. The woman who had bid $24,500 announced that she was dropping out of the bidding. Bids went back and forth between the remaining two bidders, first in $500 increments, then in $250 increments until the price settled at $29,000. At this point, the original bidder said he was finished. The auctioneer looked around the room, banged the gavel and said, "Going once at $29,000, going twice at $29,000—anyone else before I close the bid?"

Mike raised his hand. "$30,000," he said.

Everyone turned and looked at him, especially the bank officer who had rejected his $36,000 offer two months before. There were no more bids. After adding a 10 percent fee for the auction company, Mike bought the condominium for $33,000, which was $3,000 less than he originally offered. This was a case where a bank lost by trying to get a higher price for a REO property, and Mike gained because he was willing to pass on the property unless he could buy it according to his formula.

When the auction concluded, the bank officer came over to Mike, smiled, and said, "You will go ahead and give us the $36,000 you offered originally, won't you?"

"Absolutely not," Mike laughed. "You had your chance to accept the higher offer, but decided to roll the dice instead."

"We were just trying to reduce our loss," he said.

"If that's the case, then you should take me out for dinner," Mike said.

"And why is that," the bank officer asked?

"Because, if I hadn't been here you would have lost another $1,000; I was the only one here willing to pay more than $29,000 for it."

This was a funny story that Mike and the banker have chuckled about over the years, but not all auctions go that way. Most of the time lending institutions don't auction properties unless they feel they can come out better than with a negotiated sale. Mistakes made on negotiated sales aren't nearly as obvious as the mistake just described. Earlier that same year, Mike made a negotiated REO purchase in which he benefited from another bank mistake, only this one wasn't as glaring.

A small local savings bank was coming under increasing pressure from federal regulators over their growing number of bad real estate loans. They already had a number of REOs and were in the process of foreclosing several more. In the fall of the previous year, Mike had given this bank's president one of his business cards and asked him to call if he ever had any foreclosures to sell that would make good rentals. One morning in late February 1990, his phone rang.

"This is Lonnie with First Federal. Our president gave me your card and asked me to call you about a property we have that he thought might be of interest to you."

"Yeah, I remember giving him that card," Mike said. "What kind of property do you have?"

"We have two buildings located near the airport. Each one has six two-bedroom, two-bath townhouses. They were originally built as condominiums, but the builder got in trouble and ended up renting them for a few months before we finally had to foreclose. You could either sell them off individually or keep them as rental apartments."

"It sure sounds like a property I might have an interest in," Mike replied. "When can we look at it?"

"I can meet whenever it's convenient for you," Lonnie replied.

"I have to pick up someone at the airport at 3:30 this afternoon," Mike said. "If we could meet shortly after lunch, I could look at them before going to the airport. Would that work for you?"

"Unless you have other plans, why don't you let me treat you to lunch, and we can go from there," Lonnie said.

"That sounds good to me," Mike replied. "Where do you want to meet?"

They arranged to meet at a restaurant near the airport, and over lunch Lonnie told Mike about the property. The bank had financed several properties for a builder who went broke, and this was one of them. It was completed and ready to rent or sell, which is why they felt it would interest him. He went on to explain that the only problem was that the builder had taken all the appliances out of the units. Everything else was in good shape.

After lunch, they visited the property. It consisted of two buildings facing each other with a parking area in between. Each building had six two-story units, with two bedrooms and a bath upstairs; a living room, dining room, kitchen, and one bath downstairs and a nice patio and storage room in the back accessed from the kitchen. Lonnie had the keys for all 12 units, and he allowed Mike to inspect each one.

Although he had brought inspection forms with him, Mike didn't need to use them. The units were in perfect condition except for some minor touch-up painting. All they needed were new appliances, as Lonnie had pointed out over lunch. Other than that, they were ready to rent.

When Mike inquired about the price, Lonnie told him they had made the builder a construction loan for $567,000. This was based on $47,250 per unit, for the 12 units. The preconstruction appraisal was $69,500 per unit, but since none had sold, the bank still had the original loan amount in the project. He said they could probably get their money back if they marketed the units individually, but they weren't equipped to do that. He said they were willing to take some loss if they could sell all 12 units in one transaction and asked Mike to make them an offer.

Two days later, Mike delivered the bank a written offer. Knowing that all 12 units were vacant and that he would have to install new appliances, he made a very conservative offer of $411,000. He attached an earnest money deposit of $1,000 to his offer, which also asked the bank to finance the remaining $410,000 for 10 years with a favorable interest rate. He wanted payments based on a 20-year amortization, with a balloon payment at the end of 10 years. He also asked the bank to provide a survey, title insurance, termite inspections, and attorney fees. When Mike handed him the offer, Lonnie leaned back in his chair and studied it for several minutes.

"You didn't really expect us to consider this, did you?"

"You asked me to make an offer," Mike said. "That's what I did."

"Well, I know we can't do anything like this, but let me talk with our board and see if they want to make a counteroffer," Lonnie replied with a dejected look.

"That will be fine," Mike responded. "Just keep in mind that all the units are vacant and I will have to replace the appliances before I can start renting them. You don't want me to end up in the same shape in a couple of years from now that your original borrower was in, do you? If I buy the units, they will have to make money or it's not worth doing."

"I understand, and we want you to make money, but we don't want you to get rich," laughed Lonnie.

How to Find the Ideal Seller

"Take it up with your board," Mike replied. "I might be a little low, but not much. If you calculate the NOI, you'll see I've used a conservative rent amount, but you wouldn't want to deal with me if I weren't careful."

"Well . . . leave it with me, and I'll talk with them," he said.

The following morning, Lonnie called.

"I met with our board yesterday afternoon," he said, "and they've made you a counteroffer. Can you stop by my office so I can go over it with you?"

"Sure, when would you like me to come by?"

"The board has another meeting set for 2:00 this afternoon," he said. "If you could come before then, we could go over their counter, and if it is acceptable, I could report back to them today."

"No problem, I'll be there before lunch."

Mike arrived at 11:30 and went directly to Lonnie's office. He was sitting behind his desk with a big smile on his face.

"I think you will like the counteroffer the board has made," he said as Mike walked in. "Come over to the conference table, and let's go over it."

Lonnie got up and moved to the small round conference table across the office from his desk. He pulled back a chair for Mike, and they sat down. He opened the legal-sized file folder that was on the table and took out copies of the offer Mike had left the day before. He slid one across the table. Mike could see that the numbers in his offer were crossed out and new ones inserted.

"The board spent a great deal of time going over your offer," he began. "They could tell that you put a lot of thought into it, and they want to make a deal with you. They are agreeable to do everything you asked; they will finance the purchase, just the way you want, but due to reasons I'm not able to discuss, they can't sell for less than $430,000. We made that change on your offer, and they authorized me to sign the contract if this is acceptable."

At this point, Mike was shocked. He expected a counter, but he had expected it to be somewhere around $490,000, which would have been midway between his offer and the $567,000 Lonnie told him the bank had in the property. The urge to jump on the offer immediately was almost irresistible, but he remembered one of the key principles of negotiating, "Never jump at the first offer."

Real Estate Owned by Banks

Mike studied the offer for a few minutes, and then took out his calculator and a notepad. Although he knew the deal was acceptable, he asked Lonnie to give him a few minutes to see if he could make it work at their price. He spent the next 20 minutes running calculations, making notes, and giving the appearance of doing an in-depth analysis. Finally, he looked up and smiled.

"I think I've figured out how to make this work," he announced with a smile. "When I made the original offer, I planned on having $430,000 in the property, but that was after replacing the appliances. I'm not questioning the value of the property; what I'm concerned about is cash flow. I don't want to put myself in a position where I have to struggle to make the payments. I estimate it will take about $20,000 to buy new appliances, which I was planning to pay for out of pocket.

If they would agree to loan me $450,000, and lower the interest rate by one percentage point for the first two years, I could pay them $430,000 for the property. I'd use the extra money to buy the appliances and be happy to give a security interest in them in addition to the deed of trust on the property. If we can do it that way, I won't have to deplete my cash reserves and they won't have to worry about me making the payments on time."

"That's an interesting proposition," Lonnie said. "I've never heard of them doing something like that, but if you'll write a new offer with those changes, I'll take it back to the board this afternoon. Who knows, they might go along with it."

Mike wrote the new offer and left it with Lonnie. The following morning Lonnie called to let him know the board had approved his offer with the stipulation that the deal must close before the end of the month. Mike reminded him that the ball was in the bank's court. If they could get the survey and termite inspections done and the loan papers prepared, he and his attorney would have no problem closing by then.

This is a great example of why you should follow basic negotiating principles in all transactions. When the bank countered with an offer far better than anticipated, the natural tendency of most people would be to accept it. By countering with an offer to pay their price if they would finance the appliance purchase, Mike made a no-money-down deal and kept his cash to cushion the carrying cost while he got the units rented.

How to Find the Ideal Seller

The reason for the savings bank being so flexible became apparent a couple of years later when it was acquired by a larger bank. Within a year of the acquisition, Mike bought nine additional properties that the same savings bank had financed. As it turned out, Mike learned that the bank was under extreme time pressure when this transaction took place.

These two examples describe profitable transactions with lending institutions that were at opposite ends of the flexibility scale. We used these widely differing situations to help you understand that the best way to buy REO properties is to set your standards and then stick with them. If a deal is meant to be, it will happen. If it doesn't, don't get discouraged; just keep looking. Becoming a Weekend Millionaire does not depend on how many properties you buy. It depends on how many you buy that make a profit.

The better record of accomplishment you have as a real estate investor, the more advantage you will have when trying to buy real estate owned by banks. The more comfortable they become with you, the better. When you prove that you are a knowledgeable investor, you will start to find deals coming your way as simple as the one Mike made on a rural single-family home. This house was located about 10 miles outside the city limits on 1.2 acres, in an area where subdivisions mixed with small farms. The house was a three-bedroom, two-bath home, just five years old. It had a large detached two-car garage. Mike learned of it when one of his bankers called him.

"Mike, this is David with the bank. I need your help."

"What's wrong," Mike asked.

"I stuck my neck out and financed a house for one of my customers when my boss warned me not to. I should have listened to him. We just foreclosed on the property, and I want to get it off our books without the bank losing any money. You rent houses! How about if I come by and pick you up and take you to look at it. If you could pay us what we have in it, it would sure help me."

"When do you want to go?" Mike asked.

"Right now, if you can go," he said.

"I'll be waiting!"

The banker came by within the hour and took Mike to look at the house. On the way to the property, he explained that with all the expenses of the foreclosure and the unpaid interest on the loan, the bank was out almost $60,000.

"If you will give us $60,000 for the property, we won't lose any money, and I won't look like an idiot," the banker said.

Although located off a dirt road, the house was in a nice location on a hill. It had a large deck with great views of the valley below. Upon inspection, Mike found the house needed an estimated $3,000 to $5,000 worth of repairs to get it ready to rent. When he computed its value using projected NOI and allowing for repairs, he arrived at a value in its present condition that was just under $60,000.

"If I give you $60,000 for it, will you finance it for me?" Mike asked the banker.

"I will if you will put $6,000 down on the purchase," he replied.

"You've got a deal," Mike said.

They returned to Mike's office and drafted the purchase agreement. The transaction closed within two weeks. Mike got a good deal and the banker saved face. Today, the house is one of Mike's most in-demand rentals. It seems that people like its rural environment, and it is rarely vacant.

As you can see from these examples, there are many ways to buy real estate owned by banks. Set your standards, and then use persistence and creativity to find purchases that conform to them. There are many good deals if you are patient and take them as they come. Mike has bought numerous REO properties in a single year, but gone numerous other years without buying a single one. Patience is the key to success.

SECTION 4

How to Power Negotiate

In this section, we're going to focus on how to negotiate the purchase of real estate properties. We'll be drawing on Roger's experience as a negotiating expert and Mike's experience in buying millions of dollars worth of rental properties.

Knowing how to negotiate well is a key ingredient to your success as a Weekend Millionaire. When you know how to power negotiate it will help you

- Find more properties that will fit your criteria as viable purchases.
- Get sellers to accept offers from you that they refused from other buyers.
- Turn properties that are good buys into super buys.
- Produce more creative offers as you learn more about the seller's needs.
- Have fun with making low offers, because negotiating is no longer a stressful experience.
- Make win-win offers to sellers.

If you've met someone who has tried real estate investing and failed, it is probably because they didn't know how to negotiate well. They ran into a lot of resistance from sellers and failed to get offers accepted because they weren't doing it right.

As you study these negotiating tips, keep in mind that there is one underlying rule in negotiating: Power goes to the side that is able to convince the other side that they have options. Options give you power. If you say to the seller, "I have narrowed my choices down to your property and two others. Any one of the three will serve my purpose. I just need to find the seller that will give me the best price and terms," you are giving yourself power.

Conversely, if the seller has more options than you do, the seller has the power. If you're trying to buy a house for $80,000 and the seller has three other buyers waving $100,000 cashier's checks in their faces, we don't have any brilliant negotiating strategies that will make that seller accept your offer. Although there is a remote possibility that the sellers cannot accept cash due to their tax situation, or don't want cash because they have nowhere to invest it, you're probably better off to move on and find other sellers who don't have as many options.

17

Profit Is Made When You Buy

We have included an entire section on negotiating because we believe
that your ability to be a successful real estate investor and become
a Weekend Millionaire depends on how well you can negotiate.

Based on our experience, the people who get into the most trouble are
the ones who buy real estate at market price and then expect it to go up
in value so they can sell later for a profit. Do you remember the old land
sale schemes in Florida? Buyers would tell the salespersons, "That's ridiculous. This is swampland! Why would I want to own it?" To which the salespeople would patiently explain, "This land is not for owning. It's for
trading."

At real estate investment seminars, speakers touted this as the "bigger
fool" theory, which says, "If you buy for nothing down, it doesn't matter what
you pay. There will always be a bigger fool coming along who will bail you
out." These were speculators, not investors.

We don't believe in speculating when you buy real estate. We believe that
if you buy it right, you will make money even if the value never goes up. His-

tory, however, has shown that the price of real estate, with few exceptions, has risen steadily even through recessionary times.

The price of real estate goes up for two simple economic reasons, scarcity and inflation. Let's look at each of these.

Scarcity. As populations increase, the demand for housing grows. The problem is the amount of real estate remains constant. You've probably noticed that home prices soar when two factors are present:

1. The number of people wanting to live in a particular area is increasing.
2. The regulations or terrain in that area restricts new building.

Consider the Northeast corridor where prices have been skyrocketing as cities grew and available land remained the same. Consider the San Francisco peninsula, an area confined by water where thousands were moving during the dot.com boom of the 1990s. Consider the Los Angeles basin, wedged between the San Gabriel Mountains and the Pacific Ocean, where beautiful weather and immigration from Mexico and Asia has caused the population to double in the last 40 years. Limited building lots pushed prices up rapidly.

Inflation. We're sure that economists can give you a much more complex answer, but inflation occurs when there is more money available to buy than there are things to spend it on. In real estate, we call it "Too much money chasing too little property."

The Federal Reserve Board attempts to control inflation by aggressively controlling the money supply. Throughout the past decade, it has been very successful in doing so, but many of you remember when inflation reached double-digit numbers.

Real estate is an excellent hedge against inflation because of your ability to leverage large amounts of it with very little money invested. In times of high inflation, like the late 1970s and early 1980s, you wanted to own all the real estate you could buy and have the least amount of money down possible. Speculators abounded during this time. What they forgot was that the opposite is true when prices are steady or possibly declining. During these times, you want to own only real estate that produces enough cash flow to support itself. When you're highly leveraged in real estate and counting on inflation to bail you out, you are extremely vulnerable. Ask Donald Trump about what happened to him in 1991. It almost wiped him out.

You can make money speculating in real estate if you spend enough time researching your market, have the capital to risk, can cover the carrying costs, and are fortunate enough for prices to go up rapidly. Of course, you can do the same thing in the stock market too.

Become an Investor, Not a Speculator. If you're not a big risk taker, you'll be pleased to know that the Weekend Millionaire program works all the time. Periods of economic growth and recession merely change the speed at which you become a Weekend Millionaire; they don't wipe you out. If you follow our program, you make conservative investment decisions that don't rely on scarcity or inflation to make you rich. If these come, they're just a bonus.

Weekend Millionaires understand that they make their profit when they buy. They understand that by buying right, profit margins, which are small in the beginning, get bigger the longer the property is owned. This directly contrasts with speculators whose margins get smaller the longer they own their properties. The Weekend Millionaire program works for two reasons:

1. It teaches you to buy and hold and to buy so that properties show a positive cash flow from the start and don't put you in a forced sale position.
2. It teaches you the negotiating skills you will need to make these purchases.

The chapters in this section will give you negotiating techniques and gambits that will help you buy right. As you master them, you will find that you can negotiate purchases for 10, 15, or even 20 percent less than you ever dreamed possible.

You will learn that your power in a negotiation depends on the perceived alternatives that you have compared to the perceived alternatives of the seller. Obviously, a large part of buying right is searching for sellers with limited alternatives; however, when you apply the negotiating gambits we're going to give you in the following chapters, you will find your success rate improving dramatically. Mastering this section will make you a successful real estate investor.

18

Negotiating Pressure Points

I n this chapter, we're going to discuss negotiating pressure points and tell you how to use them when buying real estate. Understanding their effect on sellers and knowing when to use them will get you better buys.

Time Pressure

Time pressure plays a part in every negotiation, but it has special significance when buying real estate. Your children know about time pressure, don't they? If they want something, when do they ask for it—just at the last moment, right? Just when you are rushing out the door for an important meeting and you're already late—that's when they know they have the best chance of getting what they want. Why? Because it's easier to give it to them than take time you don't have talking about it.

People become flexible under time pressure. When sellers are not under any time pressure, it's hard to get good buys. When they are under a lot of time pressure, you can often get terrific buys.

Negotiating Pressure Points

What time pressures might sellers be under? Of course, you won't know until you have invested some time gathering information and asking questions. Here's a list of things that might cause sellers to experience time pressures:

- They are behind on their mortgage payments and don't see how they can catch up.
- They are actually in foreclosure and in danger of losing the property unless they can find a buyer.
- They need money to pay off mounting debts.
- They have contracted to buy another home and can't close on it until they sell this one.
- They need the money for other purposes such as
    - A child is going to college, and they need to pay for the tuition.
    - A daughter is getting married, and they have to pay for the wedding.
    - An accident or unexpected illness has left them with large medical bills.
- They need capital to acquire or expand a business.
- They have lost a lawsuit and don't have the money to settle it.
- They are retiring and want to move to Arizona as soon as they're through working.

This is just a partial list of the many things that put sellers under time pressure. Make your own checklist and expand it with each new situation you encounter. Keep your list in mind when you first meet with potential sellers, and see if you can spot any symptoms of time pressure they may be experiencing.

Acceptance Time. Power negotiators understand that it often takes sellers time to understand that they are not going to get as much for their property as they hoped. Never write off sellers as being hopelessly inflexible on their price. Some of the best buys we've made have been from sellers who called us back weeks after they turned down our original offer. They needed the time to see that they weren't going to get a better offer. Our advice is to always leave the door open for sellers to reopen negotiations. Instead of pressuring them by saying, "This is my final offer," leave the door open with statements like, "I hope you get what you're asking, but if you don't, call me. I'm not saying I'll be in a position to buy later, but we can always talk some more."

Spend a Lot of Time with Sellers. We have found that patience is a real virtue when negotiating. The longer you can keep sellers involved in negotiations, the better chance you have of getting what you want. Take your time inspecting the property. Ask as many questions as you can think of. Discuss things you may have in common with sellers. If you see golf clubs or a fishing rod and you golf or fish, have a conversation about it. Take a tape measure with you, measure some of the rooms, and note down the measurements. Pace off the backyard and write it down. Why do these things? For two reasons:

- The longer you spend with sellers, the more trust they will develop in you.
- The more time they spend with you, the more flexible they will become when the negotiations start. Time spent with you will affect their flexibility on price, terms, and other considerations. Why? Because mentally, they want to recoup the time spent with you. Their mind starts to tell them, "I can't walk away from this empty handed after all the time I have invested."

There is a caveat here. If you aren't careful, time can work against you in the negotiations as well. You may find yourself becoming more flexible for the same reasons sellers do. Your subconscious mind will be saying, "I don't want to walk away from this with nothing after all the time I've spent on it."

Tie Up All the Details. Don't leave anything to "we can work that out later." Sometimes an issue comes up early on and neither side wants to slow down the negotiations by taking time to resolve it. Perhaps it's an issue of a freestanding refrigerator. It's not included with the property the way the built-in appliances are. The sellers don't want to move it to Arizona when they retire, and you could use it for your rental. How much is it worth? The seller says, "That's no problem, we can work it out later." Perhaps it would not be a big problem if you worked it out now, but if you wait until you're sitting at the closing table with the attorneys; it may become a very expensive refrigerator. Our advice is to tie up all the details and avoid last-minute surprises.

Information Power

Gathering information is so important to a real estate investor that we make this statement, "When you think you know everything you need to know about a property and a seller, you probably know about half of what you really need to know." Here's a checklist of some things that are helpful to learn:

- How long has the seller owned the property?
- How long has the property been for sale?
- How many offers have been made on the property?
- What does the seller plan to do with the money from the sale?
- How much does the seller owe on the property?
- Is the seller under any pressure to sell?
- What are the seller's reasons for wanting to sell?
- Are these the real reasons for wanting to sell?
- Will the seller carry back any financing?
- If the property is listed with a real estate agent, when does the listing expire?
- Are there any hidden problems with the property?
- Are there any nearby problems that affect the value of the property?

The more information you can learn about sellers and their properties, the better insight you will have into their real motivation for selling. Any bit of information you learn could potentially lead to a creative win-win solution that will let you buy the property at wholesale.

Don't Be Afraid to Ask the Tough Questions. We used to be reluctant to ask tough questions for fear they would offend sellers. We used to preface our questions with statements like, "Would you mind if I asked you . . .?" or, "Would you be embarrassed to tell me . . .?" We've since learned to ask tough questions more directly, by professionally asking, "How much is owed on the property?" or, "Are the payments current?" Even if sellers refuse to answer the questions, you're still gathering information. Like a good investigative reporter, even if they refuse to answer, you can learn a lot by judging their reaction to your questions. Don't limit your information gathering by only asking questions that you know sellers will answer.

People Share Information across Peer Group Levels. People share information much more easily with people in their same peer group. Let's take the issue of how long a property has been on the market and how many and what type of offers the seller has rejected. Sellers may be reluctant to answer these questions if you ask them directly. The seller's broker may not want to tell you either. However, if you have your real estate broker call their real estate broker, the two of them may exchange all kinds of information because they see themselves in the same peer group. You may also gather sensitive information through mutual friends, neighbors, or coworkers of sellers.

Ask Open-ended Questions. Rudyard Kipling once wrote about his six honest serving men. He said that these six taught him all he knew. Those six serving men were Who, What, Where, When, Why, and How. Today we recognize them as the first words of open-ended questions. Questions phrased in such a way that their answers provide additional information. The opposite of these are closed-ended questions, which can be answered with a simple "Yes" or "No" without giving any additional information. Let's look at the difference between open-ended and closed-ended questions that deal with price:

- Open ended
    - How flexible would you be on your price if I could pay cash?
    - What would an offer need to contain to interest you enough to consider a lower price?
- Closed ended
    - Will you take less than your asking price if I can close quickly?
    - Are you willing to negotiate on the price?

When you're trying to gather information, use open-ended questions. These keep potential sellers talking and usually make them feel more comfortable. This interview skill takes practice to perfect, but the better you become at it, the more information you will gather.

Projecting That You're Prepared to Walk Away

This is the most important pressure point of all. If you said to us, "I'm in a big rush because I've got a meeting with a seller in 15 minutes, just give me one thing that will make me a more powerful negotiator," it would be, "Project to the seller that you're prepared to walk away if you can't get what you want."

When Roger's daughter Julia bought her first car, she went down to the BMW dealership and test-drove a really nice used BMW. She fell in love with the car, and they knew she'd fallen in love with it.

When she got home, she asked Roger to go back with her and renegotiate a better price. On the way to the dealership, Roger asked her, "Are you prepared to come home tonight without the car?" "No, I'm not!" Julia replied. "I want it! I want it!"

"If you feel that way," Roger told her "you may as well give them what they want, because you've already set yourself up to lose. You've got to be prepared to walk away."

They spent two hours negotiating the purchase and even walked out of the showroom twice during those two hours, but finally they got the car for $2000 less than Julia was originally prepared to pay. So, how much money was Julia making while she was negotiating—keeping in mind that Roger waived his normal fee? Two thousand dollars in two hours, right? We'd call that pretty good money anywhere! And it just goes to show that you can't make money faster or easier than you can when you're negotiating.

Projecting that you're prepared to walk away is the number one pressure point to use when negotiating with sellers, but how do you give yourself walk-away power? You do it by giving yourself options. Before going into a negotiation, develop some options.

Go find two other properties with which you'd be almost as happy. This doesn't mean that you won't get the one that you want, but it will make you a more powerful negotiator. When you meet with the sellers, you'll know that if they are unreasonable, you have two other properties you can look at as well. Sellers seem to be able to sense when you have other options, and this makes you a more powerful negotiator.

Study these pressure points and try them out in small day-to-day negotiations. Practice them in situations that aren't important so you can perfect them for use in ones that are. Time pressure, information power, and walk-away power are three powerful pressure points that when used properly will get you better deals in any negotiation.

19

Win-Win Negotiating

Win-win negotiating is a concept that says if you and a seller get together and learn about each other's objectives, you can come up with a magical solution that gets both of you what you want without either having to feel they lost.

An example of this would be two people with only one orange, but both want it. After they talk about it, one offers to split the orange down the middle and let each settle for half of what they really want. To be sure that it's fair, they decide that one will do the cutting and the other will get first choice of the two halves. However, as they continue to discuss the situation, they learn that their underlying needs are different. One wants the orange to make juice, and the other wants the rind to put into a cake. Magically, they have found a way that both of them can win and neither has to lose.

Note that this win-win negotiation was successful because both sides did a good job of gathering information. Initially these two people made the mistake of assuming that the other person wanted the orange for the same reason they wanted it. That's a big mistake, especially when you're buying real estate. Never assume that sellers view properties the same way you do. Doing so will often create deadlocks over issues that are completely irrelevant to the problems the sellers are trying to solve. The best way to avoid this type of complication is by sharing information and trying to learn what each party is trying to achieve.

Here are a couple of examples to illustrate how a win-win attitude can create great real estate buys. We once got a call from a developer in Seattle who had located a piece of land that he felt would make an excellent shopping center development. He could hardly believe his good fortune. He felt sure that other developers must have just overlooked it. He assembled a group of investors who agreed to syndicate the development of a shopping center on the land. He then approached the owner with an offer to buy.

What he ran into was absolute indifference to his offer. The person who owned the land didn't say it was a good or bad offer, he just wasn't interested in discussing any offer at that time.

This is always a big problem when you're negotiating. Believe it or not, you're better off to have a strong objection to what you're proposing than you are to be met with indifference.

At Roger's power negotiating seminars, he asks the unmarried people in the audience to answer this question: "What's the opposite of *love*?" Invariably, they respond, "hate." If you've ever been married, you know better than that, don't you?

The real opposite of love is *indifference*. Your spouse simply doesn't care anymore. As long as he or she is throwing plates at you, you have something with which to work! It's when they're taking the attitude of Rhett Butler in *Gone with the Wind* and saying, "Quite frankly, my dear, I don't give a damn," that you know the movie's about over!

When you're trying to buy real estate, you're actually better off to have a strong objection than you are to meet with indifference.

We said to the Seattle developer, "Quit telling us about the property; we know you're excited about it, but the answer is never with the property. The real answer is always with the person. Tell us what you know about the person."

The investor told us, "I don't know too much, except that he's an elderly man and evidently very sick. Probably going to die within a year or so, and he knows it. He's very wealthy. Money is not an issue to him at all. He's just not interested in taking time to discuss selling the land."

Well, what might interest this person? If we move around to the other side of the negotiating table and put ourselves in his position, we can start looking for something that may interest him without taking away from our position. We have to get away from the assumption that he just wants more money, before we can focus on finding creative solutions.

When we did this, we very quickly concluded that he might be interested in a monument to himself. Since he was old, wealthy, and dying, but had been very prominent in the community, preserving his name after he passed on might have some appeal. The developer was in an excellent position to provide that, by naming the shopping center after him. The old man loved the idea.

The buyer and the seller didn't want the same things. The buyer wanted the property for its development potential. The seller wasn't interested in that, but he jumped at the opportunity to create a monument in his honor.

Eventually the seller deeded the land over to the developer free and clear, in return for a share in the syndication and an agreement to name the shopping center after him. He placed his share in trust for his granddaughter with whom he was very close. That was truly a win-win solution.

Win-win solutions can only come when you understand that people in negotiations don't always want the same things. They're looking at the same situation, but they're seeing it from different perspectives.

In another instance, a man called us from Dallas. He was interested in acquiring a small business. He'd been negotiating with the sellers and had discovered that they were flexible about terms on the business. They were agreeable to a leveraged buyout, but they were rigid on the price. He called us to see if we could give him any suggestions on how to get the price down.

We said, "Don't tell us about the business; tell us about the people."

"They're a middle-aged couple with teenaged children, and that's about all I know about them," he replied.

"Do they need any cash out of the business?" we asked.

"Oh, yes," he said. "They want at least $4,000 cash when we close."

"Do you know why they need the money?"

"Their daughter's going into college this fall, and they need $4,000 for the tuition in September."

Once again, let's go around to the other side of the negotiating table and try to see things from their perspective. We want to try to find a way to solve their problem in a way that won't take away from our position. It makes sense that if they're scraping together $4,000 to pay tuition this September; they're probably going to need another $4,000 next January for the second semester, right?

Does it make any sense for them to put their daughter in a four-year college in September, if they're not sure they can maintain the tuition for the second semester? Of course not. They'd be better off to start her out in a less-expensive junior college.

But, won't they need another $4,000 the following September? And another $4,000, maybe more, the following January? In fact, they're going to need $4,000 each September and January for the next four years. Now we are starting to understand their problem.

Here's what the investor in Dallas worked out. He got the sellers to make a concession on the price and agree to carry back the financing. In exchange, he agreed to make an additional payment of $4,000 each September and January, for the next four years, thereby, assuring them that they would not only have a steady income on which to live, but also the extra money each semester to ensure that their daughter could go through college.

They didn't want the same thing, did they? They were looking at the same situation, but they were seeing it from different perspectives. The investor wanted to control the business. The sellers wanted an income on which to live and the assurance that they would have the money for their daughter to go through college.

Win-win negotiations involving real estate investing can only come when you understand that sellers don't always want what you might want if you were in their shoes.

Never assume that sellers won't do something just because you wouldn't do it. Roger once gave away a piece of land that the tax assessor valued at

$22,000. Why? Because it was an undesirable property and he felt that it would take years to find a buyer for it, plus the land was over 1,000 miles away. He decided the hassle wouldn't be worth it.

Roger once sold 20 acres of prime land in the State of Washington. (We do not recommend bare land for an investment. It's more of a speculation than an investment, but sometimes you get lucky.) The buyer assumed that Roger would want all cash. That was the last thing that Roger wanted. Cash just meant more taxes to him. He ended up accepting a small down payment, and the buyer agreed to a loan amortized over 40 years with 10 percent interest added. The payments were over $1,200 a month for 40 years and in the beginning, the payments were all interest except for less than $25 per month that went to principal. Would we ever buy property on terms like that? Absolutely not! But, it met the needs of this buyer.

Buyers do unexpected things too. Roger's neighbor recently put her home on the market for $999,000. The buyer was an immigrant from China who paid cash for the property, but told the seller, "I cannot pay you $999,000 because 9 is a very unlucky number in China. I will pay you an even $1 million if that is acceptable."

Win-win negotiating is not just a matter of getting what you want, but of helping the other person get what he or she wants also. And one of the most powerful thoughts you can have when you're negotiating with a seller is not, "What can I get from them?" but "What can I do for them that won't take away from my position?" People will give you what you want in a negotiation, if you can help them get what they want.

As you saw in Section 3, How to Find the Ideal Seller, there are all kinds of people out there who have financial problems that they need to solve. By finding out what they need and finding a way to help them get it, you'll make great buys on properties that fit perfectly into your Weekend Millionaire portfolio.

20

Beginning Negotiating Gambits

In this chapter, we're going to teach you about beginning negotiating gambits. These are the moves that you make in the early stage of the negotiation with the seller to be sure that you're setting it up for a successful win-win conclusion.

Ask for More Than You Expect to Get

The first negotiating principle is a very simple, but very powerful, one, and there are many rewards for using it. You should ask sellers for more than you expect to get.

- Ask for a lower price than you are willing to pay.

- Ask for a lower interest rate for carryback financing than you are willing to pay.

- Ask the seller to pay for attorney fees, termite inspection, home inspection fees, survey deed preparation, and title insurance.

- Ask for a later closing date if the seller wants to close the deal quickly; ask for an earlier closing date if the seller wants time to move out.
- Ask for items of personal property, such as pieces of furniture, a riding mower, or oriental carpets.

Why would you do this? Doesn't it move you and the sellers further apart? Doesn't that make it harder to make a deal? Let's consult a real expert. Henry Kissinger was one of the top international negotiators of the twentieth century. He once said, "Effectiveness at the bargaining table depends upon your ability to overstate your initial demands." Note that he says "ability." In other words, how well you can do it.

Why is this so important? For many reasons, the most important of which is that you are creating an environment where sellers can have wins as well as you. If you make your first offer your best offer, you have nothing left to give sellers to let them feel they won something in the negotiation. And remember, that's one of the key objectives in power negotiating—let the sellers feel that they won too.

Expand the Negotiating Range with Strangers

There is a corollary to this rule: The less you know about sellers, the lower your first offer should be, for two reasons:

- You may be off in your assumptions. If you don't know the sellers or their needs well, they may be willing to sell for less than you think. They may be willing to give you much better terms than you imagined.
- If you don't know the sellers, you need to be able to build rapport quickly. And, the fastest way (not the best way, but the fastest way) is to be able to make concessions to them.

Minimum Plausible Position. Your initial offer to the seller should be your minimum plausible position (MPP). This is the least that you can possibly offer and still have the sellers see some plausibility in your position. Unless you are already a very experienced negotiator, you will find that your MPP is much lower than you think it is. If you present offers the way that we will teach you, you will be able to make what appear to be outrageously low offers and still have the sellers take them seriously. All beginning real estate investors fear ridicule from sellers. They are afraid that sellers will laugh at them or get angry with them for making such low offers. Because of this intimidation, you will probably feel like modifying your MPP to the point where your offers are for more than the minimum amount that the sellers would think is plausible. Don't do that. Grit your teeth, brace yourself for rejection, and make those low offers. You will be surprised at the low offers some sellers are willing to accept.

Imply Some Flexibility. If you're presenting your minimum plausible position, imply some flexibility. If your initial position seems outrageous to sellers and your attitude is "take it or leave it," the negotiations may never get started. The seller's response may simply be, "Then we don't have anything to talk about." You can get away with outrageous opening positions if you imply flexibility.

Let's say that the sellers are asking $100,000 for the property and you need to buy it for $85,000 to make it work. You might say, "I realize that you're asking $100,000 for the property and based on everything you know that may seem like a fair price to you. Perhaps you know something that I don't know, because based on all the research that I've done; it seems to me that we should be talking something closer to $70,000." At that point the sellers may be thinking, "That's ridiculous, I'll never sell it for that, but he does seem to be sincere, so what do I have to lose if I spend some time negotiating with him, just to see how high I can get him to go?"

Other Reasons for Asking for More

Although the key reason for asking for more than you expect to get is to create a climate where the other side can win, there are also many other good reasons:

You Might Just Get It. Another reason for asking for more than you expect to get will be obvious if you're a positive thinker: You might just get it. You don't know how the universe is aligned that day. Perhaps your patron saint is leaning over a cloud looking down at you and thinking, "Wow, look at that nice real estate investor. She's been working so hard for so long now, I think I'll just give her a break." So the sellers may take the low offer, but the only way you'll find out is to ask.

It Prevents Deadlocks. If you are dealing with sellers who are proud of their ability to negotiate, the negotiations will deadlock unless you leave room for them to have a win with you. Let's say that the sellers are asking $100,000 but they've been trying to sell it for several months and haven't had an offer anywhere close to that amount. Now they need to sell and might even be willing to accept $85,000. If you make them a take-it-or-leave-it offer of $85,000, the sellers will be reluctant to accept it because it would make them feel like they lost. Offer them $70,000 and let them negotiate you up to $85,000, and they will feel much better.

It Gives You Some Negotiating Room. You can always go up on an offer to buy, but you can't go down. So, give yourself some negotiating room. It makes it easier to get what you really want. Roger tells the story of his son Dwight asking him if he could borrow his Corvette. Roger told Dwight, "No." Dwight then asked if he could borrow Roger's minivan, and Roger said, "Yes." Half an hour later Roger looked out into the driveway to see Dwight loading huge loudspeakers into the back of the minivan. Conclusion: He didn't intend to borrow the Corvette in the first place, he just knew that by asking for it and being told no, it made it a lot easier to get what he really wanted.

Bracket the Seller's Asking Price

The next question has to be, "If you're going to ask for more, how much more should you ask for?" The answer is, "Assume that you will end up midway between the two opening negotiating positions." Your initial offer should be an equal distance on the opposite side of your objective as the seller's asking price.

Of course, it's not always true that you'll end up in the middle, but that is a good assumption to make, unless you have something else upon which to base your opening position. Assume that you'll end up in the middle, midway between the two opening negotiating positions. If you track that, we believe you will be amazed at how often it happens. Watch for it in day-to-day negotiations, and prove it for yourself. Your son comes to you and says he needs $20 for a fishing trip he's planning to take this weekend. You say, "No way. I'm not going to give you $20. Do you realize that when I was your age I got 50 cents a week allowance and I had to work for that? I'll give you $10 and not a penny more."

Your son says, "I can't do it for $10, dad."

Now you have established the negotiating range. He's asking for $20. You're willing to pay $10. See how often you end up at $15. In our culture, splitting the difference seems fair.

Think of *No* As an Opening Negotiating Position

The word *no* takes on new meaning for a negotiator. It is never a refusal. It is simply an opening negotiating position, and that's all it is.

When sellers turn down your offers with a flat refusal and no counteroffer, think to yourself, "Isn't that an interesting opening negotiating position? I wonder why they decided to start with that approach."

Your children know this, don't they? You can tell your child, "I am sick of hearing about this! Go to your room! I don't want to see you until morning! And if you ever bring this up again I will ground you for a month!" Do they hear a refusal? No! They're up in their room thinking, "Wasn't that an interesting opening negotiating position?"

It's good to let the seller know that you have options by saying, "I can only afford one purchase this month, and I've narrowed it down to your property and two other properties. Frankly, I'm probably going to go with the sellers who offer me the lowest price." But, it's also good to leave the door open to future negotiations. If you get a flat refusal from the sellers, give them your business card and say, "If you decide to lower your price, I want to be the first to know about it, fair enough?"

Never Say *Yes* to the First Proposal

Saying *yes* to the first proposal from the sellers will automatically trigger two thoughts in the seller's mind:

1. I could have done better.
2. Something must be wrong.

Roger once bought 100 acres of land in the State of Washington. The sellers were asking $185,000 for the land, and Roger felt that if he could get them down to $150,000 it would be a terrific buy. (As we've said before, we don't recommend bare land as an investment. It's more of a speculation than it is an investment.) He asked the real estate agent to present an offer at $115,050. By picking that price, he was using two negotiating principles that we'll cover later:

1. Specific numbers have more credibility than rounded numbers.
2. Bracketing your objective assumes that you will end up midway between the two opening negotiating positions.

Roger knew that he was making a very low offer and thought he'd be lucky if the sellers responded at all, but to his amazement, they accepted his offer. What was Roger's reaction? Something must be wrong! He suddenly wanted to take a very close look at the preliminary title report when it came in. (You make an offer to buy subject to your approval of the preliminary title report. That's important because anybody who previously owned the property could have put a restriction on its use. We were once looking at a property that would make an excellent shopping center development. When we checked the title, we found that a former owner had put a restriction on it that there could never be any liquor sold on the property. That nixed the deal, because a liquor store not only builds traffic, but also is a big moneymaker when leased on a percentage basis.)

Roger's second thought was, "I could have done better."

Those two thoughts will go through anybody's mind whenever you say "yes" to the first offer.

Imagine if your son came to you and asked to borrow your car tonight and you said, "Sure. Take it. Have a wonderful time!" Wouldn't he automatically think, "I could have done better? I probably could have gotten $10 for the movie out of this too!" And, wouldn't he automatically think, "What's going on here? How come they want me out of the house?"

Flinch When the Seller First Tells You the Price

Power Negotiators know that you should always *flinch*—react with shock and surprise at the other side's proposals. Let's say that you are in a resort area and stop to watch one of those charcoal sketch artists. He doesn't have the price posted, and he has the shill sitting on the stool. You ask him how much he charges, and he tells you $15. If that doesn't appear to shock you, his next words will be, "And $5 extra for color." If you still don't appear shocked, he will say, "And we have these shipping cartons here, you'll need one of these too."

Perhaps you have a friend who would never flinch like that, because it's beneath his or her dignity. The kind of person who would walk into a car showroom and say to the salesperson, "How much is the convertible in the window?"

The salesperson says, "$52,000."

Your friend says, "That's not bad!"

We know it sounds dumb and ridiculous, but the truth of the matter is that when sellers tell you their price, they are watching for your reaction. They may not think for a moment that you'll pay that much. The sellers have just thrown out a high price to see what your reaction will be. If you don't flinch, they will automatically think, "Maybe I will get him to pay that much. I didn't think he would, but now I'm going to be a tough negotiator and see how far I can get him to go."

Flinching is critical because most people believe what they see more than what they hear. The visual overrides the auditory in most people. It's safe for you to assume that at least 70 percent of the sellers with whom you negotiate will be visuals. What they see is more important than what they hear. If you've ever had any neurolinguistic training, you know that people are visual, auditory, or kinesthetic (what they feel is paramount). There are a few gustatory (taste) and olfactory (smell) people around, but not many. If you find any, they're usually chefs or perfume blenders.

If you'd like to know what you are, close your eyes for 10 seconds and think of the house in which you lived when you were 10 years old. You probably saw the house in your mind, so you're a visual. Perhaps you didn't get a good visual picture, but you heard what was going on, perhaps trains passing by or children playing. That means you're auditory. The third possibility is that you didn't so much see the house, or hear what was going on, but you just got a feeling for what it was like when you were 10. That makes you a kinesthetic.

Assume that sellers are visual unless you have something else to go on. Assume that what they see has more impact than what they hear. That's why it's so important to flinch when you first hear their asking price.

Always Play the Reluctant Buyer Role

Playing Reluctant Buyer is a terrific way to squeeze the seller's expectations before the negotiations even start. Try it and you'll see how you can get sellers to drop their price many thousands of dollars in just a few seconds.

Remember that the first price sellers give you is what we call "the wish price." This is what the sellers are wishing you would pay for the property. You can't make money as a real estate investor buying at the wish price. You need to determine the seller's walk-away price—the price at which they will not, or cannot, sell the property.

Here's how you use the Reluctant Buyer gambit to uncover their walk-away price. Get the sellers to show you the property. Take all the time that you can doing this. Ask all the questions you can think of. Finally, when you cannot think of another thing to ask, you say, "I really appreciate all the time that you've taken with me. Unfortunately, I don't think I can make this work for me. Remember that I'm a real estate investor and I need to buy properties so I can rent them out and make a profit. At this price, I just don't think I can make it work. But I really appreciate all the time you've taken after me, and I wish you the best of luck."

You turn to leave and then, almost as an afterthought, you turn back and say, "I hate you had to spend so much time with me for nothing, but just to be fair, what is the very lowest price you would take for the property?"

Remember that this is not the end of the negotiation. It is not even the beginning of the negotiation. At this point, you're simply trying to squeeze the seller's expectations before the negotiations even start.

By playing Reluctant Buyer, you won't get sellers to come all the way down from their wish price to their walk-away price, but what they will typically do is give away half their negotiating range, just because you used this technique. It gives you a feel for how low they may go if you keep on negotiating.

The Vise Technique

The *vise* is another very effective negotiating gambit, and what it can accomplish will amaze you. The vise gambit is the simple little expression, "You'll have to do better than that." Here's how Power Negotiators use it: You have toured the property with the sellers. You have asked all the questions you can think of. You have played Reluctant Buyer to squeeze the seller's negotiating range, and finally the sellers give you their absolute, rock bottom, can't go a penny less, price for the property.

You pause, appear to study their offer, and then respond with the vise gambit by calmly saying, "I'm sorry; you'll have to do better than that."

An experienced negotiator will automatically respond with the *counter gambit*, which is, "Exactly how much better than that do I have to do?" trying to pin you down to a specific number. However, it will amaze you how often inexperienced sellers will concede a big chunk of their negotiating range simply because you said, "You'll have to do better than that."

One of the best examples of using the vise gambit happened to Mike before he left the business world and retired to oversee his real estate holdings. His company had advertised on the front cover of the city directory for years. One year a new salesperson called on him to renew his ad. When he told Mike how much the renewal would be, Mike flinched.

"How Much!" he exclaimed.

Immediately, the salesperson cut the price by 20 percent.

"You'll have to do better than that," Mike responded.

The salesperson cut the price an additional 10 percent.

"You'll have to do better than that," Mike said again.

The salesperson cut the price another 10 percent.

Mike couldn't believe what was happening. "You'll have to do better than that," he said again.

The salesperson cut the price another 5 percent.

By now, it had become a game with Mike to find out just how many times the salesperson would cut the price using nothing but the vise technique. Once again, he said, "You'll have to do better than that."

Another 5 percent cut, then another 3 percent cut, and a 2 percent cut later, with the salesperson almost in tears, Mike finally renewed the ad. When we discussed this incident, neither of us had ever heard of more than one or two drops in price in the same negotiation using the vise technique. This salesperson made concessions of 20, 10, 10, 5, 5, 3, and 2 percent without ever asking Mike to buy. What's ironic about this whole negotiation is that Mike was prepared to renew at the full price if necessary.

What's the best thing for you to do, once you've said, "You'll have to do better than that?" You've got it. Shut up! Don't say another word. The other side may just make a concession to you. Salespeople call this the silent close. They all learn it the first week that they are in sales. You make your proposal and then shut up. The sellers may just say "Yes," so it's foolish to say a word until you find out what they are willing to do.

Roger once watched two salespeople do the silent close on each other. As he tells the story, "There were three of us sitting at a circular conference table. The salesperson on my right wanted to buy a piece of real estate from the salesperson on my left. He made his proposal and then shut up, just as they taught him in sales training school. The more experienced salesperson on my left must have thought, "Son of a gun. I can't believe this. He's going to try the silent close on *moi*? I'll teach him a thing or two. I won't talk either."

"So there I was, sitting between two strong-willed people, who were both silently daring the other to be the next one to talk. I didn't know how this was ever going to get resolved. There was dead silence in the room, except for a grandfather clock that was ticking away in the background. I looked at each of them, and obviously, they both knew what the other was doing. Neither one was willing to give in. I didn't know how this was ever going to get resolved. It seemed as though half an hour went by, although it was probably more like five minutes. Silence makes time pass very slowly in our culture.

Finally, the more experienced salesperson broke the impasse by scrawling the word *DECIZION?* on a pad of paper and sliding it across to the other. He had deliberately misspelled the word *decision*. The younger salesperson looked at it and without thinking said, "You misspelled decision." Once he opened his mouth, he couldn't stop talking. He went on to say, "If you're not willing to accept what I offered you, I might be willing to come up another

$2,000; but not a penny more." He renegotiated his own proposal before he found out if the other person would accept it or not.

So to use the vise technique, Power Negotiators simply respond to the seller's proposal or counterproposal with, "I'm sorry, you'll have to do better than that," and then shut up.

Try it out on some minor negotiations to see how it works. This will build your confidence when you need to use it with larger negotiations.

In this chapter, we've taught you the beginning negotiating gambits that we use with the seller to get the negotiations started and headed toward a successful win-win solution. In Chapter 21, we'll teach you how to use middle negotiating gambits to keep the momentum going.

21

Middle Negotiating Gambits

As your negotiations with sellers progress, other factors come into play. Here's how you keep the momentum going toward a win-win solution with the middle gambits of power negotiating.

Use the Power of a Higher Authority

You would think that when you're buying property, you would want to have the authority to make a decision. At first glance, it would seem that you would have more power if you were able to say to the seller, "I have the power to make a deal with you."

Power Negotiators know that you put yourself in a weakened negotiating position when you do that. You should always have a higher authority with whom you have to check before you can change your proposal or make a decision. If you present yourself to the sellers as the final decision maker, you put yourself at a severe bargaining disadvantage. You have to put your ego on the back burner to do this, but you'll find it very effective.

Middle Negotiating Gambits

This method works much better when the higher authority is a vague entity such as a committee or a board of directors. For example, have you ever actually met a loan committee at a bank? We never have. Bankers have consistently told us that for loans of $500,000 or less, somebody at that bank can make a decision without having to go to a committee. However, the loan officer knows that if he or she said to you, "Your package is on the president's desk," you would say, "Well, let's go talk to the president right now. Let's get it resolved." You can't do that with a vague entity.

If you use the higher authority gambit, be sure that your higher authority is a vague entity, such as a group of business partners. If you tell the sellers that your partner would have to approve it, what's the first thought that they are going to have? Right! "Then why are we wasting our time talking with you? If your partner is the only one who can make a decision, let's get him down here." However, when your higher authority is a vague entity, it appears to be unapproachable. The use of the higher authority gambit is a way of putting pressure on people without confrontation.

Roger first learned the power of higher authority early in his career. He tells the following story in his book *Secrets of Power Negotiating* (Career Press):

> *When I first started as a real estate investor, it felt great to tell the tenants that I owned the property. It was an ego trip for me, but when my portfolio became substantial, I realized that it wasn't so much fun anymore. The tenants assumed that since I was the owner of the property, I was made of money. They would ask why it is a problem to replace the carpeting in their unit if it had a small cigarette burn, or to replace the drapes because of a small tear. Why is it a problem if the rent is late that month? In their eyes, I was rich. I must be because I owned all that property. Why was this upsetting me?*
>
> *The moment I learned the power of the Higher Authority Gambit, I formed a company that I called Plaza Properties and many of these problems went away. I became the president of a company, which was, to the tenants, a property management company han-*

dling their house or building for a vague group of investors out there somewhere.

Then when they'd say, "We've got this cigarette burn in the carpet, and it needs to be replaced," I'd say, "I don't think I can get the owners to do that for you just yet. I'll tell you what though, you keep the rent coming in on the first of the month for the next six months, and I'll go to bat for you with the owners. I'll see what I can do for you with them at that time."

If they would say, "Roger, we're not going to have the rent until the 15th of the month," I would say, "Wow, I know exactly how that goes. Sometimes it can get difficult, but unfortunately, on this property I just don't have any leeway. The owners have told me that if the rent's not in by the fifth of the month I have to file an eviction notice. So what can we do to get the rent in on time?"

This is a good example of why we recommend using a professional property manager to manage your properties. The manager automatically has the advantage of the resort to higher authority (you) when necessary.

Higher authority is also an exceptionally effective way of pressuring sellers to give you a better deal without confrontation. Look at the advantages:

- You can put pressure on sellers without confrontation: "My partners wouldn't consider an offer that high."
- It sets them up for use of the vise technique: "You'll have to do better than that if you want my partners to consider it."
- You can make suggestions to sellers without making a specific offer, "If you can come down another 10 percent, I'd be willing to recommend it to my partners."
- It sets you up to use the good guy/bad guy technique (an ending negotiating gambit that we'll teach you later), "If it were up to me, I'd pick your property, but my partners are looking at others and only care about getting the lowest price."

The Counter-Gambits to Higher Authority

You can see how using the higher authority gambit enables you to put pressure on sellers without confrontation, but what happens when the sellers use the higher authority gambit on you? You write up an offer on a property, and the sellers say, "Let me take it to my partners and see what they say" or "I'll talk to my CPA about it." What do you do then?

The best approach is to remove the seller's resort to higher authority before the negotiations even start. If you can, get them to admit that they can make a decision if the proposal is reasonable. This is what real estate agents are taught to say to buyers before putting them in the car, "Let me be sure I understand, if we find exactly the right property for you, is there any reason why you couldn't make a decision today?" It's the same thing that car dealers do when, before they let you take the car for a test drive, they say, "Let me be sure I understand, if you like this car as much as I know you're going to, is there any reason why you couldn't make a decision today?" Because they know that if they don't remove the resort to higher authority up front, then there's a danger that under the pressure of asking for a decision, the other person will invent a higher authority to use as a delaying tactic. Something such as, "Look, I'd love to give you a decision today, but I can't because my father-in-law has to look at the property (or the car)" or "Uncle Joe is helping us with the down payment, and we need to talk to him first."

Here's how you remove the seller's ability to use the higher authority gambit on you. Before you present your proposal to the seller, before you even get it out of your briefcase, you should casually say, "I don't mean to put any pressure on you, (which prepares the sellers for the pressure that you're about to put on them), but my partners are looking at another property. I think that they prefer yours but if we can't reach agreement with you, I'm sure you'll understand if they move on to the other opportunity since they do plan to buy one of them. (By saying this, you let the sellers know that you have other options, which gives you power in the negotiation.) Let me be sure I understand. If this proposal meets *all your needs* (that's as broad as any statement can be, isn't it?) is there any reason why you wouldn't give us a decision today?"

This is a harmless thing for the sellers to agree to because they think, "If the offer doesn't meet all my needs, no problem; there's loads of wriggle room there." However, if you can get them to respond with, "Well, sure if it meets *all* my needs, I'll give you an okay right now." Look at what you've accomplished:

1. You've eliminated their right to tell you that they want to think it over. If they do, you can say, "Well, let me go over it one more time. There must be something I didn't cover clearly enough because you said if the offer meets all your needs, you were ready to make a decision today. Is there something about it you don't like or don't understand?"
2. You've eliminated their right to refer it to a higher authority. You've eliminated their right to say, "I want my CPA to see the offer," or "I want my brother-in-law to take a look at it."

If you are unable to remove their resort to higher authority, then what can you do? There will be times when you'll say, "If this offer meets all your needs, are there any reasons why you wouldn't give me a decision today?" and the sellers may reply with something like, "I'm sorry, but there are tax implications here and I need to talk to my CPA before I decide. I'll have to refer it to him for a final decision" or "I have an uncle that owns an interest in the property, so I have to get his approval."

There are three steps that Power Negotiators take when they're not able to remove the seller's resort to higher authority:

Step 1: Appeal to Their Ego. With a smile on your face, you say, "But your uncle always follows your recommendations, doesn't he?" With some personality styles, this appeal to the ego is enough. They'll say, "Well, I guess you're right. It's just a formality."

But, what if they come back with, "Yes, he usually goes along with my recommendations but I can't give you a decision until I've taken it to him." Then you move to step two.

Step 2: Get the Seller's Commitment That He or She Will Take It to the Higher Authority with a Positive Recommendation. So you say, "But you will recommend it to him, won't you?" Hopefully, you'll get a response similar to, "Yes, it looks good to me, I'll go to bat for you with him."

Getting the seller's commitment that he or she is going to recommend it to the higher authority is very important. It is at this point that the seller may reveal that there really isn't a higher authority and that stating so was just a negotiating gambit that he or she was using on you.

In stage two, Power Negotiators get the seller's commitment that he or she will go to the higher authority with a positive recommendation. There are only two things that can happen now; the seller will say either, "Yes I will recommend it" or "No I won't—because . . ." Either way you've won. Their endorsement would be preferable, of course, but any time you can draw out an objection you should say, "Hallelujah," because objections are buying signals. Sellers are not going to object to your offers unless they are interested in them. If they truly aren't interested, they don't care what your offers are.

Step 3: The Qualified "Subject to" Close. The "subject to" close is the same one that life insurance agents use when they say, "Quite frankly, I don't know if we can get this much insurance on someone your age or not. It would have to be "subject to" you passing a physical exam anyway, so why don't we just write up the paper work "subject to" you passing the physical?" The life insurance agent knows that if you can fog a mirror during the physical, he or she can get you the insurance, but it doesn't sound as though you're making as important a decision as you really are.

The qualified "subject to" close, in this instance, would be, "Look, I told you about this other property that my partners are considering. They don't want to lose that opportunity, so let me suggest this. Let's just write up the offer 'subject to' the right of your CPA to reject the offer within a 24-hour period for any specific tax reason" or "Let's just write up the offer 'subject to' the right of your attorney to reject the offer within a 24-hour period for any specific legal reason."

Notice that you're not saying subject to their acceptance. You're saying subject to their right to decline it for a specific reason. If they were going to refer it to an attorney, it would be for a legal reason. If they were going to refer it to their CPA, it would be a tax reason and so on, but try to nail it down to a specific reason.

Never Offer to Split the Difference

In this country, there is a tremendous sense of fair play. This sense of fair play dictates that if both sides give equally, then it should be fair. If Joe puts his home up for sale at $200,000 and Sheila makes an offer for $180,000, and both Joe and Sheila are eager to compromise, they will both tend to be thinking, "If we settled at $190,000 that would be fair, because we both gave equally." Maybe it's fair and maybe it isn't. It depends on the opening negotiating positions that Joe and Sheila took. If the house is really worth $190,000 and Joe was offering it at an inflated price only to take advantage of Sheila having fallen in love with it, then it's not fair. If the house is worth $200,000 and Sheila is willing to pay that but is taking advantage of Joe's financial problems, then that isn't fair either. So, don't fall into the trap of thinking that splitting the difference is the fair thing to do when you can't resolve a difference in price with the sellers.

With that misconception out of the way, let us point out that Power Negotiators know that splitting the difference does not mean splitting it down the middle. If you split the difference twice, the split becomes a 75 percent/25 percent split; furthermore, it is often possible to get sellers to split the difference two, three, or more times.

Roger once negotiated with a bank that held a blanket encumbrance over several properties that he owned. He sold one property that was included under the blanket mortgage, and his loan agreement entitled the bank to a $32,000 pay-down of the loan to release it. He offered them $28,000. He got them to offer to split the difference at $30,000. Over a period of weeks, leading up to the closing on this four-unit building, he was able to get them to split the difference again at $29,000; and again at $28,500 and finally they agreed to accept $28,250.

Here's how that this gambit works. The first thing to remember is that you should never offer to split the difference yourself, but always encourage the sellers to offer to split the difference.

Let's say that you're trying to buy a single-family residence. The sellers were asking $92,000 but when you used the vise technique, they quickly offered to take $89,000, if they could get a quick sale. You ran the NOI and found that you could make the property work if you could buy it for $86,000.

You bracketed your objective and offered the sellers $83,000 but implied flexibility to encourage them to negotiate with you. Since then, the sellers have come down to $87,000 and you have raised your offer to $85,000. You're only $2,000 apart, and your target price of $86,000 is in the middle. Getting the seller to agree to split the difference should be easy.

Instead of you offering to split the difference, here's what you should do. You should say, "Well, I guess this is just not going to fly. It seems like such a shame though, when we've both spent so much time trying to put this together, and now it looks like it's all going to collapse, when we're just $2,000 apart."

If you keep stressing the time that you've both spent trying to reach an agreement, and the small amount of money that you're apart on the price, eventually the sellers will say, "Look, why don't we just split the difference."

When they make this offer, you act a little dumb and say, "Let's see, splitting the difference, what would that mean? I'm at $85,000, and you're at $87,000. What you're telling me is you'd come down to $86,000, is that what I'm hearing you say?"

"Well, yes," they respond. "If you'll come up to $86,000, then we'll settle for that." At this point, you say, "$86,000 sounds a lot better than $87,000. Tell you what, let me talk to my partners" (or whatever other higher authority you've set up) "and see how they feel about it. I'll tell them you came down to $86,000, and we'll see if we can put it together now. I'll get back to you this afternoon."

That afternoon you get back to the sellers and say, "Wow, are my partners tough to deal with right now. I felt sure that I could get them to go along with $86,000, but we spent two hours going over the figures again, and they insist that we'll lose money if we go a penny above $85,000, but my goodness, we're only $1,000 apart now. Surely, we're not going to let it all fall apart when we're only $1,000 apart?"

If you keep that up long enough, eventually they may offer to split the difference again. If they do, this gambit has made you an extra $500; however, even if they won't budge and you end up paying the $86,000 that you would have done if *you* had offered to split the difference, something very significant happened.

The significant thing that happened was you let them feel like they won because they proposed splitting the difference at $86,000. Then you appeared to struggle to get your partners to go along with their proposal. If, on the other hand, you suggested splitting the difference, then it would put the sellers in the position of having to come down to meet your price. That may seem like a very subtle difference to you, but it's significant in terms of who felt they won and who felt they lost. Remember that the essence of power negotiating is to leave the other side thinking that they won, so the rule is, "Never offer to split the difference, but always encourage the other person to offer to split the difference."

Always Ask for a Trade-Off

The *trade-off gambit* tells you that any time the sellers ask you for a concession in the negotiations, you should automatically ask for something in return. The first time you use this gambit, you'll get back the money you invested in this book many times over. From then on using it will earn you thousands of dollars every year. Let's look at a couple of ways of using the trade-off gambit:

Let's say that you've contracted to buy a house. The sellers ask if they can leave some of their furniture in the garage for three days after closing, until they can borrow their brother-in-law's pickup to move it. That's not a big problem, but we want you to remember this rule, "However small the concession they want, always ask for something in return." Say to them, "Let me check with my family (vague higher authority) and see how they feel about that, but let me ask you this, "If we would be willing to do that for you, what will you do for us?"

One of three things is going to happen when you ask for something in return:

1. *You might just get something.* The sellers may be willing to clean the windows, put the storm windows on, or pass out your business cards at their social club.
2. *You elevate the value of the concession.* When you're negotiating, why give anything away? Always make a big deal out of it. You may need it later. You may have trouble getting your financing completed on time, and you need to delay the closing for a few days. Now you're able to say,

"We went along with you when you wanted to leave your furniture in the garage. I need you to go along with me on this." When you elevate the value of a concession, you set it up to use as a trade-off later if necessary.

3. *It stops the grinding away process.* This is the key reason why you should always use the trade-off gambit. If they know that every time they ask for something, you're going to ask for something in return, then it stops them constantly coming back for more. I can't tell you how many times students of ours have called with examples like, "Can you help me? I thought I had a sweetheart deal put together. I didn't think there were any problems at all, but in the very early stages, the sellers asked me to make a small concession. I was so happy to be buying the property that I told them, 'Sure, I'll do that.' A week later, they called again for another small concession, and once again, I said, 'All right, I guess I can do that too.' Ever since then, it's been one darn thing after another. Now it looks as though the whole deal is going to fall apart." They should have known up front that when the sellers asked for that first small concession, they should have asked for something in return. "If I can do that for you, what can you do for me?"

We recommend that you use these gambits word for word the way that we're teaching them to you. If you change even a word, it can dramatically change the effect. If, for example, you changed, "If I can do that for you, what can you do for me?" to "If I do that for you, you will have to do this for me," it becomes confrontational. You will weaken your position if you become confrontational at a very sensitive point in the negotiations—when the other side is under pressure and needs a favor. In fact, you could even cause the negotiation to blow up in your face.

We realize it's tempting to ask for specific concessions because you think that you'll get more that way, but we disagree. We believe you'll get more in the end by leaving the suggestion up to them.

In this chapter, we've taught you the middle negotiating gambits that we use to keep the momentum going with sellers. In Chapter 22, we'll teach you how to put the deal together with ending negotiating gambits.

22

Ending Negotiating Gambits

As you get closer to the end of your negotiations with the sellers, other factors come into play. Here's how you conclude the negotiation using the ending gambits of power negotiating.

Good Guy/Bad Guy

Using the *good guy/bad guy* gambit is a very effective way of putting pressure on people, without confrontation. I'm sure you've seen the good guy/bad guy gambit used in the old police movies. Officers bring a suspect into the police station for questioning, and the first detective to interrogate him is a rough, tough, mean-looking guy. He threatens the suspect with all kinds of things that they're going to do to him. Then he's mysteriously called away to take a phone call, and the second detective, who's brought in to look after the prisoner while the first detective is away, is the warmest, nicest guy in the entire world. He sits down and makes friends with the prisoner. He gives him a cigarette and says, "Listen kid, it's really not as bad as all that. I've taken a liking to you. I know the ropes around here. Why don't you let me see what I can do for you?" It's a real temptation to think that the good guy's on your side when, of course, he really isn't.

Then the good guy would go ahead and close on what salespeople would recognize as a minor point close. "All I think the detectives really need to know," he tells the prisoner, "is where did you buy the gun?" What he really wants to know is, "Where did you hide the body?"

Starting out with a minor point like that and then working up from there works very well, doesn't it? The car salesperson says to you, "If you did invest in this car would you get the blue or the gray?" "Would you want the fabric upholstery or the leather?" Little decisions lead to big ones. The real estate salesperson who asks, "If you did invest in this home, how would you arrange the furniture in the living room?" or "Which of these bedrooms would be the nursery for your new baby?" Little decisions grow to big decisions.

So how would this work in buying real estate? You've made an appointment to meet with a seller to discuss a purchase. When you get there, you find that the seller has his brother-in-law with him, who evidently has a small financial interest in the property. The brother-in-law has clearly convinced the seller that he's an expert in real estate. You present your offer, and everything seems to be going along fine until the brother-in-law starts getting irritated. Suddenly he stands up and says, "This person isn't interested in making you a serious offer. I don't have time for this," and storms out of the house.

This really upsets you if you're not used to negotiating. Then the seller says, "Sometimes he gets that way, and he's hard to deal with. But I'd really like to see us put this together if we can. If you can come up a little on your price, I still think we can make it work. Tell you what, why don't you let me see what I can do for you with my brother-in-law?" Unless you realize what the seller is doing to you, you'll hear yourself saying, "What do you think you could get him to go along with?" And soon you'll have the seller negotiating for you—and she's not even on your side! But keep reading, because on page 132 we'll give you several ways that you can counter the good guy/bad guy gambit.

The good guy/bad guy gambit works because, in a tense negotiation, you are drawn to the good guy. When you create a bad guy in the seller's mind, it draws the seller to you. You are the one who wants to make the deal. You are the one who wants to solve the seller's problems. Who would your bad guys be? You have several choices:

- The lender who won't make a loan at the seller's price.
- A spouse who thinks you're spending too much time investing in real estate.
- Your partners, who think you'd be paying too much.
- Your property manager who is telling you it won't rent for that much or that the repairs will cost more than you think.

So you say to the seller, "I'd love to put this together with you. Selling this house is the only thing that's stopping you from retiring to that condo in Florida. But my partners are telling me that we can't make it work at this price. Come down another couple of thousand, and I'll go to bat for you with my partners."

In Roger's book *Secrets of Power Negotiating,* he tells the story of using the good guy/bad guy gambit on a landlord when he was the president of a large real estate company in California:

We had one branch that consistently lost money. The branch had been open about a year, but we had signed a three-year lease on the premises, which committed us to try to make it work for two more years. No matter how hard I tried, however, I couldn't find a way to either increase the income or decrease the expenses of the office. The biggest problem was the lease. We were paying $1,700 a month, and that one expense was killing our profit.

I called the landlord and explained my problem to him and tried to get him to reduce the rent to $1,400 a month, a figure at which we could have eked out a small profit. He said, "You have two more years on that lease, and you're just going to have to live with it." I used every other Gambit I knew, but nothing would budge him. It looked as though I would just have to accept the situation.

Finally, I tried the Good Guy/Bad Guy Gambit combined with a great deal of time pressure. Several weeks later, I called him up at 5:50 in the evening. "About that lease," I said. "A problem has come up here. I want you to know that I really agree with your po-

sition. I signed a three-year lease, there are more than two years left on it, and there isn't any question that we should live with it. But here's the problem. I have to go into my board of directors meeting in half an hour, and they're going to ask me if you've been willing to reduce the lease to $1,400. If I have to tell them no, they'll tell me to close the office."

The landlord protested, "But I'll sue."

"I know. I agree with you entirely," I said. "I'm squarely on your side, but the problem is the board of directors with whom I have to deal. If you threaten to sue, they'll just say, 'Okay, let him sue. This is Los Angeles County, and it will take him two years to get into court.' "

His response demonstrates how effective the Good Guy/Bad Guy Gambit can be. He said, "Would you go into that board meeting and see what you can do for me? I'd be willing to split the difference and reduce the lease to $1,550, but if they won't settle for that, I could drop it as low as $1,500." The Gambit had worked so well that he actually asked me to negotiate for him with my own board of directors.

See how effective it can be in putting pressure on the other person without confrontation? What would have happened if I had said to him, "Go ahead and sue me. It'll take you two years to get into court"? It would have upset him so much that we would have spent the next two years talking to each other through attorneys. By using a vague higher authority as my bad guy, I was able to put incredible pressure on him without having him get upset with me.

As you can see from this story, by blaming a bad guy, you can put enormous pressure on the other side without confrontation.

A big benefit of knowing about this gambit is that you'll easily recognize it when sellers use it on you. Don't buy into it when you hear comments like this from the seller:

- "My husband (or wife) is so upset by your low offer that he's not even speaking to me anymore."

- "I ran your offer by our accountant, and he says I'd be crazy to accept it."
- From a real estate agent, "My seller is a tough business person. I don't have the nerve to take him an offer this low."

All these expressions are indications of the good guy/bad guy being used on you. Here are some counter-gambits to use when that happens:

- The first counter-gambit is simply to identify the gambit. Although there are many other ways to handle the problem, this one is so effective that it's probably the only one you need to know. The good guy/bad guy gambit is so well known that it embarrasses people when they are caught using it. When you catch the sellers doing this to you, you should smile and say, "Oh, come on—you're not going to play good guy/bad guy with me are you? Come on, sit down, let's work this thing out." Usually their embarrassment will cause them to retreat from the position.
- You could respond by creating a bad guy of your own. Tell them that you'd love to do what they want, but you have partners involved in the purchase who insist that you stay within the parameters of their investment program. A bad guy who is not in the negotiation can beat one who is every time!
- Sometimes just letting the bad guy talk resolves the problem, especially if he's being obnoxious. If the husband is ranting and raving about your low offer, sooner or later his wife will get tired of hearing it and tell him to knock it off.
- You can counter the good guy/bad guy gambit by saying to the good guy, "Look, I understand your strategy here. From now on anything that he says, I'm going to attribute to you also." Now you have two bad guys to deal with, so it diffuses the gambit. Sometimes just identifying them both in your own mind as bad guys will handle it, without you having to come out and accuse them.
- If the seller shows up with an attorney who is clearly there to play bad guy, jump right in and forestall the bad guy role. Say to the attorney, "I'm sure you're here to play bad guy, but let's not take that approach. I'm as eager to find a solution to this situation as you are, so why don't

we all take a win-win approach. Fair enough?" This really takes the wind out of their sails.

Nibbling

The *nibble gambit* tells you that you can get things toward the end of the negotiation that you can't get earlier. Initially, for example, the sellers may be adamant that they will not carry back any financing. Later on, when they know you better and trust you more, they may well change their mind.

Children are brilliant nibblers, aren't they? If you have teenage children living at home, you know that they don't have to take any courses on negotiating. But you have to—just to stand a chance of surviving the whole process of bringing them up—because they're naturally brilliant negotiators. Not because they learn it in school, but because when they're little, everything they get, they get with negotiating skills.

When Roger's daughter, Julia, graduated from high school, she wanted to get a great high school graduation gift from her parents. She had three things on her hidden agenda. Number one, she wanted a five-week trip to Europe. Number two, she wanted $1,200 in spending money. And number three, she wanted a new set of luggage.

She was smart enough not to ask for everything up front. She was a good enough negotiator to close Roger first on the trip. She then came back a few weeks later and showed him that the recommended spending money was $1,200 and got him to commit to that. Then, right at the last minute, she came to Roger and said, "Dad, you wouldn't want me going to Europe with that ratty old set of luggage would you? All the kids will be there with new luggage." And she got that too. Had she asked for everything up front, Roger would have negotiated out the luggage and negotiated down the spending money.

What's happening here is that a person's mind will always work to reinforce earlier decisions. Our minds do a flip-flop when we make a decision. We fight the decision up until we make it. Then we want to do things to reinforce that decision. Power Negotiators know how this works and use it to get the sellers to agree to something that they wouldn't have agreed to earlier in the negotiation.

Why is nibbling such an effective technique? To find out why this works so well, a couple of psychologists did a study at a racetrack in Canada. They studied the attitude of people immediately before they placed their bet and again immediately after they placed their bet. They found out that before the people placed their bet, they were uptight, unsure, and anxious about what they were about to do. Compare this to a seller when you first start to deal with them: They may not know you, they don't know whether to trust you, and they don't know if you can do the things you're promising to do. Chances are they're uptight, unsure, and anxious.

At the racetrack, the researchers found out that once people had made the decision to go ahead and place their bet that suddenly they felt very good about what they had just done and were tempted to double their bet before the race started. In essence, their minds did a flip-flop once they had made the decision. Before they decided, they were fighting it; once they'd made the decision, they supported it.

If you're a gambler, you've had that sensation, haven't you? Watch them at the roulette tables in Atlantic City or Vegas. The gamblers place their bets. The croupier spins the ball. At the very last moment, people are pushing out additional bets. The mind always works to reinforce decisions that it has made earlier.

So one rule for Power Negotiators is that you don't necessarily ask the seller for everything up front. You wait for a moment of agreement in the negotiations and then go back and "nibble" for a little extra.

You might think of the power negotiating process as pushing a ball uphill, a large rubber ball that's much bigger than you. You're straining to force it up to the top of the hill. The top of the hill is the moment of first agreement in the negotiations. Once you reach that point, then the ball moves easily down the other side of the hill. This is because people feel good after they have made the initial agreement. They feel a sense of relief that the tension and stress is over. Their minds are working to reinforce the decision that they've just made, and they're more receptive to any additional suggestions you may have.

Countering the Nibble Gambit When the Seller Does It to You

The counter-gambit to the nibble gambit is to make the other person feel cheap. You have to be very gentle in the way you do this because obviously you're at a sensitive point in the negotiation. Let's say that at the last minute the seller is saying to you, "You will pay all the closing costs, won't you?" You smile sweetly and say, "Oh, come on, you negotiated a fantastic price with me. You know that we can't afford to pay your share of the closing costs too." That's the counter-gambit to the nibble gambit when it's used against you. Be sure that you do it with a big grin on your face, so that the seller doesn't take it too seriously.

Consider these points when you go into negotiations:

- Are there some elements that you are better off bringing up using a nibble gambit, after you have reached the initial agreement?
- Have you made a plan to try a second time to get something to which you can't get them to agree the first time around?
- Are you prepared for the possibility of them nibbling on you at the last moment?

The Walk-Away Gambit

We discussed this gambit in Chapter 18, but we will mention it again briefly, because not only is it an ending gambit, it is the number one pressure point in negotiations.

As we explained earlier, your job is to convince the sellers that you are prepared to walk away if they won't accept your offer. The best way to do that is to develop options, because options give you power. Find two or three other houses with which you'd be almost as happy as the one the sellers own. This doesn't mean that you won't get the one you want, but it does mean that you'll be a more powerful negotiator. When you present your offer, you'll be thinking, "I hope these sellers will come down in price (or give me the terms that I want) but if they don't, I've got these other properties I can fall back on and I may even get a better deal on one of them." The sellers can always sense when you have options.

Sometimes, you need to tell the sellers about your options. You need to say something like, "We can only buy one property this month, and we've narrowed it down to your house and two others. I prefer yours, but frankly, my partners like one of the others better. In reality, any one of the three will work, and we can only buy one of them."

Conversely, of course, the seller's job is to convince you that he or she has options. The seller says, "I've already turned down one offer for $120,000; why on earth would I accept your offer of $110,000?" That may or may not be true, but it's an excellent negotiating strategy and usually nothing more. Don't allow it to cause you to give up trying. The truth is that, even if they really did turn down an offer for $120,000, it may have been an offer with completely unacceptable terms, such as dependent upon the sale of another property or involved with taking other property in lieu of a down payment.

The Positioning for Easy Acceptance Gambit

This is a very important gambit, particularly if you're dealing with sellers who have studied negotiating. If they're proud of their ability to negotiate, you can get ridiculously close to an agreement and then have the entire negotiation still fall apart on you. When it does, it's probably not the price or terms of the offer that caused the problem, it's the ego of the sellers as negotiators.

Let's say that you have a seller who was asking $100,000 for a property. It was on the market for six months without an offer, and the seller has now dropped the price to $90,000. You have calculated the NOI and can make the property work if you can get it for $80,000. You've made an appointment to meet with the seller at 3:00 this afternoon. What you may not realize is that just before you show up the husband says to his wife, "You just watch me negotiate with this buyer. I know what I'm doing, and I'll get us a good price."

Suddenly, he's not doing as well as he hoped in the negotiation, and he's reluctant to agree to your proposal because he doesn't want to feel that he lost to you as a negotiator. That can happen, even when the buyer knows your proposal is fair and it is the best that he will be able to do.

When this happens, you must find a way to make the seller feel good about giving in to you. You must *position for easy acceptance*. Power Negotiators know that the best way to do this is to make a small concession just at the last moment. The size of the concession can be ridiculously small, and you can still make it work because it's not the size of the concession that's critical, but the timing.

You might say, "We're only $2,000 apart on price here. We just can't budge another dime on the price, but I tell you what. If you'll go along with the price, I'll raise the earnest money from $2,000 to $5,000" or "We'll close in 30 days instead of 45 days."

Perhaps that's not a big consideration to you, but the point is that you've been courteous enough to position the sellers so they can respond, "Well all right, if you'll do that for us, we'll go along with the price." Then they don't feel that they lost in the negotiation, they feel that they traded off with you.

Positioning for easy acceptance is another reason why you should never go in with your best offer up front. If you have offered all your concessions already, before you get to the end of the negotiation, you won't have anything left with which to position the other side for acceptance.

Remember that it's the timing that counts, not the size of the concession. The concession can be ridiculously small and still be effective. Using this gambit, Power Negotiators can make the other person feel good about giving in to them.

In this chapter, we've taught you the ending negotiating gambits that we use to get the seller to agree to accept our offers. We have made millions of dollars using them, but we didn't learn them overnight. It takes constant practice to be a Power Negotiator. We suggest that you practice these gambits in all areas of your life. If you go into a store to buy a newspaper, see if you can get a nickel taken off because the corner is torn. By practicing in little things, you gain confidence. Don't wait until you're with a seller and there are thousands of dollars at stake.

23

You're Negotiating All the Time

In this section on negotiating, we have given you several examples of how to negotiate with sellers. It's very critical for you to learn to negotiate well, for when you buy you make money at the time of the purchase. You can't depend on making money when you sell, because if you follow the Weekend Millionaire program, you may never sell a property.

A s we conclude this section on negotiating, we want to emphasize the fact that you are negotiating all the time, not just when you're with sellers. Here is just a partial list of the other people with whom you will do business and will attempt to negotiate better deals:

- *Property managers*. You will negotiate management contracts and possibly even teach your managers how to be better negotiators. This will benefit you when they hire people to work on your properties.
- *Tenants*. You will occasionally have to get involved in negotiating with your tenants if issues arise that your property managers can't handle.

- *Maintenance workers*. You will negotiate fees, charges, and response times that will save you money on your maintenance work and improve your relations with your tenants.
- *Roofers, carpenters, plumbers, electricians, landscapers, and others*. You will negotiate with all the tradespeople that you use to build, refurbish, and repair your properties.
- *Real estate agents and brokers*. You will negotiate commissions and finders fees and the method in which you will pay these.
- *Attorneys*. You will negotiate legal fees, closing dates, and other services.
- *Accountants*. You will negotiate accounting fees and tax planning services.
- *Stores*. You will negotiate purchases of appliances, carpeting, and other materials you use in the course of business.
- *Car dealerships*. You will negotiate vehicle purchases, including trucks and other equipment you may ultimately use in your business.
- *Local governments*. You will negotiate with city and county governments over fees, charges, permits, inspections, etc.
- *Utility companies*. You will negotiate with electric, water, sewer, garbage, telephone, and cable companies that provide services to your properties.

Once you commit to becoming a Weekend Millionaire, you become a businessperson. The sooner you get in the habit of trying to negotiate better deals on everything you do, the sooner you'll see substantial increases in your income.

A negotiating dollar is not a gross revenue dollar to a businessperson—it's a bottom line profit dollar. If you practice your negotiating skills on small everyday negotiations, you will develop the skills to become successful in big negotiations like buying property.

Just keep in mind that you're negotiating all the time in everything you do. If you aren't getting what you want out of life, it's possibly because others are out-negotiating you without you realizing it.

SECTION 5

How to Structure the Offer

In the previous sections, we introduced you to the fundamentals of real estate investing. We say introduced, rather than taught, because it's truly difficult to learn a skill until you do it. To be a successful Weekend Millionaire you must have both knowledge and skill: the knowledge to analyze properties and structure offers, and the skill to get sellers to accept your offers. You can learn knowledge by reading this book; you develop skill when you put this knowledge to work and actually start making offers.

Whether it's the skill of playing golf, flying airplanes, or buying real estate, you have to tee up a ball, crank up an engine, or write a few offers. You have to get started.

That's what this section will help you do. In this section, we will show you how to structure the offer so that your property will generate an income stream for you.

First, in Chapter 24 we'll revisit the concept that we told you about in Chapter 5. We told you that the NOI that the property generates is far more important than the price of the property. We'll revisit that concept and show you in detail how to calculate the NOI. We'll also cover another very important point: You need to get a return on investment on any cash that you put into the property. That may be cash for the down payment, or it may be cash to fix up the property so you can get a higher rent.

Then you need to learn how to structure your first offer. You'll see how you determine the wholesale value of properties by a combination of the price that you pay and the terms under which you pay it. You may be surprised to learn that how you pay for your properties is far more important than what you pay for them. We'll show you in Chapter 25 how to establish a range of offers from all cash to all financing and show you how to use this range to write offers that meet the needs of many sellers.

Buying at Wholesale Prices. Keep in mind that the Weekend Millionaire method of real estate investing is all about making purchases at wholesale values. If you were going into the shoe business, you could not pay retail for your shoes, and then sell them at retail, and stay in business. There would be no margin of profit. Similarly, you cannot pay market value for real estate, and then rent it for market value, and expect to be successful. There's just no margin of profit. Please, do not make the mistake of thinking that the terms price and value are interchangeable. Price alone determines what is wholesale in the shoe business because shoes are expendable commodities that you pay for in full at the time of purchase. Real estate, on the other hand, is a long-term investment, so terms are as important, and perhaps more important, than price. You determine real estate's value by using a combination of price and terms.

In Chapter 27 we'll talk about nothing-down deals that work. Can you really buy real estate without paying any cash down? Will those deals be a good value for you? Our friend Robert Allen, author of the best-selling book *Nothing Down* (and his follow-up book *Nothing Down for the '90s)* led the field in this area. Our good friend and golfing buddy Carleton Sheets has an excellent program entitled *How to Buy Your First Home or Investment Property with No Down Payment*. We'll show you how you can do this and still stay within the Weekend Millionaire's goal of generating a cash flow in the first year.

Finally, in this section, we'll teach you the incredible tax advantages that you get from owning real estate. Our government wants you to own real estate, and it gives you some great incentives to do so.

24

Valuing Single-Family Properties

Back in Chapter 5, we told you that the biggest problem we hear from beginning investors is, "I can't figure out how to make money on rental property because prices are so high these days. I can't get enough rent to make the numbers work."

We also introduced you to the concept of buying a property based on its NOI. Being able to calculate the NOI of a potential purchase is critical to your success. In this chapter, we're going to go into detail about how to calculate the NOI.

Calculating the Net Operating Income (NOI)

Once you have determined what the property will rent for and the amount of money it will take to put it in marketable condition as a rental, you can then determine its worth. By filling in the blanks on the form in Appendix B, at the back of this book, you will be able to establish a good estimate of

Valuing Single-Family Properties

the NOI you can expect the property to generate. Let's look again at the calculation of NOI for 114 Elm Street that we showed you in Chapter 5.

Net Operating Income Calculation Form		
Property Address:	**114 Elm Street**	
Income	Monthly	Annually
Gross rent	$ 1,100.00	$ 13,200.00
Vacancy factor	($ 55.00)	($ 660.00)
Net rent	$ 1,045.00	$ 12,540.00
Expenses		
Management fee	($ 104.50)	($ 1,254.00)
Maintenance reserve	($ 104.50)	($ 1,254.00)
Utilities	($ 0.00)	($ 0.00)
Taxes	($ 50.00)	($ 600.00)
Insurance	($ 25.00)	($ 300.00)
Other expenses	($ 11.00)	($ 132.00)
Net operating income	$ 750.00	$ 9,000.00

Before we continue, let's discuss certain assumptions that we made in the above example. Keep in mind that these factors will vary from market to market, neighborhood to neighborhood, and property to property.

Vacancy Factor. The factor we used here is 5 percent. This is an allowance for the time between when one tenant moves out and a new tenant moves in. A 5 percent vacancy factor estimates that there will be a loss of income for a little over 18 days per year while the property is being re-rented. Some markets won't take this long, while others may take longer. Until you have experience, a professional property manager will be able to give you a good estimate of the time required to re-rent the property. Be aware that you will run into some real estate agents who will tell you that you don't need to consider a vacancy factor. They'll tell you that rental demand is so high you will always have the next tenant waiting to move in the same day the previous one leaves. Some will even tell you that your vacancy factor should

145

be a plus because you will have tenants move out before the end of the month even though they have paid through the end of the month. Don't be fooled by this kind of naively optimistic thinking. It could happen, but don't count on it. Better to be safe than sorry!

Management Fee. The management fee we projected at 10 percent of the net rent. This is an estimate of the amount a property manager will charge you to handle the property. Again, 10 percent is only a typical management expense. The property managers with whom you plan to work will let you know what they charge. Ten percent is typical, but your rate may vary from 4 to 12 percent depending upon your market, the number of properties you own, the competition among property managers, and your ability to negotiate a better deal with the property manager you decide to use. If you plan to manage the property yourself (although we don't recommend it), you still want to include a management fee in your calculations unless you plan to work for free. Just to be safe, always include a management fee when calculating NOI.

Maintenance Reserve. Our example uses 10 percent of the net rent, but depending on the age and condition of the property, you may want to vary this reserve from 5 to 30 percent or more. Regardless of how good the property's condition may be in the beginning, you need to set up a reserve fund for maintenance. Even if the property is brand new, the roof, paint, carpet, appliances, heating and air conditioning systems, and other items start wearing out as soon as you purchase the property. If the property has some age on it, part of the useful life of these items will already have been consumed. This means that repairs or replacement will come sooner rather than later. On older properties, you can allow for this deferred maintenance by increasing the percentage you put into reserve. To avoid getting into a cash flow bind, it's very important that you set aside a reserve for maintenance so you can pay for these expenses when they arise.

Utilities. We show these as zero in our example, because tenants typically pay them directly when renting single-family homes. If you will have to pay utilities, you will need to estimate their expenses and insert them in your calculations. Always check to see who pays the utilities when you are looking at properties. Don't make assumptions. In some areas, owners are required to pay for things like recycling and trash collection because they are included on the property tax bill. You will want to look very closely at utilities if you are calculating NOI for larger multifamily properties.

Taxes. You can estimate property taxes by using the tax rate for the taxing district where the property is located and applying this rate to your offering price. If a recent reassessment has occurred, you may be comfortable using that figure, even though it's lower than your purchase price. Don't rely on prior years' tax bills, because some states automatically reassess property following a sale. If this happens, you could be in for a very unpleasant surprise. In California, for example, the property tax is 1 percent of the purchase price plus any special assessments that voters have approved.

Insurance. You can get insurance quotes from any of the property and casualty insurance agents in your area, so shop around because these can vary widely. Some insurance companies may have had a bad experience in some parts of town or with some types of property, and they have deliberately priced themselves out of the market.

Other Expenses. We show this as a token amount because there aren't many hidden expenses on single-family homes. If, however, you are calculating NOI for larger multifamily properties, there will be a number of other expenses such as common area maintenance, grounds maintenance, area lighting, and snow removal.

Calculating Return on Investment

Now that you understand how to calculate the NOI for a property, let's use this to compute your return on investment (ROI). This is a standard business term that means exactly what it says. If an investor pays cash for the property, what will his or her return on the investment be?

If our property at 114 Elm Street generates $9,000 per year in NOI and the purchase price of the property is $90,000, then you would get a 10 percent return if you paid all cash. That's what investors call return on investment. It's an important figure because it gives you a chance to compare this investment to other investments such as stocks, bonds, or precious metals.

Remember that ROI in real estate assumes that you pay cash for the property. You're not going to do that, but it's the standard way that an investor calculates return on investment. Then what becomes important to you is the spread between the ROI if you did pay cash and the cost of borrowing the money. A 10 percent return on investment may be a very good deal if you can borrow the money to purchase the investment at 6 percent. You would be making a 4 percent spread on the money. It would be a bad deal if you had to pay 12 percent to borrow the money, because then you would have to pay the 2 percent loss from other funds. We call this latter type of property an *alligator*, because you have to keep feeding it.

How Changing the Financing Affects the Price You Can Pay for a Property. In our example, we calculated the NOI for the property at 114 Elm Street and determined that it represented a 10 percent return if you paid the $90,000 asking price. Probably not a bad deal, but let's look at some other scenarios:

Suppose you could purchase the property for cash and only pay $75,000 for it? The $9,000 annual NOI would then represent a 12 percent return.

On the other hand, if you paid $120,000 for the property, but were able to finance 90 percent of the purchase price at 6 percent interest, the interest on the loan for the year would cost you $6,480. When you subtract this from the $9,000 NOI, it leaves you with $2,520, or a 21 percent return on the $12,000 cash down payment you made.

In this example, you would have an ROI of 12 percent if you paid $75,000 cash, or an ROI of 21 percent if you paid $120,000 by putting $12,000 down and financing the $108,000 balance at 6 percent. Which would be the better deal? Of course, earning 21 percent on your down payment and letting your tenants buy the rest of the property for you would be a much better deal.

We don't mean to confuse you with this comparison, but it demonstrates why price may not be the most important thing when buying real estate. If this seems confusing, read it over a few more times until you grasp the concept. Once you understand the point we're making, you'll understand why so many people say they can't find property that will generate cash flow. You will also understand how we can give sellers a higher price and still generate income.

Now that you understand this concept, let's look again at the 114 Elm Street property, which we have determined has an annual NOI of $9,000. We're going to calculate the value of the property using different ROIs.

Calculating the Value Using Different ROIs. It's easy to see that $9,000 would be a 10 percent return on $90,000, but let's calculate the value of the property using other rates of return to establish a range of prices at which the property might be a good deal. To do this, you will divide the $9,000 by the different rates of return: $9,000 divided by 6 percent (0.06) = $150,000.

In case it's been a while since you had to crunch numbers on a calculator, we'll stop here for a quick math lesson. You can use a simple calculator to compute the value at specific ROIs in two ways. First, you can put the NOI, in this case $9,000, into the calculator; hit the divide key; and then enter the percentage amount, in this case 6; and then hit the percentage key. This produces a value of $150,000. Or, you can convert the percentage into its decimal equivalent by dividing it by 100, in this case 6 divided by 100, which produces 0.06. Then enter the NOI ($9,000); hit the divide key; and then enter the decimal equivalent of the percentage (0.06); and hit the equal key. This also produces a value of $150,000. It's not that complicated when you think about it. You can use either of these methods to compute values at various percentages of ROI.

What we've shown you here is that $9,000 is a 6 percent return on $150,000. Can you see how there might be a scenario where you would pay this much for the property if it could be purchased with long-term financing at less than 6 percent interest?

The following is a wide range of amounts that when invested at the rates shown, all produce a $9,000 annual ROI:

$180,000.00 @ 5% = $9,000
$150,000.00 @ 6% = $9,000

$128,571.42 @ 7\% = \$9,000$

$112,500.00 @ 8\% = \$9,000$

$100,000.00 @ 9\% = \$9,000$

$90,000.00 @ 10\% = \$9,000$

$81,818.18 @ 11\% = \$9,000$

$75,000.00 @ 12\% = \$9,000$

$69,230.77 @ 13\% = \$9,000$

$64,285.71 @ 14\% = \$9,000$

$60,000.00 @ 15\% = \$9,000$

This example shows how the $9,000 is simply a different rate of return on wide-ranging amounts of money. This is important when evaluating investment real estate, because it demonstrates how you can use NOI to structure a range of offers that balance price and terms, yet do not exceed the cash generated by the property. In other words, any deal you can make that lets you purchase the property with its NOI is a good deal. That's how you buy investment real estate you can afford to own. The key to becoming a Weekend Millionaire is understanding why terms play a larger role than price when buying investment real estate. In reality, you can let the sellers set the price if they will let you set the terms of payment, or vice versa. This phenomenon produces the give and take needed to negotiate wholesale purchases.

Consider the Length of the Loan in Your Calculations. If you truly want to purchase the property with the NOI, you will need to consider the length of the loan as well. Going back to the $9,000 annual NOI we've been discussing, that's $750 per month, so you need to make offers that a payment of this amount will cover. Unlike the prior example, which only shows the annual rate of return at varying rates, the following chart takes into consideration the time to pay off the loan as well as the rate of return. It shows the different loan amounts you can pay off with $750 per month payments, over 15, 20, and 25 years, at the interest rates shown in the left-hand column.

Valuing Single-Family Properties

Amounts You Can Pay Off with a $750 Mortgage Payment.			
Rate, %	15 Year	20 Year	25 Year
3	$108,604.00	$135,233.00	$158,157.00
4	$101,394.00	$123,766.00	$142,089.00
5	$ 94,841.00	$113,644.00	$128,295.00
6	$ 88,878.00	$104,686.00	$116,405.00
7	$ 83,442.00	$ 96,737.00	$106,115.00
8	$ 78,480.00	$ 89,666.00	$ 97,173.00
9	$ 73,945.00	$ 83,359.00	$ 89,371.00
10	$ 69,793.00	$ 77,718.00	$ 82,535.00

By using this chart, and knowing that the asking price of the Elm Street property is $90,000, you can see that you can pay this asking price under the following conditions:

- 15-year financing at a rate between 5 and 6 percent
- 20-year financing at a rate between 7 and 8 percent
- 25-year financing at a rate between 8 and 9 percent

By adjusting the length of the loan, you can pay sellers their asking price and still stay within the NOI. This chart also shows you that you could pay considerably more than $90,000 and keep the loan at 15 years if you could find financing at rates in the 3 to 5 percent range.

Don't panic! This is not as complicated as it looks! When you determine the NOI for a property and use it to calculate the variables under which you can pay the asking price, you have a simple formula that will let you purchase properties that you can afford to own and that will make the money you need to become a Weekend Millionaire.

In later chapters, we'll explore the variations of this method you will need to consider when evaluating multifamily and commercial properties.

Before we leave this lesson on the importance of running the numbers, let's consider another factor: the ROI on the cash that you put into the deal as a down payment or to fix up the property. Unless you include that, you're not getting an accurate picture of your ROI.

Including an ROI on the Cash Down Payment. This is fairly straightforward. If you made a $10,000 down payment when you bought the Elm Street property and you want to earn a 6 percent return on that money, you must keep $600 ($10,000 × 0.06 = $600) a year or $50 ($600 ÷ 12 = $50) a month of the $9,000 NOI to give you a 6 percent return on your down payment. This means the money you will have to make loan payments will be reduced from $9,000 to $8,400 or $700 per month instead of $750.

Including Rate of Return on the Cost of Repairs. Another factor you must take into consideration once you determine the NOI and are ready to make an offer is repair costs. This is a little more complicated than figuring your ROI on the down payment, because you have to estimate what it will cost you to bring the property up to prime rental condition.

Remember the inspection form (Appendix A) that we recommended you use to examine the condition of properties? If your inspection reveals repairs that you need to make, you need to consider the estimated cost of these when formulating an offer. Since you asked the property manager to tell you how much the property would rent for in good marketable condition, you will have to reduce your offers by the amount it will take to put the house in that condition.

If the property needs $4,000 worth of repairs, you will have to reduce the NOI by the amount of return you want to earn on this money just as you did with the money for the down payment. If you want a 6 percent return on your $4,000, then you will need to deduct another $240 (or $20 a month) from the $9,000 annual NOI.

Most investors overlook ROI on their down payment and the cost of fixing up the property. That's not good enough for a Weekend Millionaire. We want you to become a real numbers person when it comes to calculating your NOIs and ROIs.

Going back to our Elm Street property example, the true NOI available for new debt coverage is $9,000 less the $600 return on your down payment and less the $240 return on the repair costs. You now have only $8,160 to cover the payments on a new loan ($9000 − $600 − $240 = $8,160).

This means you must structure your offers based on $8,160, or $680 per month. Since the sellers want $90,000 for the property and you are putting $10,000 down, you need to figure out the conditions (interest rate and length of loan) under which you can borrow the remaining $80,000 and pay it off with monthly payments of $680. To help you out with this one, the number of months to pay off $80,000 with a $680 monthly payment at various rates is as follows:

131 months @ 2%

139 months @ 3%

150 months @ 4%

162 months @ 5%

178 months @ 6%

199 months @ 7%

231 months @ 8%

286 months @ 9%

If you want to look at more conventional loan terms of 15, 20, and 25 years, the $680 monthly payment will pay off $80.000 in 15 years @ 6.113 percent; in 20 years @ 8.217 percent, and in 25 years @ 9.157 percent. We'll tell you in Chapters 25 and 26 where you can get tools to help you with the more complicated calculations.

If we have confused you, please don't give up. Just reread this chapter, do some of the calculations on your calculator, and keep at it until the light goes on and you say, "Oh yes, now I've got it!" Knowing how to run the numbers is critical to your success.

25

Structuring
Your First Deal

As a beginning investor, you need a simple way to get started. You need to know how to write offers at wholesale prices that sellers will accept. Let's begin by using the home at 114 Elm Street that you analyzed in Chapter 5. This property had an asking price of $90,000. Now you need to determine the income and expenses.

Income. You met with a property manager who told you what the property could rent for.

Expenses. You looked up the taxes, you contacted your insurance carrier to get an estimate of the insurance premium, and after careful study, you estimated the maintenance reserve needed to keep the property in first-class condition. Based on your findings, you determined that the property would produce an NOI of $750 per month. With this work completed, it is now time to make an offer to purchase.

The Weekend Millionaire method of buying defines a wholesale purchase as one that will let you buy the property for the NOI of $750 per month or less and pay for it in 15 to 20 years. This takes into account that history has proven that real estate tends to go up in value while mortgages go down as payments are made.

Running the Numbers. You now need to get a good financial calculator, a computer with one of the many fine mortgage calculation programs, or a mortgage payment calculation book that you can find at most bookstores. Any or all of these tools will be useful in helping you identify and analyze your options. Let's look at some potential offers you might make using the Weekend Millionaire method.

> *Offer 1. Conventional Bank Financing.* You could go to a bank and seek conventional financing. The loan officer will probably want you to put down 20 percent of the purchase price and will finance the balance—if your credit is good and you have the income to support it. Assuming the bank's interest rate is 8 percent and you would like to earn a 10 percent return on the cash you put into the deal, the offer you might make could be $80,500 structured as follows:
>
> Monthly payment for $64,500 bank loan at 8%
> for 15 years   = $616.40
>
> Monthly cost of $16,000 cash down—yielding 10%
>   annually   = $133.33
>
> Monthly cash required for this deal   = $749.73

> *Offer 2. Seller Carries Back All the Financing.* You could simply offer to pay the seller $750 per month for 15 years with no interest. This would result in a purchase price of $135,000.

How to Structure the Offer

$$\$750 \times 180 \text{ months} \qquad\qquad = \$135,000$$

Monthly cash required for this deal $\qquad = \$750$

Both of these offers are virtually the same; i.e., they both require you to pay $750 per month for 15 years. But are they realistic? Offer 1 requires a substantial amount of cash and good credit, which you may not have. It also is $9,500 below the seller's asking price. Offer 2, which appears to be $45,000 more than the asking price, may be impossible for the sellers to accept, even if they want to, because they may not own the property free and clear. Even if they do, they still will probably be reluctant to turn their property over to you without a substantial down payment or additional security. Although both of these offers *have* worked for investors, we use them to illustrate the wide range of "prices" which you could offer without getting out of wholesale value range.

Value Is a Combination of Price and Terms. As we explained earlier, the value of real estate is derived from a combination of price and terms. These two offers, which range from $80,500 to $135,000 in price, and from 8 to 0 percent in interest, yield virtually the same value for the long-term investor. If you purchase properties using the NOI, it makes little difference whether the payment is all principal or part principal and part interest, if you only have to make it for the same number of months.

This concept is very important because of the way people in this country tend to negotiate. Most sellers are so bottom-line oriented that when someone mentions negotiating a purchase, the first thing most of them think about is price. This fixation on price can work in your favor as you set out to purchase investment properties. Let's go back to the hypothetical property with the $750 per month NOI. You could offer almost any price short of $135,000, and there would be an interest rate at which $750 per month would pay off the note. For example, by rounding to the nearest $100, the amount this payment would pay off in 15 years would be

$116,500 @ 2% interest

$101,400 @ 4%

$88,900 @ 6%

$78,500 @ 8%

$69,800 @ 10%

$62,500 @ 12%

etc.

As interest rates increase, the amount you can pay off decreases.

With the wide price range you have to work with on this hypothetical property, and knowing that the sellers asking price is $90,000, what do you do? If the sellers are presented with two offers at the same time, one for $60,000 cash from an investor looking for a 15 percent return on cash ($750 per month equals a 15 percent return on $60,000) and another from an investor offering $135,000 payable $750 per month for 180 months, what are they likely to do?

Who knows! That's what makes real estate investing fun. Because of their individual circumstances, one seller might take the $60,000 cash, while another might prefer the income stream from the $135,000 offer. Between these extremes are hundreds of combinations of price, terms, and financing sources that allow you to structure purchase offers to meet a wide range of seller needs. As we will teach you in the chapters that follow, there are specific reasons why offers all across this spectrum may be attractive. You seldom know the sellers' motivations until you present them with a written offer. As you learn more about the relationship between price and terms, you will learn how to make offers that stay within the range that best fits your personal financial situation.

If you are fortunate enough to have excellent credit and excess cash to invest, you definitely have more options. However, if your credit isn't the best and you don't have a big stash of cash, this is no excuse to stay broke for the rest of your life. No matter how bad your circumstances, you will learn that there are also people who own real estate that need to sell just as much as you would like to buy. Let's look at some other offers for the $90,000 property with the $750 NOI; ones that you may be able to handle and that may be attractive to a number of sellers.

How to Structure the Offer

Offer 3. Seller Carries Back a Second Mortgage. You may offer the
sellers $54,000 cash at closing and ask them to take back a
subordinated or second mortgage for $42,111 payable in 180
direct principal reduction payments of $233.95 per month.
Since you will need the cash to give the sellers, your offer will
also need to contain a clause making it conditional upon you
obtaining a $54,000 loan at a rate not to exceed 8 percent in-
terest for 15 years. The monthly payment on this loan will be
$516.05, which coupled with the $233.95 payment to the sellers, just happens to total $750, or exactly the amount of the
NOI.

The "price" in Offer 3 falls between Offers 1 and 2. It is closer to the asking price, and it still meets the goal of buying with the NOI of $750 per
month. The offer is more conventional, and it totals $96,111, or $6,111
more than the $90,000 listing price. This alone will cause the sellers to take
a closer look. The $54,000 loan is just 56 percent of the offering price or 60
percent of the asking price, which should make it more attractive to a
lender. But, you say, "My credit is not good enough to get a bank loan."
Don't worry; the lender doesn't have to be a bank. Individuals with cash present a wide variety of possibilities. A $54,000 first mortgage, that pays 8 per-
cent interest, and which is secured by a $96,111 property may be very
attractive, especially when rates on certificates of deposit may only be 2 to
5 percent.

This offer may also be attractive to sellers who have substantial equity
in the property and do not need all their cash at once. The $54,000 loan pro-
vides enough cash to pay off a small mortgage, pay a real estate sales commission, and still have some money for the sellers to take away from the
closing. This offer will not work with sellers who have little or no equity or
who need all cash at closing, and these people *may* simply reject your offer.
You don't know which sellers are which until you make the offer and give
them the opportunity to respond.

At this point, you may be thinking, "No one is going to sell property and take back financing at 0 percent interest." People thought the same thing about automobile manufacturers. They never dreamed these companies would sell new vehicles and finance them at 0 percent interest, but that's exactly what they did following the events of September 11, 2001. The decline in sales and burgeoning inventories that followed the terrorist attack in New York caused companies to become motivated. Suddenly they became very flexible sellers. And it must have worked because according to the National Automobile Dealers Association, October 2001 was the best October on record for new car sales.

Fortunately, it doesn't take major terrorist attacks, killing thousands of people, to produce motivated real estate sellers. Personal situations ranging from death of a loved one, to divorce, loss of a job, illness, aging, overextended credit, and a myriad of other personal crises produce motivated sellers. As we discussed in Section 3 you saw that purchasing someone's property can be a blessing in disguise rather than taking advantage of the person's unfortunate situation. Now let's look at one more offer that you might make for the hypothetical property we have been discussing.

> *Offer 4. Blended Rate.* Here you will use a blended rate offer that still falls within the criteria of letting you buy with the NOI. In this tender, you will offer the sellers $30,000 cash at closing and ask them to carry a subordinated or second mortgage for $60,000 at 4.64 percent interest for 15 years. Once again, you will need to make the offer contingent upon obtaining a $30,000 loan at 8 percent interest or less for 15 years. This offer gives the sellers their full asking price of $90,000 and is structured as follows:

> Monthly payment for $30,000 third-party loan
> at 8% for 15 years   = $286.70

> Monthly payment for $60,000 seller loan at 4.64%
> for 15 years   = $463.30

> Monthly cash required for this deal   = $750.00

How to Structure the Offer

In Offer 4, you will be paying 8 percent for part of the money and 4.64 percent for the other part of the money. This produces a blended rate of 5.8 percent, which is the same as financing the entire $90,000 in one loan at this rate. Again, all you are going to pay is $750 per month for 180 months. In order to meet the seller's cash needs, you juggle the amount of the third-party financing with the amount of seller financing and use the interest rate you have to pay the third party to determine the interest rate you can offer the sellers.

At this point, you might feel like this is a game where each time you give in one area you take away in another, and it is. You could easily restate Offer 2 with an offering price of $90,000, an interest rate of 5.8 percent, and payments of $750 for 180 months. Believe it or not, there are sellers who would be attracted to the offer stated one way who would not be interested in it stated the other way.

So far in this chapter, we have talked theory and hypothetical situations. We have tried to help you grasp the concept of making multiple offers that meet a wide variety of seller needs, yet all fall within the guidelines you have set for yourself. You may even want to take a columnar pad and create a rates versus amounts comparison chart to help you see the relationship even more clearly. You can look at our hypothetical example by entering amounts starting with $60,000 in the second row of the far left-hand column, and increasing by $5,000 increments up to $135,000 in each subsequent row. Then across the top, start with the second column and enter an interest rate beginning with 0 percent and increasing by 0.5 percent increments up to 12 percent as headers on each column. Now take your financial calculator and compute the payment amount that would be required to amortize the amount in the left column over 180 months at the interest rate in the column header. This will produce a grid more detailed than the one shown below, and you will easily be able to see how the relationship between price and terms (or rates versus amounts) affects payments.

Rates versus Amounts Comparison					
Payments required to pay off amounts in the left-hand column in 15 years at the rates shown in the column headers					
	0%	**2%**	**4%**	**6%**	**8%**
$ 60,000	$333.33	$386.11	$443.81	$506.31	$573.39
$ 65,000	$361.11	$418.28	$480.80	$548.51	$621.17
$ 70,000	$388.88	$450.46	$517.78	$590.70	$668.96
$ 75,000	$416.66	$482.63	$554.77	$632.89	$716.74
$ 80,000	$444.44	$514.81	$591.75	$675.09	$764.02
$ 85,000	$472.22	$546.98	$628.73	$717.28	$812.30
$ 90,000	$500.00	$579.16	$665.72	$759.47	$860.09
$ 95,000	$527.77	$611.33	$702.70	$801.66	$907.87
$100,000	$555.55	$643.51	$739.69	$843.86	$955.65

Writing Up Your First Offer. Once you have completed these exercises, the next step is to obtain a real estate Offer to Purchase and Contract form. These are available from real estate companies, title companies, attorneys' offices, and some office supply stores. Make copies of the form, and practice filling out a variety of offers. Find a real estate broker or attorney friend who will review these sample offers with you to make sure you are completing them properly. Continue doing this until you feel comfortable that you can write offers and can explain how they work.

Fear and anxiety keep the vast majority of people who purchase how-to books from ever actually putting the techniques contained in the material into practice. Don't become entangled in the paralysis of analysis that keeps so many people from reaching their full potential. Don't be afraid of getting a "No!" (Maybe even an occasional "Hell no!") Think of it as a game. When you start to view making offers to purchase real estate as a game, it becomes fun. If an offer gets turned down, and most will, don't panic. Just remember, unless you can buy the way *you* want to buy, don't buy. You are the one who will have to pay for the property for years to come, not the seller or the real estate broker. *Every purchase should work for you, not the other way around.*

How to Structure the Offer

The negotiating sections of this book will teach you how to structure offers that give you room to negotiate with sellers and still stay within the range of values you determine a property to be worth. Each time you make an offer, you will get better, you will feel more comfortable, and you will hone your skills. All you have to do now is make that first offer.

Practice, Practice, Practice. It's simple to make your first offer! Go find a property, use what you have learned up to this point to evaluate its income potential, and then fill out an Offer to Purchase and Contract form with an offer that will let you buy the property with its NOI or less. Make a good-faith deposit with an escrow agent and then present your offer to the sellers together with the receipt for your deposit. If you are working through real estate agents, they can handle much of this for you, but don't be afraid to simply hand the offer to the sellers yourself, and then give them time to look it over and respond. Making your first offer is that simple. If you get a "no," and chances are good that you will, no big deal. At least you will have taken the first step toward financial independence, which is getting started.

Patience, Patience, Patience. Each time you make an offer; you will learn and get better. If it takes 20, 30, 40, or more offers before you buy your first property, chances are excellent that you will buy it in a way that will give you an income for as long as you own it. Just don't get impatient and buy properties that fall outside the range of values you established. We call these alligators because they take a bite out of your wallet each month you own them.

26

How to Write the Offer

In Chapter 25, we suggested that you go to a real estate office, title company office, attorney's office, or office supply store to obtain an Offer to Purchase and Contract form, and then make copies and practice filling out offers. These forms may vary slightly from state to state, but all of them should address certain important items. An excellent resource that we highly recommend is the Carleton Sheets Real Estate Toolkit, available from The Professional Education Institute; 7020 High Grove Boulevard; Burr Ridge, Illinois 60527 (630-382-1000). This toolkit contains a huge variety of items you will use in analyzing and managing properties as well as planning your investing career. It also contains calculators, reports, and forms including an excellent generic Real Estate Purchase Contract. You can order it online at www.carletonsheets.com.

What All Offers Should Include

Whichever form you decide to use, there are certain items that should be included in each written offer. Among these are the following:

- *Buyer and seller information.* In this section, you will need to enter the full legal name of the buyer(s) and the name in which the property is currently titled.

How to Structure the Offer

- *Property description.* In this section, you should include both the street address and legal description of the property. If you don't have the full legal description, you may substitute a property identification number (PIN), lot number from a recorded plat, or the book and page number where the deed is recorded in the county registry. Any of these references may be used to locate the full legal description.
- *Purchase price.* In this section, you will enter the total price you are offering for the property.
- *Payment of purchase price.* In this section, you will specify the way in which you propose to pay the purchase price. This is where you will record the amount of deposit you are making with the offer, the amount of cash you will pay at closing, any existing financing you propose to assume, any new financing you propose to acquire, and any other consideration you will be giving.
- *Condition of property.* In this section, you will record the condition the property must be in for you to purchase it. This may be a statement as simple as, "As inspected on _____ date," or as detailed as necessary to describe repairs you want sellers to make prior to closing.
- *Closing date.* In this section, you will enter the date on which you are proposing to close the transaction.
- *Occupancy.* In this section, you will specify the date the seller is to deliver occupancy of the property. This is usually on the date of closing; however, if the property is a rental, you will want to identify the tenants and require a copy of the lease. You will also want to give yourself the right to withdraw from the contract if the lease(s) contain provisions not acceptable to you.
- *Deed and warranties.* In this section, you will specify the type of deed with which you expect the sellers to transfer the property. You will also include the warranties you expect the sellers to make concerning the title. This list may include exceptions such as easements of record, liens for taxes not yet due, and zoning restrictions.
- *Title review period.* In this section, you will specify the amount of time, following acceptance of the offer, you will need to have the title

and exceptions reviewed and the amount of time you will allow the sellers to cure any defects found during this examination.

- *Closing costs.* In this section, you will specify the costs associated with the closing that the buyer will pay and those which the seller will pay. Some items to be addressed in this section are

    1. Revenue stamps
    2. Title examination
    3. Title insurance
    4. Survey
    5. Appraisal fee
    6. Real estate commission
    7. Home inspection
    8. Termite inspection
    9. Recording fees
    10. Mortgage satisfaction fees
    11. Mortgage discount points
    12. Photographs
    13. Repairs
    14. Attorney's fees
    15. Lead paint inspection fee
    16. Other miscellaneous fees and charges

    Not all these costs and fees will be applicable in every transaction, but this partial list gives you an idea of expenses that can be paid for by the buyer or the seller or split between the two.

- *Prorated items.* In this section, you will address ongoing income and expense items that will continue after the closing and specify the date to which these items will be prorated. Usually these are prorated as of the date of closing, but other dates such as the end of the month can also be used. Among these items are

    1. Rents
    2. Utilities
    3. Taxes

How to Structure the Offer

4. Assessments
5. Interest on assumed mortgages
6. Heating oil or gas
7. Prepaid service contracts
8. Homeowners association dues
9. Prepaid mortgage insurance

- *Default and remedies.* In this section, you will specify what remedies the buyer and seller may seek from each other in the event either party fails to perform under the contract. Usually the buyer's liability is limited to the deposit made at the time the offer to buy was made.
- *Risk of loss.* In this section, you will clarify which party suffers the loss, and to what degree, in the event the property is damaged or destroyed prior to closing.
- *Miscellaneous.* This section encompasses several items that are usually referred to as "boiler plate" in a contract. Among these are

   1. *Governing law.* The state whose laws will govern the contract.
   2. *Binding effect.* A statement that makes the agreement binding on the respective heirs, successors, and assigns of each party.
   3. *Captions and headings.* A statement explaining that captions and headings used in the contract are for reference only and are not to be taken into consideration when interpreting the contract.
   4. *Survival.* A statement specifying that any provision of the contract requiring performance after the closing will survive the closing and remain in effect.
   5. *Entire agreement.* A statement that acknowledges that there are no outside agreements that are not included in the contract, and that any changes, additions, or deletions must be put in writing and agreed upon with the same formality as the original agreement.
   6. *Notices.* A statement that spells out how and where to send required notices to both buyer and seller.

- *Termination clause.* A clause in which the buyer gives the seller a specific time in which to accept an offer or it will expire or terminate.

- *Signature block.* This is the last section of the offer to purchase where the buyer and seller each sign the agreement. Typically, the buyer signs the offer and sends it, together with an earnest money deposit, to the seller. If acceptable, the seller then signs the offer and it becomes a legal contract. If the seller wishes to make a counteroffer, this is often done by modifying the original offer, signing it and initialing the changes, and then returning it to the buyer to initial the changes if they are acceptable.

Optional Items That You May Want to Consider

The preceding items should be included in all offers to purchase; however, there are others to consider as well. These items aren't required, but you should give them consideration. Among these are

- *Assignment.* This is a statement giving you the right to assign your rights under the contract. This can be done by simply including "or assigns" after the buyer's legal name. This is useful if you think that you might sell your position in the contract to someone else prior to the closing. Buyer's agents often use this technique to protect the identity of their clients.
- *Apportionment of purchase price.* This is an agreement between the buyer and seller as to the portion of the purchase price that is for land, buildings, and personal property. This allocation is important to Weekend Millionaires because depreciation is different for buildings and personal property and there is no depreciation on land. Since you are buying wholesale, it may be advantageous for you and the sellers to agree upon where the price reduction was made.
- *Survey.* Although not necessary unless required by a lender, we strongly recommend that you require a survey of the property prior to closing. As a negotiating tool, you can ask the seller to pay for the survey, but even if you have to shoulder this expense, it is worth it to confirm that property lines are where they were represented to be and that there are no adverse encroachments on the property.
- *Title insurance.* Like a survey, title insurance is not a requirement un-

less you are going to be getting a bank loan, but we strongly recommend that you never buy a property without it. As careful as most title examiners are, occasionally they miss things. Title insurance is cheap compared to the protection it buys. This insurance is another item you can use as a negotiating tool by asking the seller to pay its cost.

- *Inspections.* Termite, home, mold, and lead paint inspections are not required for property transfer, although some lenders may require one or more of these. The better you get at inspecting properties, the less important these inspections will become, but like surveys and title insurance, they make excellent negotiating tools when you ask the seller to pay their cost.

- *Condominium/homeowners association provision.* This is a clause you will want to include in offers on condominiums or homes in areas with homeowners associations. It should be drafted to give you the right to inspect the written declarations to ensure that there are no provisions that would prevent or unduly restrict you from using the property the way you plan.

- *Third-party financing.* If your offer is dependent on obtaining financing from a bank, mortgage company, or private individual other than the seller, you will want to give yourself the right to withdraw from the contract if you are unable to obtain the financing under the terms and conditions you used to calculate the offer.

- *Seller financing.* If your offer is dependent on seller financing, you need to make it subject to the seller agreeing to your specific terms and conditions.

- *Use restrictions.* Although not required, it is a good idea to make your offer conditional upon the property complying with building codes, zoning, and other local ordinances.

- *Personal property.* In this section, you will specifically identify any personal property your offer includes. When you include furniture, vehicles, carpets, drapes, appliances, and other items of personal property in the purchase price, it gives you many things you can trade away for other concessions when negotiating.

Miscellaneous Considerations

You may feel just a bit overwhelmed after reading this list of items to consider when writing offers to purchase. Don't be! Once you start writing practice offers, you will quickly discover that many of these are consistent from one offer to another, and with practice, they will come easily. The items that vary from offer to offer will give you the biggest challenges.

Keep in mind that there is no such thing as a standard way of making an offer. Whatever you and a seller agree upon, as long as it isn't illegal, constitutes a contract. We have seen real estate contracts that included plowing fields, delivering groceries, painting a car, permission to hunt and fish, paying off a credit card, putting up a billboard, and numerous other odd things that made deals come together.

Don't be afraid to ask for anything when presenting an offer. You never know what sellers will do until you ask. What's important is getting a dialogue started, and that's what written offers will do.

27

Nothing-Down
Deals That Work

In almost every book, audio, or video program on real estate investing, there is a section, often a very large section, on how to buy property with no money down. This technique is included because it is the most profitable way to invest in real estate. When you can acquire an income property without having to use any of your own money, any gain you receive from the property gives you a rate of return that is so big there is no way to measure it. That's why the no-money-down technique is so popular. No-money-down transactions are not only for investors who don't have any cash. Because they take ultimate advantage of the principle of leverage, even investors with plenty of cash should consider them.

However, you must be very cautious when you consider property you can buy without a down payment. Many properties that you can buy for no money down are ones you can't afford to own once you buy them. Often, the condition or problem that makes a seller willing to accept a no-money-down offer transfers with the property and leaves the new owner taking on the same problems that defeated the seller.

Nothing-Down Deals That Work

As we do throughout this book, we want to give you the knowledge you need to become a successful, long-term investor, but we also want to caution you about the pitfalls into which many new investors fall. That's why we have titled this chapter Nothing Down Deals That Work. The key word here is *work*. There are many ways to buy property with no money down. If you are committed to becoming a long-term investor whose goal is to build a substantial stream of passive income, there are only a few that actually work.

Many no-money-down deals depend on your ability to flip the property to another buyer quickly before the cash flow requirements of ownership kick in. We consider these deals speculations rather than investments. If new buyers can't be located quickly enough, these alligators can deplete your cash reserves and make you a prime candidate to offer someone else a no-money-down deal. You can quickly become like the mouse that says, "To heck with the cheese, just let me out of this trap."

As you strive to become a Weekend Millionaire, you need to be aware of four criteria, at least one of which must be present for a no-money-down deal to work. You must do at least one of the following:

1. Get enough cash at closing to cover any negative cash flow while you get the property in condition to support itself
2. Get an immediate income stream from the property that will cover cash flow requirements from the time you acquire it
3. Defer payments until you can get the property rented
4. Have enough cash reserves to support the property until you can get it rented

Without at least one of these conditions and preferably a combination of two or more of them present, you should pass on the deal, because you won't be able to meet the cash flow requirements of ownership.

Let's look at the kind of no-money-down deal that you as a beginning investor may encounter. The second of the four criteria identified above, which is an existing income stream sufficient to cover cash flow requirements, is easiest to find in single-family homes. Even though they may be vacant when you put them under contract, single-family homes usually rent quickly. Often, you can find a renter prior to closing the purchase.

How the Due-on-Sale Clause Changed No-Money-Down Deals

In the late 1970s and early 1980s interest rates were soaring. The prime rate peaked at 21.5 percent in 1980. Buyers of property clearly preferred to assume a low-interest-rate loan from the seller rather than borrow the money at a much higher rate from banks and savings and loans. Banks started adding due-on-sale clauses in their contracts as a way of "calling in" those low-interest-rate loans. Consumer groups filed lawsuits against the lenders, claiming unfair business practices. The banks started to lobby Congress to pass a federal law that would override court cases. The banks won the battle, and Congress passed the Garn-St. Germain Federal Depository Institutions Act in 1982. It gave lenders the power to enforce due-on-sale clauses, and it changed real estate investing forever.

Before the advent of the due-on-sale clause, investors made no-money-down deals by assuming a mortgage and then getting the seller to finance the difference between the mortgage balance and the selling price. To give you a simple example: The seller owes $80,000 on a $100,000 home. The seller lets the buyer assume the $80,000 loan and carries back a $20,000 second mortgage. If the seller needed cash, the buyer would take out a $10,000 second mortgage, pay the seller the $10,000 cash, and then the seller would carry back a third mortgage for $10,000.

Investors in those days sought properties with little or no equity to turn into no-money-down deals. Today, when we can't assume the underlying mortgage, it's just the opposite; we look for properties with large equities or no mortgage at all. The greater the seller's equity, the more options we have.

Sellers Who Own the Property Free and Clear

Sellers with no mortgage on their properties have many options; including taking back a mortgage for the full sales price. There are many reasons why a seller might want to do this. Let's explore some of them:

1. A seller may be at or past retirement age and be more interested in converting a house into an income stream rather than cash.
2. You may be in a position where you can give the seller a security interest in other property in addition to the purchase money mortgage as an enticement to get full financing.
3. The house could be an inheritance. The person inheriting it may prefer to convert it to an income stream in the form of note payments rather than trying to rent it, especially if it is located a considerable distance away.
4. It may be a property that can be lease/optioned. In this scenario, you would lease the property for a period with a portion of the lease going toward the down payment on a loan you will obtain later.

These are just some of the ways you can make no-money-down deals directly with sellers that have no mortgage. If they need some cash, or have a small mortgage that needs to be paid, you may have to bring in third parties to get no-money-down deals. When we talk about no-money-down deals, what we mean is none of *your* money. You use other people's money (OPM). By getting a small first mortgage from a private investor, you can make a no-money-down purchase and get operating funds at closing as well. With single-family home purchases, it is not only easier to find private funds, but the need to get cash at closing is less because this type of property is much easier to rent than commercial or industrial properties.

Structure the Purchase So That the NOI Covers Your Acquisition Costs

The important thing to remember when making a no-money-down purchase of a single-family home is to structure the deal so that the NOI you expect to receive will cover the payments. Don't forget that NOI is the money left over after allowing for vacancy, management, maintenance reserve, utilities, taxes, insurance, and any other recurring charges you will have to pay when you own the property. This will probably prevent you from financing a large portion of the purchase at market interest rates. For this reason, you should limit your third-party debt to the minimum amount necessary to make the purchase. You will want the seller to carry as much of the financing as possible and to do so at low or no interest so you are not put into a negative cash flow position.

A Typical No-Money-Down Purchase of a House

A typical transaction may look like this. You locate a home that you can purchase for $100,000. There is a $20,000 mortgage on the property. You determine that the house will rent for $995.00 per month. After deducting expenses, you determine that the NOI is $605.00 per month. You offer the seller $100,350 payable $30,000 cash at closing, which you will get by obtaining a 15-year private mortgage at 7 percent interest with payments of $269.65 per month. You then offer the seller a second mortgage payable $335.00 per month for 210 months, which totals $70,350. This offer gives the seller the cash needed to pay off the first mortgage of $20,000, an additional $10,000 with which to pay a real estate commission or use in some other manner, and eliminates the payment the seller has been making on the small first mortgage. *(Although the mortgage may be small, the payment may not be, because the original loan may have been for a much larger amount.)* This is important, because by eliminating the expense of the old first mortgage and adding the income from the payment on the new second one, you create a significant change in cash flow for the seller. For you, the two payments combined total $604.65, which is within the NOI you expect to get from the property.

When making an offer like this, three things should be included in the offer to purchase:

1. The right to show the property to prospective renters prior to the closing
2. The right for a new buyer to assume the second mortgage in the event of a sale of the property
3. The right to transfer the mortgage to another property of equal or greater value

This third option gives you a way to keep a low- or no-interest mortgage even if you sell the property.

The more successful you become as a real estate investor, the more options you have to make no-money-down deals. As your portfolio of properties grows, the combination of inflation growth and mortgage reductions will result in substantial equity growth. It may take you a few years, but if you periodically evaluate your positions, you will eventually be able to refinance some of your properties and pay off others. Once you get one or more properties free and clear, another more conventional way to make no-money-down deals becomes available. You can borrow against a free-and-clear property and pay cash for the new purchase; then it becomes a free-and-clear property. This not only gives you a way to make no-money-down deals, but also allows you to negotiate from the strongest of all positions *cash*.

The Value of Owning a Property Free and Clear

Just getting one property free and clear can open the door for you to make many no-money-down purchases. Here's how it works. Let's assume you own a property appraised at $100,000, free and clear. Given that you already own the property, you can probably get a loan on it for 90 to 95 percent of its value. This gives you a source of cash with which to make future purchases. Since cash is king when buying real estate and you will be looking to make wholesale deals, this gives you the advantage to negotiate future purchases for as little as 60 to 80 percent of appraised value. This doesn't mean that just because you have access to cash, you can buy everything wholesale. It simply means that you are in the strongest of all positions to negotiate wholesale purchases, and you should continue making offers until you find one.

Once you find wholesale opportunities, let's see what having just one $100,000 free-and-clear property can do for you. Since you can borrow against it to get cash, you are now in a position to make wholesale offers of $60,000 to $80,000 cash for other properties that appraise for $100,000. When you find sellers whose circumstances cause them to accept your offer, you borrow the money against your existing property, buy the new property, and still have a $100,000 free-and-clear property you can use to make another such deal. Banks will loan you up to 90 to 95 percent on property you already own, but they won't loan you 100 percent to purchase the same property even though you are buying it wholesale. By having a property free and clear, you can repeat this process over and over as you acquire additional properties, and the equity you gain from these wholesale purchases solidifies your financial position and builds your net worth.

Using Your Home Equity to Finance Purchases

Another source of funding you can use to make no-money-down deals is a home equity loan. If you are fortunate enough to have a large equity in your home and good credit, you can obtain a home equity line of credit. You can draw funds from this line of credit to purchase a new investment property, and then after you close on the property and get it rented, you can obtain a mortgage on it and use those funds to repay your line of credit. In the end, you have a no-money-down deal and, since you only pay interest on home equity lines of credit, you will have the advantage of interest-only financing while you get the property rented.

Anatomy of a Commercial No-Money-Down Purchase

Can you use no-money-down techniques to purchase large properties? Absolutely! Here's how Mike used the techniques to purchase a commercial property. Is this a typical no-money-down deal? Absolutely not! Deals like this are rare, but it doesn't take many of them in a lifetime to make you wealthy.

This involved a commercial building listed for sale at $242,000. The tax value assigned to the property by the county tax assessor was $243,100. The owner had operated a small manufacturing facility in the building, but had since closed the operation and retired. It was located in an industrial area with much larger manufacturing buildings on each side.

A real estate broker who had sold Mike several other properties brought this property to his attention. The broker said it had been on the market for some time and that the seller may be flexible and willing to provide part of the financing for a purchaser. After inspecting the building, Mike informed the broker that he felt it would be difficult to rent the property for enough to support a purchase price much over $150,000.

Nothing-Down Deals That Work

The broker consulted with the seller who said he might consider an offer of $200,000, but no less. The owner indicated a willingness to finance part of the purchase and casually mentioned that it would be nice to have an extra $1,000 per month during his retirement. There was a small existing mortgage on the property that would have to be paid, and it, along with the commission due the broker, would require Mike to come up with $60,000 cash to complete the purchase.

Mike didn't want to pay much over $150,000 and the seller was adamant about not selling for less than $200,000. Since he would have to pay $60,000 of this in cash, it would appear that a no-money-down deal was out of the question.

Mike's first thought was, "How can I give the seller what he wants and at the same time get what I want?" A major consideration was the fact that the building was vacant and producing no rental income. If he purchased the property, he would have an immediate negative cash flow. Whatever offer he made would have to address that problem.

One of the factors that Mike considered in making his target price $150,000 was the going market rate for rental of small manufacturing buildings. When he checked out similar buildings, he learned that the going rate was between $2.25 and $4.00 per square foot per year. Since this building was not quite as attractive as some others due to its location and condition, if he purchased it, he wanted to be able to offer it at a below-market rate in order to get it rented quickly. A rate between $1.50 and $1.80 per square foot would give him this advantage. How could he structure an offer like this and still meet the seller's expectations?

Mike went to work with his financial calculator to see if there was some combination of price and terms that would allow him to pay $200,000 for the building and still make the numbers work even if he had to rent it at a reduced rate. He knew he would need $60,000 cash at the closing. He had a good indication that the seller would finance the remaining $140,000, but this would still leave him with a cash flow problem. He estimated it would take at least $20,000 to cover the negative cash flow that would accrue while he marketed the property and located a suitable tenant. To make this purchase, he would need $80,000 cash plus $140,000 in seller financing.

How to Structure the Offer

Here's an analysis of the offer Mike made and the thinking behind it:

He began by taking the square footage of the building (12,000 square feet) and multiplying it by $1.50 and $1.80 (the rate range that would give him a competitive advantage in the market). This produced a potential annual rent of $18,000 to $21,600 or between $1,500 and $1,800 per month. Mike knew he would have to have $80,000 cash at the closing, which he would have to borrow.

The going rate of interest at the time was 8 percent, so the first thing he did was calculate what the payment would be on $80,000 financed at 8 percent interest for 15 years. This came out to be $764.52 per month. He recalled the real estate broker's comment that the seller said he would like to have about $1,000 per month income for his retirement. If he could pay the seller $1,000 per month for 140 months, it would pay off the $140,000 balance, but without any interest.

Again using his financial calculator, Mike computed the amount of money he could pay off with payments of $1,000 per month for 11 years 8 months (140 months) at the going rate of 8 percent. This calculation gave him the present value of the income stream. Amazingly, this came out to $90,830.91, which when added to the $60,000 the seller needed at closing totaled $150,830.91 or exactly the amount he originally thought the property was worth. If he could get the seller to accept an offer like this, his total payments on both loans would be $1,764.52, which was within the $1,500 to $1,800 per month range he felt the property would produce in rent. Not only would this be a no-money-down deal for Mike, but it would also let him finance the $20,000 he figured he would need to cover the carrying cost while he marketed the property.

Mike wrote an offer to purchase the property for $200,000, payable $60,000 cash at closing, and he asked the seller to take back a purchase money note for $140,000 payable $1,000 per month for 140 months. He also asked the seller to subordinate his note to a senior encumbrance or a first mortgage. (Subordinate means to put the note in second place in the event of a foreclosure.) In addition to this, he also asked the seller to pay for a title search, title insurance, a survey, termite inspection, an appraisal, the real estate commission, and a Phase I environmental inspection.

When he presented this offer to the real estate broker, the broker read it over and began to laugh. "No one in their right mind would accept something like this," he said.

"Why?" asked Mike.

"Well, for starters, you're asking him to finance $140,000 at no interest, put himself in a second position to another mortgage, plus pay all these other costs, many of which you should be paying," the broker replied.

Very calmly, Mike responded, "Let's look at the big picture. First, the seller is retired, but he still has to make payments on the existing mortgage. We're going to take that burden off him. Second, we're going to give him an income stream of $1,000 per month for 140 months that he can count on for his retirement. Because I'm not paying any interest, he doesn't have to worry about the loan being refinanced if rates drop a couple of points, which would mean he would get all the money in one lump sum and be taxed on it in one year. The combination of payment relief from the existing note plus the proceeds from the new note could amount to $1,500 per month or more in income he doesn't now have. Third, the offer I am making totals the $200,000 he wants. Finally, you'll be getting a commission on $200,000 rather than $150,000, which is all I can pay if I have to finance the full purchase at today's rates. As for the other items, I may have some flexibility on them, but let me call your attention to an important point. Won't it benefit both of us in the end for me to be able to buy the property and make a profit from renting it? Isn't that also what will give your seller the most security?"

"I guess I never thought of it that way," replied the broker. "Let me talk with the seller and see what he thinks."

Two days later the broker showed up with a somewhat sheepish grin on his face. "You aren't going to believe this," he said. "Not only do you have a deal, but it's just the way you wrote it up. I still can't believe he accepted it."

Mike and this broker still laugh and talk about that transaction, years later. The broker will readily admit that this transaction taught him not to try to think for other people. However, there's still more to this story.

With the contract accepted, Mike now had to find a lender willing to loan him the $80,000. At the time, rates on certificates of deposit were paying around 4 percent. Mortgage loan rates for real estate investors were at 8 percent. This spread, which is always there no matter what the rates, creates an excellent opportunity. Mike took his accepted contract to an individual he knew who had several hundred thousand dollars in certificates of deposit. He offered the individual a first mortgage on a property (that had a tax value of $243,100) in exchange for an $80,000 loan at 8 percent interest. He pointed out that currently the individual was loaning his money to the bank at 4 percent and the bank was in turn loaning it out at 8 percent and keeping the difference. Why not just loan the money directly to the investor and get the full return, especially when the security was as good as it was in this deal? The investor agreed!

Mike went to the closing with no money and left the proud owner of a 12,000 square foot industrial building plus a check for $20,000. It took him nearly a year to lease the property, but when he did, he hit another home run. He got a 10-year, triple net lease beginning at $2,250 per month and escalating by 3 percent per year for the full 10 years. The tenant invested over $300,000 of its money renovating the building to suit its needs, which raised the value of the property to over a half million dollars.

Since Mike put no money into this transaction, it's impossible to measure his rate of return. Deals like this are not for the beginning investor. We use this example to illustrate the importance of taking into consideration the cost of ownership before entering into a no-money-down deal. If Mike had failed to consider the $20,000 carrying cost he included in the purchase, he would have had to fund this from his personal cash reserves. While in his case he could have done so, many buyers would have defaulted on the loans and lost the property before securing a tenant.

We could fill an entire book with methods and case studies of how to structure no-money-down deals. Remember that, to become a Weekend Millionaire, you must keep your cash flow requirements at or below NOI. If you do this, you will be successful. There are excellent sources of information about no-money-down techniques; two of the best are Carleton Sheets's course titled *How to Buy Your First Home or Investment Property with No Down Payment* and Robert Allen's best-selling books *Nothing Down* and *Nothing Down for the '90s.*

28

Tax Benefits of Owning Real Estate

If you've ever driven past one of those huge government housing projects in New York or Chicago, you understand why the government wants housing to be in private hands. When you own real estate and make it available to renters, you perform a valuable service for your community, and the government rewards you with some impressive tax benefits.

Real estate is still one of the best, if not the best, tax sheltered investments you can own. Although not the gravy train it was prior to the 1986 tax law revisions, when it could shelter all of the income it produced plus substantial portions of what you earned on your job, real estate still enjoys many tax benefits. In its heyday, people used real estate to shelter incomes in excess of a million dollars a year and paid no federal taxes at all.

Unfortunately, those glory days are over, but let's review some of the benefits that remain for real estate investors today. We do not claim to be tax advisors, and the information in this chapter is not tax advice. We are providing the information solely for the purpose of giving you topics you can discuss with professional tax advisors to determine what works best for you.

Favorable Income Tax Treatment. When you work for money, you must pay Federal Insurance Contributions Act (FICA) taxes on your wages. There is no way around this unless you make more than a certain maximum income. If you work for someone else, your employer has to match whatever taxes are deducted from your paycheck. If you work for yourself, you have to pay both the employee and employer shares. FICA taxes and the maximum amount on which you must pay them have been steadily rising ever since the passage of the Social Security Act in 1935. There is strong reason to assume they will continue to increase as the baby boom generation ages and greater numbers of people start collecting social security.

The rents you collect from real estate are not subject to FICA taxes. No matter how large your rental income grows, it is exempt from both the employee and the employer share of FICA taxes. This is a tremendous tax break afforded to real estate investors.

Passive Loss Deductions. You may use all expenses associated with investment real estate to reduce rental income and shelter it from taxes. This means you get to deduct management fees, taxes, insurance, repairs, homeowner's dues, utilities, legal and accounting fees, and any other expenses incurred from owning and renting property. You even get to deduct a portion of the cost of the property each year in the form of depreciation. (We further discuss depreciation later in this chapter.) If after taking all these deductions, your income is zero or you show a loss, you will pay no ordinary income tax. If, you have a loss, you can use a limited amount of this to reduce your income tax liability on other income including your wages. Under certain circumstances, you may have to pay Alternative Minimum Tax, but you should seek counsel from a reputable tax advisor to make this determination.

Interest Deduction. Throughout this book, you will be learning how to use other people's money (OPM) to build a portfolio of investment properties. Whether OPM is from banks, mortgage companies, private individuals, or other sources, the Internal Revenue Service (IRS) allows you to deduct the interest charged, when you use OPM to purchase or upgrade investment real estate. Since leverage plays such an important role in becoming a Weekend Millionaire, interest is usually a major expense. Having this deduction is extremely important, especially in the early years when cash flows are tight. Over time, as you reduce your mortgages, the interest deductions decline and larger portions of your rental income become subject to taxes, but by that time your cash flow position should be such that taxes will not be a burden.

An important point to keep in mind is that while interest deductions help you avoid taxes in the beginning when your equity is low, as it grows, and you owe less, you will eventually have to pay taxes. That's not all bad though, because taxes only take a percentage of each dollar while interest takes a dollar spent to get a dollar deduction. When you pay off your mortgages and owe no money, you have no interest deductions, but you get to keep a substantial portion of the money that was all going to pay interest.

Depreciation Deduction. Even though appreciation increases the value of your property, the Internal Revenue Service allows you to deduct what you paid for the buildings from your income. You don't get to deduct it all at once; you have to do it over a period of years.

You can deduct the cost of residential buildings like houses and apartment buildings over 27.5 years. This is done by dividing the cost of a building by 27.5 if you elect to use straight-line depreciation, and the resulting number, known as depreciation, may be deducted from your income each year for as long as you own the property, up to 27.5 years. For example, you pay $100,000 for a rental house in a subdivision. Of this purchase amount, you decide to allocate $15,000 to the cost of the land and $85,000 to the cost of the house. Dividing the building cost of $85,000 by 27.5 gives you $3,090, which is the amount you can deduct from your income annually for up to 27.5 years. Accelerated depreciation is also available, but you should contact your tax advisor for advice on the best method to use in your personal situation.

Commercial buildings, on the other hand, are depreciable over 39 years. The process is the same as with residential properties, except the time is longer. This makes the percentage of cost you deduct each year smaller; however, you still get to depreciate the cost of buildings that due to appreciation are more than likely going up in value.

As good as depreciation can be, there is a potential downside for some investors. If you sell a property upon which you have taken depreciation, you not only pay tax on the profit you make over and above your initial cost, but in addition, you have to recapture the depreciation you have taken and pay income tax on this amount as well. This will be of little concern to people following the Weekend Millionaire program, because you will be buying and holding properties, not buying and selling.

Tax Deferral on Exchanges. If you sell an investment property, you can reinvest the money in other investment real estate and pay no taxes on the sale regardless of how great your profit is. Known as 1031 Exchanges, after the section of the Internal Revenue Code that permits them, these types of exchanges allow you to roll profits from one transaction into another, and then another, tax-free.

However, like with most tax breaks, the IRS makes rules that define the parameters you must follow in order to take advantage of them. One of the rules governing 1031 Exchanges is that the properties must be "like kind" properties. In other words, you must invest the profits from one investment property into another investment property. Some people take this provision to mean that you have to invest profits from a single-family house into another single-family house, an apartment building into another apartment building, a commercial property into another commercial property, etc. This is not the case. Whether the property you sell is single-family, multifamily, or commercial, you may invest the profits into any other type of investment real estate. Investment property is any property held as an investment. If you invest in raw land with the intention of developing it and selling lots, houses, condominiums, or other type of buildings, this will not qualify unless you continue to hold and rent the property after it is developed. If you simply develop and sell the property, it is inventory and does not qualify for a 1031 Exchange. In addition, there are specific guidelines you must follow concerning time between a sale and a reinvestment. As with all aspects of tax law, you should contact a competent tax law professional for advice if you plan to do a 1031 Exchange.

Tax-Free Sale Potential. Under the current Internal Revenue Code, you can avoid paying taxes altogether on up to $250,000 of profit when you sell your personal residence. (Double that if you're filing jointly!) All you have to do is live in the property for at least two of the five years immediately prior to selling, and you get this tax break. Although the Weekend Millionaire program teaches you to buy and hold properties, we want you to know about this opportunity, because you can do it every two years, simply by living in the house. Potentially, this could allow you to generate cash or upgrade to a nicer home without having to paying any taxes.

Capital Gains Tax. Ordinary income tax rates can be as high as 39 percent. If you sell a property you have owned for more than 12 months, the profit from the sale is long-term capital gain. The top rate for long-term capital gain income is 20 percent and under certain circumstances can be as low as 10 percent. This rate gets even better if you own the property for more than five years. Again, this tax break is available only when you sell properties. Our goal is to teach you how to buy so you can build an ongoing stream of income and don't have to sell.

Continued Ownership is Even Better for the Weekend Millionaire. As we'll show you, Weekend Millionaires don't have much use for the tax breaks that come from selling because they rarely sell properties. They use the equity that builds up to buy more properties and increase their income stream.

Roger was once in Atlanta, getting ready to give a seminar to several hundred real estate investors. Before the meeting started, he called Mike and said, "I want to be sure that I'm quoting the right number. What's the current tax rate when you sell a property?" Mike replied, "I don't know. I've never sold one!"

Summary. The bottom line is that government wants the ownership of real estate to be in private hands. It gives some impressive tax benefits to encourage you to own property. In this chapter, we have touched briefly on some of the tax advantages available to real estate investors. As we said at the beginning of this chapter, we are not tax advisors; therefore, before taking advantage of any of these, you should meet with professional advisors who know the Internal Revenue Code far better than we do and let them advise you on tax decisions.

SECTION 6

Moving into Larger Properties

As you've seen, we believe that all beginning investors should start out investing in single-family homes. There is a greater selection from which to choose, you're diversifying your holdings instead of putting all your eggs in one basket, and they are easier to finance and manage. Also, you have much greater liquidity because if you need to raise cash you can always find a buyer for a single-family home.

As you build your portfolio though, you will probably want to consider acquiring some multifamily properties (apartment houses) and perhaps even some commercial properties (retail space, office buildings, and warehouses).

In this section, we're going to give you some tips about buying and leasing out these properties. You'll see that there are many differences from investing in single-family homes, and much more specialized knowledge is required.

We'll also show you in this section how important it is to build great relationships with what we call your support team: your attorney, your certified public accountant (CPA), your property manager, and especially your bankers.

29

Valuing Multifamily Properties

In Chapter 24, we discussed valuing single-family properties. These are the safest real estate investments you can own, but they are more difficult to find and are usually purchased one at a time. Apartment houses and commercial properties offer greater opportunities, but these tend to come with higher risks, more problems, and require greater knowledge.

First, let's define apartment houses and commercial properties. Apartment houses mean residential property such as an apartment building where the landlord owns the entire building. You could own a condominium apartment and rent it out but that would be considered a single-family residence. Commercial real estate means shopping centers, offices, industrial buildings, factories, and warehouses. We'll teach you how to value apartment buildings in this chapter and commercial properties in Chapter 30.

Before discussing the differences between the way you value single-family properties versus apartment buildings we want to caution you: *Stay with single-family properties until you have the experience to handle larger projects.* We suggest that you stick with single-family properties until you acquire enough of them to get the feel for real estate investing, establish a track record with lenders, build a substantial cash flow, and experience a few tenant problems. You need to gain first-hand working knowledge about evaluating properties and making deals before you move into larger apartments. And above all, be patient. Successful Weekend Millionaires build a solid base of knowledge and experience with single-family properties before they graduate to the bigger projects. Just as pilots learn in small single-engine airplanes before moving into multiengine and jet aircraft, we want you to learn the basics before moving to the bigger stuff. We want you to become a Weekend Millionaire, not a high-flying casualty.

How to Put a Price on Apartment Buildings. You establish a net operating income on apartment buildings in much the same manner we discussed in Chapter 24 on valuing single-family properties. You calculate your net rental income after an allowance for vacancies and deducting the expenses of management, maintenance, utilities, taxes, insurance, and other expenses.

Gross Multipliers. Beware of real estate agents who describe the price of an apartment building in terms of a gross multiplier. A gross multiplier is a quick gauge that is not nearly accurate enough for our purpose. Here's how it works: Take the gross annual rents and divide them into the purchase price. Let's say you have a 16-unit building, where each unit rents for $400 per month. The gross annual rent is 16 units × 12 months × $400 for a total annual income of $76,800. If the building were priced at $768,000, it would have a 10 times gross multiplier. If the gross multiplier were 9 times, the price would be $691,200. An 11 times multiplier would put an $844,800 price on the building.

This may have some value in comparing properties that are in the same part of town and are similar in their operating expense structure, but it is far too vague to be of much value to the Weekend Millionaire. For one thing, gross multipliers vary widely according to the area of town. In the most desirable part of town, gross multipliers may be 15 times or more. In the areas of town where you have to collect rents with a gun, a gross multiplier may be only 6 times and the building still would not be a good buy.

The other thing that a gross multiplier does not take into consideration is the cost of managing the building, a factor that can vary widely and may be completely different from single-family properties.

Expenses for Apartment Buildings

There are additional expenses that you must take into account when considering the purchase of an apartment building over a single-family residence. Here are the key differences.

Utility Costs. Tenants in single-family properties usually pay for utilities, such as water, electricity, gas, and sometimes sewer. In apartment buildings, owners are more likely to pay the bills. This can be a critical issue for you. One of the first things that you look for when you visit a potential apartment building are rows of electric and gas meters on the outside of the building. If they are there, they indicate that each apartment is metered separately and the tenants pay for their own utilities. If not, chances are that the owner is paying for the tenants' gas and electricity. That expense must be factored into your purchase. As you can imagine, tenants whose landlords pay their utilities are less likely to conserve. Your utility costs could become excessive, and you wouldn't even be able to identify the culprit. In addition, tenants who have to establish an account with the gas and electric providers tend to be more stable.

Yard Maintenance. This is another expense that is usually handled by the tenant in single-family properties but is almost always an expense of the landlord in apartment buildings. Common area maintenance (such as cleaning of hallways), pool maintenance and the care of other recreation facilities, area lighting, and other such expenses must also be taken into consideration when establishing NOI for apartment buildings. On average, expenses on apartment buildings will be 15 to 30 percent greater than that on single-family properties. Unless you consider these additional expenses, it is very easy to pay too much and find out after the fact that you can't afford to own the property.

Management Costs. Many states require you to have a resident manager in apartment buildings. Check the rule in your state, but a typical state regulation is that if you have 16 or more units in one location you must have a resident manager. The good news is that you may not have to pay that manager a salary. Perhaps offering a couple a 50 percent discount on their rent will induce them to take on the job. Perhaps you'll have to give them a rent-free apartment. They don't have much to do. They pick up trash, discipline disruptive tenants, collect the rents, and show units to prospective tenants. You have to figure the lost rent that their unit would otherwise generate as a cost of management.

A friend of ours sank his investment program by buying an apartment building without realizing the difference in costs between owning an apartment building and a single-family residence. When he first started investing, he was buying single-family homes and doing quite well. He told us several times how well his rental houses were doing and how his cash flow was growing. Then one day, he mentioned that he had finally found a buyer for the apartment building he owned. He went on to say that he had purchased a 20-unit building about a year and a half earlier and really thought he had gotten a good deal, but had been totally surprised at how much more expensive it was to own than the houses. He told us that after six months he realized that, not only was the apartment building not cash flowing, it was eating up all the cash flow from his houses plus part of his salary from his job. When the deal closed, he told us that he was never so glad to get rid of a piece of property in his life and that he would not be buying any more apartment buildings.

Well, it wasn't the apartment building that was the problem; it was buying it without considering the additional expense items that made it a bad deal. Multiunit properties are great, so long as you buy them right. Let's look at the advantages and disadvantages of investing in apartment buildings versus single-family houses.

Advantages of Buying Apartment Houses

The cost of buying an apartment building as a multiplier of the total rents is much less than for single-family residences. If you have your expenses under control and factored into your purchase price, they could show a better cash flow.

You acquire tenants much faster. You can buy a 16-unit apartment building in one transaction. It might take you years to purchase 16 separate houses. It's a quick way to generate more people sending you a monthly check and contributing to your retirement fund.

It's easier to raise the rent in apartments. Once a year or so, you can raise everybody's rent by $20 or $30 a month. In a 16-unit building, raising everyone's rent by $20 a month puts $3,840 a year into your pocket. Raising the rents at 16 different locations would be harder.

Disadvantages of Buying Apartment Houses

It's harder to arrange creative financing. With single-family homes, it's much easier to structure no-money-down purchases using seller financing.

You lose liquidity. In a down market, you may not be able to find a buyer for a 16-unit building at any price. With 16 individual houses, you will always be able to sell some of them.

You may be putting too many eggs in one basket. Let's say that you own a 36-unit apartment building, and it represents 75 percent of your real estate investment portfolio. It's a Hawaiian motif, a style that was very popular when it was built but is now out of style. Additionally, it's in a neighborhood that was once chic and upscale but is now declining. Suddenly you find that 75 percent of your portfolio is shrinking in value, cash flow, and marketability.

Apartment house dwellers tend to be more transient than home dwellers. That's particularly true if the apartments are furnished. For that reason we recommend that you stay away from furnished apartment buildings entirely.

House renters tend to be more stable than apartment dwellers. They have children in school. They've decorated their house, filled their garage with tools, and made small improvements that they are reluctant to leave.

Our Recommendation

Stay with single-family homes until you have a few years' experience under your belt. Then begin building a diverse portfolio that includes single-family homes and apartment buildings.

30

Valuing Commercial Properties

In Chapter 29, we discussed valuing apartment buildings. In this chapter, we'll talk about valuing commercial properties. We don't intend to give you all the information you need to invest in commercial properties. We'll save that for a later book. However, once you become known as a real estate investor, you will probably be approached about buying commercial properties. You need to know that there are major differences in the valuation of commercial properties.

Commercial Properties. Shopping centers, offices, industrial buildings, factories, and warehouses give you a unique challenge. Leases on these properties are very different from residential leases, taking on many of the characteristics of loan documents rather than a simple rental agreement. In fact, lenders often rely on these documents to collateralize loans. That means that the bank will want a security interest in the leases as additional collateral for the financing. They want the leases written to a much higher legal standard than you would need for residential property leases.

Valuing Commercial Properties

Commercial lease contracts may contain widely differing provisions that vary from one tenant to another and from one property to another. Virtually anything agreed upon between the parties may be included, and residential landlord-tenant laws in most areas do not govern these contracts. Remedies available to a landlord in the event of a default are also much greater. Because of this difference, commercial properties offer opportunities that residential properties do not.

With commercial property, you will see leases that range from simple month-to-month rentals where the landlord pays maintenance, taxes, insurance, utilities, and every other expense; to sophisticated long-term recorded leases where the tenant pays everything. When the tenant pays all the expenses, the leases are called *triple net leases*, meaning that the tenant pays the three major expenses, maintenance, insurance, and property taxes. In that case the rent is truly the NOI on the investment.

Commercial properties offer a wide range of leasing options, which require you to have greater knowledge and a better understanding of financing alternatives to be successful with them. Properties with triple net leases are very attractive to own and require little attention while they are under lease, but when they go vacant, it can take months or even years to get them re-rented. In some cases, a building may even have to be demolished and a new one constructed to make the property marketable again. This is often because many commercial buildings are built to suit a specific tenant and have little or no use for other activities. Unless a commercial building is constructed in such a manner that it is suitable for many applications, you must be extremely careful not to get caught with a property that becomes obsolete before it can pay for itself and produce a return on investment.

Let's now explore some of the possibilities you may want to consider if you decide to purchase commercial properties.

Generic Commercial Properties. First, if the property is especially generic, if its construction and location will accommodate multiple applications, it can be valued more like a residential property. You can estimate a reasonable vacancy factor based on market conditions. You wouldn't need to budget much money to make it suitable for the new tenant, and you could lease it on shorter terms with less stringent conditions. Should a tenant move out, a new one could be found in a reasonable period of time, much as happens with residential property. With such a property, you could use a simple lease or rental agreement rather than the sophisticated commercial lease you would need if the property were a special-use property or if the tenant wanted you to spend big money customizing the property for its needs. In either case, you could always make the tenant responsible for those expenses. That would be part of the negotiation with the new tenant.

Customizing Commercial Property to a Tenant's Needs. Even if the property is generic in nature, there will probably be situations where a tenant will want you to do some customizing to suit its needs. In cases like this, you will want to assume that the tenant's improvements or changes will have no value to you beyond the tenancy. So, make sure that the cost of these improvements gets amortized within the term of the lease and that you can make a profit on the money you invest on these improvements. We suggest that you do this by calculating the amount the lease will need to increase for each $1,000 you invest. The figure you set should allow you to completely pay for the improvements and make a profit on the money you invest over the term of the lease. Therefore, it's important to evaluate the creditworthiness of the tenant. Do you really want to invest your money for the tenant's benefit? In effect, you're making the tenant a loan. You need to be sure that you're getting a good return on your investments.

Banks obtain money either from people who maintain deposit accounts with them or the Federal Reserve Bank. In turn, they loan the money out at rates higher than they are paying. You will be doing the same thing when you invest in tenant-specific improvements to commercial properties. What's important is that you not only get your money back, including the interest you have to pay on the money, but that you make a profit on it as well. The following chart shows what the monthly payment would be to pay off a $1,000 loan at interest rates of 6 and 12 percent over periods ranging from 3 to 10 years. The column at the right shows the monthly difference between these payment amounts. If you could borrow money at 6 percent and increase the monthly amount of your lease by the amount in the 12 percent column, you could make a 6 percent spread on the money you invest in addition to having it paid back during the lease term. Here's what the numbers look like:

Valuing Commercial Properties

Monthly Payment Amount per $1,000			
Years	@6%	@12%	Difference
3	$30.42	$33.22	$2.80
4	23.49	26.34	2.85
5	19.33	22.25	2.92
6	16.57	19.56	2.99
7	14.61	17.66	3.05
8	13.14	16.26	3.12
9	12.01	15.19	3.18
10	11.10	14.35	3.25

You can create a chart like this to fit your particular needs. Simply use a financial calculator to compute the payment amount for each $1,000 at whatever rates and whatever spread you want to use. When determining the spread you will use, consider the creditworthiness of the tenant. The stronger a tenant's credit, the less risk you will be taking; therefore, the less spread you may be able to get. The rate you charge the tenant is negotiable, but the spread you establish should give you a profit on the money you invest and take into consideration the credit risk you will be taking.

Adjusting Rents Using the Adjustment Rental Clause. Leasing commercial property that the tenant wants customized offers some unique opportunities. A lease negotiated under these circumstances does not have to be limited to a fixed lease amount. It can contain a flexible Adjustment Rental clause that increases the monthly rental amount in accordance with the amount you invest in tenant-specific improvements. Using the above chart, an Adjustment Rental clause for a five-year lease under which the tenant wants improvements that will cost between $20,000 and $30,000, may read like this, "Lessor agrees to make tenant-directed improvements in an amount not to exceed $30,000. When such improvements are made, the Lessee agrees to pay, in addition to the Base Rental, an Adjustment Rental in the amount of $22.25 per month for each $1,000 invested by the Lessor. After completion of such improvements, the Adjustment Rental calculated under this clause shall be added to the Base Rental and the total of these two amounts shall become the New Base Rental."

In this example, if the Lessor spends the full $30,000, the monthly rental would increase by $22.25 × 30 = $667.50 per month. Assuming that the Lessor borrows the $30,000 at 6 percent interest for five years, the payment on the loan would be $579.90 per month giving a profit of $87.60 per month on the improvements. At the end of the initial five-year lease, if the lease is renewed, there is an excellent opportunity for greater profits because the improvements have been paid for in the initial five-year term.

Build-to-Suit Commercial Properties. Opportunities abound in commercial build-to-suit properties, which have unique uses. These are buildings for tenants, such as fast-food chains, service stations, or other businesses, that require custom-built, unique buildings that have little or no use except for that specific tenant. The design of these types of buildings is often trademarked and legally cannot be used for anyone except that tenant. In these situations, you will need to give even more careful consideration to the creditworthiness of the tenant and be sure the lease term is long enough or the rental rate high enough to pay for the building and make a profit within the original term of the lease. Not only does the contract need to be legally binding so that if the business closes the tenant will still be obligated to pay the lease amount, but the tenant's creditworthiness needs to be strong enough to ensure that in such a case the tenant will continue to make payments.

This section merely scratches the surface of the many possibilities that exist with commercial properties. The examples used here are for illustration purposes only to give you ideas as to the range of deals that you can structure when acquiring commercial properties. There are as many possibilities in this area of real estate investing as there are combinations of people and properties. That's why we advise you that commercial properties do offer greater opportunities, but tend to come with higher risks, more problems, and require greater knowledge. Don't be afraid of these properties, but seek the advice and counsel of a good attorney, accountant, and banker before delving into them. These professionals will become more and more valuable to you as your portfolio grows. In Chapter 31 we'll discuss the importance of building relationships with professional advisors.

31

Building Your Support Team

As you begin your real estate investing career, you will quickly realize the value of developing a support team of professionals. Establishing solid working relationships with good title companies or real estate attorneys, accountants, savvy real estate brokers, and bankers who know and understand your goals is vitally important to success in real estate investing.

Sometimes You Need Special Services from Your Support Team.
If you are like most people, your understanding of the legal and accounting aspects of owning income-producing properties is limited. That's where the professional advice of attorneys and accountants enters the picture. Often, especially with small residential properties, decisions have to be made at night or on weekends to get the best deals, and closings have to occur quickly. When you are trying to put deals like these together, there will be times when you will want legal or tax advice before entering into a contract. Having an attorney or accountant you can call after hours can

often mean the difference between making a good deal and getting into a situation you regret later. The only way to get this kind of response is to build strong personal relationships with your advisors. Let's explore some of the situations where good relationships with these people can play a very important role.

The Value of Being Able to Close Quickly. When attempting to buy property at substantially reduced values, two things are most likely to produce favorable responses from buyers: cash and rapid closings. If you can offer both, it makes sense that you will find more deals than someone who can offer only one of them. However, if you are just getting started on the road to becoming a Weekend Millionaire, you may not yet have the option of paying cash, which is why building relationships with the professionals who can give you the option of offering quick closings is so important. When a seller is hurting, the quicker you can ease his or her pain, the better deal you can get.

Imagine finding a seller who is hurting enough that he offers to sell you his property for 50 to 70 percent of appraised value, but you lose the deal because he has to close in a week. Can you see how upsetting this could be? You found the property first but had to watch another investor close the deal because it would take you 60 days or more to get financing approved, legal documents drawn up, and a closing date set.

On the other hand, imagine having the ability to move rapidly and be the first to have opportunities like this brought to you by real estate agents who know you can solve their client's problems quickly and efficiently. That's the benefit of building a good support team.

Imagine having a title company or real estate attorney you know will be able to close a transaction within a week if you put this option into a purchase offer. Imagine banking relationships strong enough that you could get a loan commitment in a day or two or even better still, that give you a preapproved line of credit to purchase investment properties. Imagine having access to legal or tax advice at night and on weekends to keep you from missing deals when you aren't quite sure how to structure them. These kinds of resources move from imagination to reality when you build personal relationships with a strong support team.

Building Your Support Team

So, how do you do it? Like becoming a Weekend Millionaire, developing relationships like this does not happen overnight. The burden is on you to convince members of your support team that you are different from the average person who may only buy one or two properties in a lifetime. It's up to you to get them to see that it will be advantageous for them to work with you and provide you the services you request. This is where communications enters the picture. By opening an honest dialogue in which you share your goals, ambitions, objectives, expectations, requirements, and above all the plan you have for reaching them, it gives prospective team members an opportunity to see the benefit of being a part of your team. It also gives them a benchmark to measure how well you perform over time. When you begin these discussions, don't get discouraged if you run into some doubters with tough questions. Remember, the burden is upon you to prove that you are for real, that you have the desire, commitment, and stick-to-itiveness that make you worthy of special treatment.

Be Willing to Reward People Who Help You. You will need to assure each of them that you will not abuse their generosity if they agree to meet your expectations. You will need to allow them to handle your other normal transactions and not just the special rush jobs. Title companies or real estate attorneys feel much better about helping you close a transaction quickly when they know they will get to handle a few others at their leisure. Those special real estate agents that bring you super deals are likely to bring you more if you reciprocate by including them in other transactions that may not be their listings. Also, refer clients to your professional advisors every chance you get. Your referrals will mean more as your real estate investment portfolio grows. The more success you have, the more other people will seek your advice and guidance and the more weight your recommendations will carry. Just remember that every time you help a member of your support team, the strength of your relationship grows.

It is never too early to start building your support team. In the beginning, you may not see the importance of cultivating these relationships, but don't wait until you own 10, 20, or 30 properties to get started. It takes years to develop and solidify them, so you should start building these relationships as soon as possible.

Moving into Larger Properties

Building a Relationship with Your Bankers. Of all the relationships you will build, banking relationships are the most important. They take the longest to establish, so you should start as soon as possible. Although you will use numerous sources of funds to purchase real estate, banks without a doubt provide the largest financing source for individual investors. While not mandatory, good credit definitely makes buying investment properties easier. However, building good credit takes time—lots of time. It requires establishing a bond of trust, demonstrating responsibility, and developing a good record of accomplishment. One of the reasons it takes time is the cyclical nature of the economy. Just because you have a great track record through a boom period does little to establish your ability to perform during recessions, and recessions are usually when the best real estate deals can be found. Establishing good credit and building strong banking relations will put you in position to take advantage of these good deals. For this reason, we would like to give you a checklist of things you can do to build strong banking relations.

1. *Be honest.* Don't pad your financial statements and paint rosy pictures that you can't deliver. You only have to give a false statement once to make your future statements suspect for years to come. Furthermore, providing false statements to secure credit is illegal.

2. *Pay in a timely manner.* Establish a record of paying on time and regularly. Everyone knows that you need to pay your bills before they become past due to build good credit, but paying in a timely manner is just as important. Establish a record of paying at a consistent time each month. A record of paying 10 days early one month, the day before going past due the next, then on the due date the next, is not as good a payment record as paying within a couple of days of the same date each month. A consistent payment record shows discipline and demonstrates that your ability to pay is not influenced by fluctuations in your monthly cash flow. Granted, whether you pay 10 days before or 10 days after the due date probably won't affect your credit report, but we're talking about building long-term banking relations, not getting first-time credit. In most cases, a payment is not reported as late or charged a late fee unless it is paid more than 15 days after the due

date, but internal documents within the bank tell a different story. While the time may vary from bank to bank, watch lists are generated 5 to 10 days past the due date showing those customers that still haven't paid. This watch list, which may not cause concern, gets circulated not only to your bank officer, but to the bank's credit administrators as well. When your loan officer submits a loan request, you definitely don't want your name recognized by members of the loan committee because of your appearance on watch lists. This can't help but taint their thinking and cause your loan officer to have to answer unnecessary questions. Your loan officer may be able to approve your early requests under his or her own lending authority, but as you add properties and your debt grows, it will require approval from a growing number of people to approve your loan requests. Having a consistent payment record is just another way of impressing those bankers you will never see, and it gives your loan officer more ammunition with which to support your request.

3. *Keep your bankers informed.* Whether its good or bad, let them know how you're doing. Don't make them have to ask for financial information. There are so many mistakes made in real estate investing that bankers tend to be extremely cautious about letting new investors get too leveraged, even when the debt is well secured. To ease their minds, give them a report of income and expenses quarterly until you acquire five properties. After you have five or more, give them the report monthly. Even include photos of the properties so they can see that you have nothing to hide. You may think this is overkill, but there is a reason for doing so. When you have four or fewer properties, the Federal Deposit Insurance Corporation (FDIC) views you as a passive investor and it classifies your loans differently than it does after you have five or more. At this level, your loans become investor loans and are viewed as having higher risk than the first four. For this reason, you will want to keep your banks informed about how your properties are performing, which will in turn help them do a better job for you.

4. *Build cash reserves.* As quickly as possible, build up a cash reserve that will let you make payments on time even if rents are late. A good rule of thumb is to maintain enough cash to cover 3 to 6 months of ex-

penses even if you have no income. This may seem like a lot, but you can do it in a few short years by simply allowing your profits to accumulate. Continually monitor your reserves and make sure you increase them as you add properties.

5. *Maintain your properties.* By following the recommendations contained in the Weekend Millionaire, you should be able to set aside reserves for maintenance. Be sure to use this money to keep the properties well maintained. Certain maintenance items like paint, carpet, roofs, heat and air conditioning systems, only have to be replaced every several years. These are big-ticket items that must be planned for in advance, and money must be reserved to cover the costs when they occur. By demonstrating that you have the discipline to set aside money for these expenses, you will make your bankers feel much more comfortable that you are a knowledgeable real estate investor. As a word of caution, don't be tempted to use the money for other things and then come up short when the need arises.

6. *Take your bankers for a ride.* Literally! As you build a real estate portfolio, periodically invite your bankers to go with you to inspect the properties. By doing so, you will be showing them that you are acquiring good properties and keeping them in good condition. If you buy run-down properties that you fix up, be sure to make before and after pictures. If you take a banker by a property you have refurbished, it makes a better impression if you can show a picture of what it looked like when you got it, and it gives you the opportunity to describe the improvements you have made. The better condition in which you can keep your properties, the more comfortable it will make your bankers when you take them on these inspection rides. Conducting inspections with your bankers every year or two shows them that you are serious about long-term investing, not just bleeding properties for what you can take out of them.

7. *Be fair.* Understand that bankers are businesspeople just like you. They have to make a profit too. Their job is to get the best return for their bank, while yours is to get the best deal for you. While you may be able to shave an extra quarter of a point off the interest rate occasionally, deals that benefit only one party don't build good relationships. What-

ever you do, don't ask banks to bid against each other for the business. If you are going to shop more than one bank, negotiate your best deal on its own merit with each bank and don't make your banker feel like price is the only thing important to you. It's far more important that you focus on structuring loans to fit the cash flow of the properties than to simply focus on getting the best rate. Remember, in real estate, terms are just as important, if not more important than price.

8. *Don't put all your eggs in one basket.* Again, keep in mind that banks are businesses. Smaller community banks may have more flexibility since credit decisions are usually made locally, but these banks also have smaller lending limits. Larger national banks can handle any size transaction but tend to be less flexible because credit decisions are often made by analysts who never meet a customer. Whether large or small, banks have their cyclical periods just as the economy does. A bank that has a very large appetite for real estate loans one year may have little or none the next. This has nothing to do with your credit rating, your net worth, your cash flow, or anything else about you. It has everything to do with a bank's position in relation to its capital base, the amount of cash it needs to put to work, the number of problem real estate loans in its portfolio, and many other such factors that have nothing to do with you. For this reason, you should build relationships with more than just one bank. Often, when one bank is shying away from real estate loans, another is seeking them. When you establish good relationships with your bankers, they can be honest with you. If they know they can't handle a transaction due to no fault of yours, they will tell you so rather than having you jump through the hoops of applying for a loan and then giving some lame excuse for why it can't be approved. Another reason for building multiple banking relationships is the fact that a particular deal may fit one bank's portfolio better than another's. As you get to know your bankers better, you will learn which ones like what kinds of deals.

As you can see, these actions take time. The longer you follow these suggestions, the stronger your banking relationships will be. Don't think of bankers as adversaries. Many people's first reaction when a bank denies their loan request is to blame the banker. The truth is, bankers want to make loans as much as you want them to; but they want to make good loans, and good loans are ones they can make and then forget about. Just because a loan is well secured with real estate does not mean it is a good loan. Believe us, bankers do not want to collect their loans by having to foreclose on properties and then sell them to get their money. By far the most important thing you can do to strengthen your banking relationship is to embark on a course of actions that demonstrates your ability to perform as agreed. The suggestions we have given you tell you what these actions need to be.

The better you understand and follow the advice contained in this chapter, the quicker you will establish the good credit and build the solid professional relationships it takes to enjoy success in real estate investing. Following this advice will produce lifelong behavior changes that will establish you as a knowledgeable professional with the commitment it takes to build a great future. It will give your support team members the confidence they need to grow with you.

SECTION 7

Getting Started

Yου've read the book so far, and you're ready to become a Weekend Millionaire. Now what do you do? The next eight short chapters will show you exactly how to get started; step by step, weekend by weekend, including checklists to mark off when you've completed each week's assignment.

Before you jump to the next chapter, we want to remind you of the advice we have been giving throughout the book—be patient. Becoming a Weekend Millionaire is not a get-rich-quick proposition. The last thing we want you to do is to go out hyped up on enthusiasm and start making mistakes. In this final section we give you a step-by-step guide to take you through the "in the field" learning that you need to build your knowledge and hone the skills that will lead to making your first purchase.

Don't become discouraged because you don't see immediate results. Stay calm, remain positive, and follow the steps we give you. Don't let your family or friends discourage or distract you. See yourself as the wealthy real estate investor that you will become. Imagine yourself driving down the streets of your neighborhood pointing out all the houses that you own.

We want you to think of real estate investing as a long-term, steady-growth proposition. Many people work 40 hours per week, 50 weeks per year, for 40 years and end up in retirement with only a small social security check to show for their efforts. If you spend four hours each weekend, for just one year, you should have no problem buying at least one rental house. In 15 to 20 years, this one house will probably provide you with more income than you will draw from social security when you retire.

What if you continued doing this for 15 years and bought just one house per year? If you started at age 30, by age 45, you could be retired and living the good life with many times what social security would pay you. That's why we want you to keep farming your neighborhoods and making offers. Don't get discouraged if things seem slow at times. When you're waiting for whole-sale deals, you must have the endurance to stay the course until the time is right. The best part is that when you land one, it will pay you for the rest of your life, and unlike social security and retirement plans, it will be there to provide for your family long after you are gone.

Now, turn the page, and let's get started!

32

What to Do Your First Weekend

It's Saturday morning, and you're ready to get started; what do you do first? This weekend, you're going to start learning your market. We want you to allocate at least four hours to survey your surroundings. Your only task this weekend is to familiarize yourself with the area near where you live. Once you get started, you may want to spend more time, but just four hours will give you a good start. In most cases, there is enough investment potential within a 10-mile radius to make you rich. You may think you already know the area quite well, and this may be the case if it's just road names and the ability to navigate without getting lost. What we're talking about is much different.

We want you to take along a pad to make notes. You're going to be looking for basic starter homes, the type that attracts first-time homebuyers. These are usually 900 to 1,200 square feet in size with two to four bedrooms and one or two baths. Probably, you will find these in subdivisions containing many similar type houses. Occasionally you may find them scattered about, but most will be located in subdivisions where developers have subdivided a large tract of land and built them to sell. Often these are called tract homes. People will have bought many of them and financed the purchase with Veterans Administration (VA) or Federal Housing Administration (FHA) loans. This is important, because these loans are still assumable.

On this first weekend, thoroughly explore the area within a 10-mile radius of where you live. You will need a detailed map of the area if one is available. As you drive around, get off the main roads. Go down each side street and back road looking for subdivisions. Consult your map to locate street grids that look like subdivisions. Each time you find one containing a number of these basic starter homes, make a note of it and mark it on your map. You will come to view these target subdivisions in much the same way that farmers view their fields. Just as the farmer cultivates and harvests crops from the ground, you will cultivate and harvest your first real estate investments from these neighborhoods.

The reason we suggest looking down side streets and back roads is that there are many small neighborhoods containing 10 to 20 homes that meet our criteria, but don't show up on the map as a subdivision. The size of the subdivision is not nearly as important as locating the homes that fall into the basic starter home classification. The more of these you can locate on this first weekend, the better. By the end of the weekend, you should have a list of the potential neighborhoods you want to farm.

As you can see, your first assignment is pretty simple; but as simple as it is, we're still going to provide you with a checklist so you can mark off each task as you complete it. We will provide a similar checklist for each chapter in this section.

What to Do Your First Weekend

CHECKLIST
Weekend One

_____ I have gotten a map of my city and drawn a circle covering a radius 10 miles around my house.

_____ I have driven the area for four hours looking for subdivisions or neighborhoods with houses that meet my criteria.

_____ I have marked the potential tracts of starter homes I located on the map.

Kick back, relax, and congratulate yourself. You have started, and getting started is half the work! You're now on your way to becoming a Weekend Millionaire!

33

What to Do Your Second Weekend

Your second weekend has arrived, and you're ready to continue learning. This weekend, you're going to take the list of neighborhoods you compiled last weekend and learn more about them. Pick one—any one—it doesn't matter, because eventually you will work your way through all of them. Go to your selected neighborhood and ride around. Observe how the properties are maintained and the lawns kept, watch for signs of children, look for vacant houses, and For Sale signs, survey the age and condition of vehicles parked in driveways or on the streets, and most importantly, look for people with whom you can talk. What you'll be doing during this exercise is determining whether the neighborhood is a place where you will want to invest.

Properly maintained homes and well-kept lawns are a good indication that most of the residents are homeowners that take pride in their community. Swing sets, bicycles, and toys are indications of families with children. If you find only a few vacant houses, it shows that the neighborhood is desirable. A shortage of For Sale signs indicates a stable neighborhood.

What to Do Your Second Weekend

Clean, well-maintained vehicles indicate that the residents take pride in their personal possessions as well as their property. Investing in neighborhoods like this has many advantages. They are easier to rent, easier to finance, and you enjoy the benefit of having neighbors who will let you know if your tenants are not well behaved or are not taking care of your property.

On the other hand, poorly maintained houses, overgrown or barren yards, numerous vacant houses, a predominance of For Sale signs, and disabled or unlicensed vehicles give you important warning signs. Neighborhoods in this condition are often declining in value, and the unattractive surroundings make it difficult to attract desirable tenants. Many times, these neighborhoods contain unusually high percentages of rental properties owned by proprietors who invest little in maintenance and upkeep. Buying in areas like these can be very risky business, unless you are able to buy enough of the houses to change the direction of the neighborhood.

Ideal properties for beginning investors are ones that need attention, like the ones in the risky neighborhoods, but are scattered throughout desirable communities. Look for these telltale signs of owners who are neglecting their properties:

- Unattended lawns, especially in the summer
- Christmas decorations still up long after the season is over
- Peeling paint
- Trash piled up
- Run-down cars parked in the driveway
- Advertising flyers scattered in the entryway
- A general appearance that is noticeably inferior to other properties in the neighborhood

All of these are indicators that may point to flexible sellers.

Continue Exploring Your Farm. Get a Multiple Listing Service (MLS) book from a real estate agent or property manager. Some Boards of Realtors publish a book each week that lists all the properties for sale and includes pictures of most of them. It's called the MLS book. Some Boards of Realtors have discontinued these in favor of Internet listings, but there is always a way for real estate agents to look up properties for sale. Ask a real estate agent which method her board uses. If it's a book, ask her if you can have or borrow her previous week's book for your research. Real estate agents are not supposed to give it away, but we've never had a problem getting one. Also, learn how to research properties for sale on the Internet. Try www.Realtors.com , which is the website for the National Association of Realtors. It contains a wealth of information. Try doing a search for real estate and your city name. Also, many real estate brokers in your area will have their own websites.

Although you can read newspaper ads and look through other listings of properties for sale, these sources don't usually give information about a property's surroundings. This is the reason we want you to get out, ride, and visually inspect the properties.

Whenever you locate a property in a desirable neighborhood that doesn't seem to fit with the surrounding properties, write it down. Whether it is for sale or not, it is worth checking out because it may be an opportunity that just hasn't surfaced yet.

As you ride your targeted areas, stop and talk with people you see in their yards or on the streets. Ask if they live in the neighborhood. Let them know that you are interested in buying in the area and were riding around looking at houses. If they are residents, ask them what they like best about the community. Ask what they like least about it. Ask if there are any problems that you should know about. Ask if they know of any houses for sale that might be good deals. Ask about the neighbors. Find out if most of them own their homes. Are there many rental properties in the neighborhood? If you have spotted some potential investment properties in the area, ones that do not seem be up to par with the rest of the neighborhood, ask about them. Some of these may be great investment opportunities that simple have not hit the market yet. If you can find these before other investors do, your chance of making a good deal is greatly improved.

It is amazing what you can learn by talking to people about their neighborhood and showing an interest in buying in it. They will view you as a potential neighbor and want to know as much about you as you want to know about the area. It makes for good conversation and allows them to open up with information that may be hard to get otherwise. Let them know that you will have to find a very good deal before you can buy. You may learn about someone who is being transferred and is willing to take a big discount if they can get a quick sale or be told about someone who has lost a job or suffered another financial distress and needs to sell, but hasn't listed the property for sale yet. People can become very flexible when going through a divorce or trying to settle an estate. Many times the houses you spot that need attention need it because the owners are experiencing problems. These offer excellent opportunities not only to help you, but to help the owners as well. The more you ride, look, and talk, the more of these opportunities you will find.

CHECKLIST
Weekend Two

_____   I have ridden through _____ neighborhoods in the area I am farming.

_____   I have spoken to _____ people who live in the areas through which I rode.

_____   I have asked _____ neighbors in these areas about homes that might be for sale.

_____   I have found _____ potential investment houses in these areas and have found out who owns them.

_____   I have checked the Internet to see if it will help me locate homes for sale in the area I am farming.

_____   I have obtained an old Multiple Listing Service book from a real estate agent or property manager and reviewed it to learn about the homes for sale in the area I am farming.

34

What to Do Your Third Weekend

You have spent your first two weekends getting familiar with the area you will be farming, locating neighborhoods with a high predominance of basic starter homes, talking with residents, and identifying potential investment properties. It is now time to get ready to start inspecting these properties and making offers. To prepare for this weekend, you will need to do a little homework. Start by going back and reviewing Chapter 6, Finding a Property Manager. In preparation for this weekend, get out the phone book and check the yellow page listings under Real Estate Management. You should also check the newspaper classified ads under Houses for Rent and Apartments for Rent. Property management firms primarily use the yellow pages to attract owners and the classifieds to attract renters. By cross referencing the companies advertising property for rent in the classifieds with the companies in the yellow pages that claim to be property managers, you will learn which seem to be the more active and aggressive companies. For this third weekend, make a few calls and try to find two property managers willing to spend a couple of hours riding with you on Saturday. Explain that you are planning to buy several investment properties within the area and are looking for a manager with whom you will feel comfortable managing them for you.

Once you have lined up two property managers, take the map you have been using and the notes you have compiled during the first two weekends and select a group of properties, preferably properties for sale by owner (FSBO), that you can ride by within two hours or less. You will want to take both property managers on the same ride, but not at the same time. By doing this, you can compare the information you get from one, with the information from the other. You will be conducting drive-by inspections and asking each property manager to give you an estimate of the range of rents they feel each property could bring. Since you will have few if any details of the interior layout of the houses, ask for rent estimates for two, three, and four bedrooms and one, one and a half , and two baths. Make notes on their estimates as you visit each property. You will need these notes next weekend. (If there is a wide disparity between the rates you get from each property manager, you may want to repeat this exercise the next weekend with different property managers before moving on. You must have reliable data to make good offers.)

When you ask the property managers for rental rates, be sure to explain that you want estimates based on the houses being in good condition, even though they may be run down when you look at them. This is important, because you will want to use these estimates to make offers that will allow you to fix up the property and get a return on both the purchase price and the repair costs.

As you ride with these property managers, pick their brains. Ask for references, preferably in the form of names and phone numbers of the owners of properties they currently manage. Ask if they know of any properties that may make good investments. Ask if any of the people for whom they are currently managing properties are interested in selling. Find out how many homes they are currently managing in the areas where you are riding. If possible, ask them to show you some of these properties. Note their overall condition and general appearance. Granted, owners often tie the hands of property managers when it comes to making repairs and doing maintenance, but if they show you run-down properties, they will let you know if the owners are refusing to let them make needed repairs. If they don't comment on the condition, it could be an indication that they are not keeping the owners informed. Throughout your ride, you will be evaluating them and they will be sizing you up, but the most important part of this exercise is developing a feel for rental rates in your targeted neighborhoods. If you get good feelings about a particular property manager in the process, that's an added bonus.

When you complete this weekend's work, you should be familiar with your target areas, have a list of properties for sale, and have a good idea of the rent these properties could produce. Be sure that you have looked at a minimum of three FSBO properties, because you will be working with these during your fourth weekend.

CHECKLIST
Weekend Three

_____ I have researched the classified ads for homes and apartments for rent.

_____ I have located two property managers who are willing to ride with me on the weekend.

_____ I have ridden with the property managers and gotten a good feel for the range of rents for _____ houses we visited.

_____ I have asked the property managers if they have owners who want to sell.

_____ I have developed a list of properties for sale in the areas where we rode.

_____ I have identified at least three FSBO properties in the areas where we rode.

35

What to Do Your Fourth Weekend

The reason we suggested that you look at several FSBO properties during your rides with the property managers on your third weekend was because this weekend you will conduct detailed inspections on some of these properties. Review your notes from previous weeks, and select three FSBO properties that you feel have the most potential. Sometime during the preceding week, we want you to call the owners of these properties and schedule appointments to inspect them on the weekend. Explain that you work during the week and would like to look at the houses on Saturday if possible. Allow yourself about an hour to inspect each one. You can maximize the use of your time by scheduling inspections of three properties within close proximity of each other.

Prior to visiting the properties, turn to Appendix A and review the sample inspection form. Make copies of it if you wish or use it as a guide to set up your own inspection form. It's not important which form or method you use; what is important is that you have a checklist to guide you through the inspection process. Using this checklist, you will inspect each item and rate it as being excellent, average, or poor. If you rate an item as poor, estimate the cost of repairing it. If some of the items are large-ticket items like the roof, paint or siding, heat or air conditioning systems, or carpet, and you don't feel comfortable estimating costs, you may want to call vendors that do the specific work and ask them for an estimate range.

For example, if you think the roof needs replacing, you may want to call a couple of roofing companies, tell them the approximate size of the house (32' × 38', 28' × 40', etc.) and ask them to give you the minimum and maximum amounts it may cost to replace the roof. If you explain that you are thinking about buying a house that needs a new roof and you need an approximate range of what it may cost to replace it, most companies are happy to help. Of course, they will tell you that they can't give you a firm estimate without actually looking at the job. This is fine, because all you need to know at this point is the maximum it may cost. You will use this higher figure when making a purchase offer, but by requesting a range of estimates, you have something to negotiate with if you buy the house and actually have to do the work. You can use this same technique to get estimates on any of the other large-ticket items.

When estimating smaller items like door locks, screens, and minor repairs, use your own best judgment. Since the cost of these type items is small, even if you miss with your estimate, the impact will be minimal. The more experienced you become, the more accurate your estimates will be.

What to Do Your Fourth Weekend

CHECKLIST
Weekend Four

_____ I have located _____ FSBO properties and made appointments with the owners to inspect them this Saturday.

_____ I have familiarized myself with the property inspection form in Appendix A.

_____ I have inspected _____ of the FSBO properties.

_____ I have obtained rough estimates on the cost of any necessary major repairs such as roofs, heating and air conditioning systems, and carpet.

_____ I have estimated the total cost of repairs to bring each inspected property into good condition.

36

What to Do Your Fifth Weekend

During the week prior to your fifth weekend, you have another home-work assignment. Go back and review Chapter 24, Valuing Single-Family Properties, and Chapter 25, Structuring Your First Deal. These are important chapters because this weekend you will actually be presenting offers to purchase the properties you inspected last weekend. You will use the information in Chapter 24, the rent ranges from the property managers who rode with you, and the cost estimates for any needed repairs from your inspection form to determine the value each property has to you. Forget about appraisals; they are for banks and people buying a home in which to live. Appraisals are estimates of "market value." Remember, you can't pay market value for a property and rent it for market value and stay in business—there is no margin of profit.

By taking the NOI a property will generate, assuming the property is in good condition, and using it to back into a value, you will be determining a wholesale price for the property. From this price, you will want to deduct the cost of any needed repairs to put it in good condition.

What to Do Your Fifth Weekend

At this stage of the game, you may be reluctant to present an offer for what you have determined the value to be. Don't worry if most of your offers are rejected. What's important is that the ones sellers do accept are profitable. Realize that public perception is against you. Homeowners, real estate brokers, banks, and almost anyone else involved with real estate use appraisals to establish values. That's the norm. Making wholesale offers for real estate goes against this norm. There's really no difference, however, between you making a wholesale offer to buy a piece of property and car dealers making you a wholesale offer for your car that's $1,000 to $2,000 less than they will put it on their lot for sale. The difference is that people are accustomed to getting wholesale offers for their cars on trade, but they aren't familiar with wholesale offers for a house.

We want to emphasize the importance of making offers that will allow you to purchase properties with the NOI. Granted, this is more difficult when buying single-family homes, but it's not impossible. Understanding this, we want you to calculate the amount you are willing to offer and the way you are willing to pay it for the three properties you inspected last weekend. Remember if you are able to pay cash, ask for the lowest possible price; if not, raise the price and ask for favorable terms. Just be sure the income from the property will give you the return you want on your cash or will pay off the mortgage if you request terms.

Once you have completed your calculations and made a determination about the kind of offers you will make, you need to put them into writing. Go back and review Chapter 26, How to Write the Offer. In case you didn't do so earlier, we would like to recommend again that you order the Carleton Sheets Real Estate Toolkit that we told you about in Chapter 26. This user-friendly program, available on CD, can be loaded onto your computer and will allow you to print purchase contract forms and give you all the other forms and tools you will need to analyze, purchase, and manage properties. It even gives you the option to customize all the forms by adding names, dates, addresses, and dollar amounts and anything else you want to include, prior to printing.

Once you have your offers in writing, your task for the fifth weekend is to present them to the sellers. You will begin by contacting the sellers and letting them know that you would like to bring them an offer to purchase their property. When you get in front of them, before going into the offer, explain that you are an investor and that you have carefully analyzed their property to determine what you can pay for it. Put in plain words the fact that as an investor, you must structure your offers so that you can receive a return on your investment or you cannot buy the property. You may even want to acknowledge the fact that they might be able to get more for the property if they can find a buyer who wants to live in it. You're looking for the sellers who do not have the option of waiting to find a retail buyer.

As you present your offer, tell the sellers that you do not expect them to make a decision on the spot. Suggest that they study your offer overnight before making any comment about it one way or another. Since your offer will be a wholesale offer, it will probably be for much less than what the sellers expect. This is understandable. It is also the reason you will be asking them to study the offer before making any decisions. Written offers are one of the best ways of finding sellers that due to personal circumstances may need to rid themselves of a property even at a wholesale price. If their problems are embarrassing or ones they do not want to discuss, they may be able to solve these by simply accepting your offer. As the old saying goes, "You never know until you ask."

Once you have presented your three offers, your assignment for the weekend is complete. If any of them are accepted, great. If not, it's no big deal because you will have just made your first offers and that's what getting started is all about. This exercise is designed to take you from the "thinking" to the "doing" phase of becoming a Weekend Millionaire. If you're like most people, making these first offers will be the toughest steps you will take. You will be nervous, maybe a little scared, and not quite sure of yourself. That's only normal, but you will have taken your first step. As you go forward, your confidence will grow with each offer you write. Now go to the checklist, and as soon as you have completed it, let's move on to the sixth weekend.

What to Do Your Fifth Weekend

CHECKLIST
Weekend Five

_____ I have reviewed Chapter 24, Valuing Single-Family Properties.

_____ I have reviewed Chapter 25, Structuring Your First Deal.

_____ I have calculated the NOI and used it to establish a value on each of the three target properties.

_____ I have reviewed Chapter 26, How to Write the Offer.

_____ I have written up offers on my three target homes.

_____ I have presented those offers to the sellers.

Take yourself out to dinner and celebrate. You have just completed the toughest part of becoming a Weekend Millionaire—making the first offer!

37

What to Do Your Sixth Weekend

This weekend will be similar to weekend four, but easier. Once again, you will be inspecting properties, only this time they will be properties listed for sale with real estate brokers. The brokers will show you the properties rather than the owners. As you are going through the houses, the brokers will more than likely point out the positive attributes and leave it up to you to find the negatives. Listing brokers work for and are paid by the sellers, so their fiduciary duty is to them. Their job is to get the best deal for their clients.

Many investors are reluctant to work through listing brokers for this reason. Our experience is that good brokers do what is best for their sellers and that doesn't mean automatically discouraging them from accepting wholesale offers. Naturally, if sellers are able to wait for the right buyer to come along, they will get a better deal. However, if they don't have the time and financial ability to wait, their broker can be very instrumental in getting them to accept your offer.

When inspecting properties with brokers, follow the same procedure you would use if you were with the owners. Use a checklist so that you don't miss items. Work at your pace when conducting inspections, even if the broker tries to rush you. Once again, it's up to you to identify those items that are not satisfactory so you can review them later and estimate their repair costs. You will find that inspections will be much quicker once you have done a few of them. You may even want to try to inspect four properties this weekend rather than three as you did on the fourth weekend. Remember, the more properties you inspect and the more offers you make, the better your chances of making wholesale purchases.

CHECKLIST
Weekend Six

_____ I have identified _____ houses in the area I am farming that are listed with real estate brokers and arranged to inspect them with the brokers on Saturday.

_____ I have reviewed and made copies of the inspection form in Appendix A or prepared my own inspection form to use.

_____ I have inspected _____ of the properties I found that were listed with real estate brokers.

_____ I have obtained rough estimates on the cost of any necessary major repairs such as roofs, heating and air conditioning systems, or carpet.

_____ I have estimated the total cost of repairs to bring each inspected property into good condition.

38

What to Do Your Seventh Weekend

Just as we did for weekend five, we suggest that you go back and re-view Chapters 24 and 25. Until you become thoroughly familiar with the process, you will benefit greatly by reviewing these chapters each time before making new offers. This weekend, you are going to make offers on the properties you inspected the previous weekend with the listing brokers.

Once again, after you have completed your calculations and made a determination about the kind of offers you want to make, you need to put them into writing. You familiarized yourself with this process in week five by reviewing Chapter 26 and writing offers to purchase the FSBO properties you inspected. You did this on Offer to Purchase and Contract forms designed for that purpose. You can handle the offer to purchase properties listed with brokers in the same way, but the brokers will usually want to help you prepare the forms and present the offers to the owners for you. You have the right to ask to accompany brokers when your offers are presented, but this often makes them feel a need to display their fiduciary duty to the owners by finding fault with your offers. We suggest that you allow the agent to present to the seller without you if they prefer, but reserve the right to meet with the seller if the agent can't get the offer accepted. This challenges the agent to push for acceptance.

Another, and often less controversial, way to present wholesale offers through brokers is the use of a *letter of intent* rather than a contract form. These are simply letters expressing your interest in purchasing the property, briefly outlining what you are willing to pay, the method of payment, and any other pertinent terms or conditions. Address these letters to the brokers, asking them to contact the owners to see if they are interested and if so propose to transfer the offer immediately to a more formal contract form. A typical letter of intent might look like this:

Dear Broker,

This letter of intent is to convey my sincere interest in purchasing the house you showed me at 114 Elm Street. When I inspected the property, I found that it needed approximately $6,300 worth of repairs. I would be happy to share my list of work that needs to be done if you think it would be important.

I am very interested in the property and would be willing to purchase it in its present condition under either of the following scenarios:

1. $79,250 cash at closing. Buyer and seller to pay own closing costs except that seller will provide a current survey and a title insurance policy in the amount of the purchase.

2. $103,600, with $10,000 being paid in cash at closing and the seller to take back a purchase money mortgage payable in 180 direct principal reduction payments of $520 per month. Buyer and seller to pay own closing costs except that seller will provide a current survey.

Would you please discuss this offer with the owners, and if either scenario is acceptable, I will show good faith by immediately transferring it into contract form and make a $1,000 earnest money deposit to an escrow account. I look forward to hearing from you with a favorable response to one of these proposals.

Sincerely,

Your name

Signature

Address

Phone Number

Letters of intent give you another tool with which to work. Something as simple as a letter like the one above can get the ball rolling. In this example, the seller is given two options that basically are the same offer; just different in the way they are presented. (Review Chapter 25, Structuring Your First Deal, to better understand this concept.)

Letters of intent speed up the process of getting offers in front of sellers, especially with brokers involved. They provide you with a way to reach agreement in principle and still leave plenty of room to improve the deal with negotiations on minor points.

Remember the more offers you make, the better your chances of success. Review the checklist that follows, and make sure to complete each item before moving on to the eighth weekend where we give you another strategy to locate potential wholesale purchases.

What to Do Your Seventh Weekend

CHECKLIST
Weekend Seven

_____ I have reviewed Chapter 24, Valuing Single-Family Properties.

_____ I have reviewed Chapter 25, Structuring Your First Deal.

_____ I have calculated the NOI and used it to establish a value on each of the properties I inspected.

_____ I have reviewed Chapter 26, How to Write the Offer.

_____ I have prepared _____ offers on the properties I inspected last weekend using a contract form to present the offer. (Make at least one offer this way.)

_____ I have made _____ offers on the properties that I inspected last weekend using a letter of intent to present the offer. (Make at least one offer this way.)

Treat yourself to another dinner and celebration. You have just completed the second toughest part of becoming a Weekend Millionaire.

39

What to Do Your Eighth Weekend

We hope that when we told you in the preface to Section 3 about the importance of having business cards that proclaim you are a real estate investor, you immediately went out and ordered some. The story in Chapter 11 of Mike's $42,000 business card demonstrated this importance. Business cards are one of the cheapest ways to get the word out that you are a real estate investor. Don't let it bother you if you haven't bought the first property yet. You are a real estate investor the moment you decide to buy investment property. You're simply an investor who hasn't yet found the right property to buy.

The first weekend we told you that you would come to view your target subdivisions in much the same way that farmers view their fields. That just as the farmer cultivates and harvests crops from the ground, you would cultivate and harvest your first real estate investments from these neighborhoods. You've plowed the ground; it's now time to start planting the seeds. This weekend we want you to revisit your target neighborhoods. Take along a stack of your business cards and start passing them out. Give one to everyone you see. Ask them to call you if they hear of any properties getting ready to go on the market in their neighborhood. If people aren't at home, leave a card on their door or taped to the outside of their mailbox. You may want to put a note on the back that says, "I'm interested in buying in this neighborhood. If you know of any properties for sale, please give me a call." The more of these cards you have floating around in your target neighborhoods, the better chance you have of finding out about properties before they ever go on the market for sale. They are like the seeds in the farmer's field; they sprout, grow, and eventually become a harvest for you to reap.

You have no way of knowing when a seller may need to sell quickly and will take a wholesale offer. As unfortunate as it may be, death, divorce, loss of employment, bad investments, and many other events happen in people's lives that can cause them to become flexible sellers almost overnight. People who are incredibly inflexible one month can become extremely flexible the next. The more people who have your business card, the better your chance of them turning to you for help rather than giving other investors the great deals.

As you are riding through the neighborhoods passing out your cards, keep your eyes peeled for new For Sale signs, ones that were not there when you first rode through. As you can probably guess, you've come full circle. You're back riding your neighborhoods as you were on the first weekend, and you're probably noticing that new properties are now for sale and ones you saw on the first trip have sold. As you make these repeated rides, be aware of properties that remain for sale trip after trip. The longer properties are on the market, the more flexible their sellers become.

Getting Started

CHECKLIST
Weekend Eight

_____ I have revisited the neighborhoods in the area I'm farming and handed out my business card to everyone I met.

_____ I am building a file with many notes on houses I have inspected in my area.

_____ I have a list of all the potential investment properties that are for sale in my area.

_____ I am paying special attention to all the FSBO properties in my area.

_____ I am watching and researching the run-down properties in the nicer neighborhoods in my area that aren't listed for sale.

_____ I understand that if I just keep doing what I've been doing for the last eight weeks I will buy my first investment property soon.

_____ I understand that if I continue devoting four hours a week to my real estate investing career, I will become a Weekend Millionaire.

_____ I understand that becoming a Weekend Millionaire takes time and commitment, and I agree to give both.

Your First Eight Weeks in Review

The eight-week exercise you have just completed has given you a feeling for what it takes to become a Weekend Millionaire. You have familiarized yourself with neighborhoods, inspected a few properties, made some offers, and gotten a general idea of what it takes to become a real estate investor. You may or may not have purchased your first property; what's important is that you have started the process.

Stay positive and don't let anything or anyone stop you from spending four hours each week on the Weekend Millionaire program. Your four hours don't have to be on the weekend. If you cherish your weekends and want to invest the time during the week, that's fine. What's important is that you work on becoming a Weekend Millionaire consistently week after week. Patience, persistence, and discipline are the keys to wealth. Buying one house won't make you wealthy, but buying one or two a year, year after year, will.

If you haven't already done so, you're only a few weeks away from buying your first investment property. If you buy it in the way we have taught you, it will start a trickle that will grow with each subsequent purchase until it becomes a rivulet and eventually a river of passive income. And, the amazing thing is, you can accomplish this by simply repeating and getting better at the eight steps we have just shown you.

Chapter 40 is our bonus to you. It will address some of the common mistakes that new investors make. Now that we've taught you what to do; it's only right that we close by summarizing what not to do.

40

The 14 Biggest Mistakes New Investors Make

(Bonus Chapter)

Many people view success as an event rather than a lifestyle change. They talk about becoming wealthy, but instead of investing, they speculate. You see these people lined up buying lottery tickets at convenience stores or feeding money into slot machines at casinos. They hear about someone's uncle's, brother's cousin who found a million dollar gemstone panning dirt at a gem mine, so they flock to the mine and buy buckets of dirt to wash hoping the same thing will happen to them. These people will spend their grocery money to buy some harebrained get-rich-quick scheme off the Internet or from a TV infomercial.

Have you ever wondered why so many of these schemes come and go? How can something that is supposed to make you rich in two weeks not earn enough to keep the advertising on TV? The reason is simple: These schemes appeal to people who lack the three D's of success—discipline, desire, and dedication. They lack the discipline to make small investments and then allow these investments to mature; they lack the desire to stay the course when the going gets a little rough; and they lack the dedication to continued learning, which is required to make lifestyle changes.

When you bought this book, you set yourself apart from the get-rich-quick crowd. You're willingness to sit down with a book and study it is an excellent first step. Your decision to explore real estate as a way to wealth will be highly rewarded. As our friend Carleton Sheets quoted Marshall Field, founder of Marshall Field & Company, in the foreword to this book, "Real estate is not only the best and quickest way to make you wealthy, for the average person it truly is the only way." The fact that Carleton's program *How to Buy Your First Home or Investment Property with No Down Payment* has been on television continuously for over 20 consecutive years, speaks volumes to this fact.

We know what real estate investing can do for you. We know that even average people can become millionaires investing in real estate. Granted some get there faster than others do. In this book, we've given you tools and ideas with which to work. What you do with them is up to you. Fear of failure keeps more people from getting started than any other single cause.

We want to close by making you aware of the common mistakes new investors make and hope that by doing so you will guard against making them and be on your way to becoming a Weekend Millionaire.

1. Being Impatient

As we've said all along, the Weekend Millionaire is not a get-rich-quick scheme. Although many of our students have achieved rapid success, we don't expect you to buy a house every month. Even if you only bought one a year you would still become wealthy over time as the rents keep rising, mortgages start paying off, and larger and larger amounts of the rent money go straight into your pocket. Neither do we expect you to get your first offer accepted (if you do, you probably paid too much). You may not get the tenth or the twentieth offer accepted. Remember, "inch by inch, anything's a cinch," or if you prefer, "meter-by-meter, everything's sweeter." Be patient!

2. Commingling Your Accounts

Keep your investment income separated from your earned income. Right from the first day, we want you to open up a bank account to handle your real estate investments. Think of this account as an individual retirement account (IRA) or other retirement account that you will not touch until you are ready to retire. You may feel silly going into a bank and opening up an account under John Doe Investments and depositing only $100, but it's the principle that's important. Never take money from your investment account for personal expenses. If you have to put earned income into the account, treat it as a capital investment or a loan. If it's a capital investment, you will leave it in the account just as you would a contribution to an IRA. If it's a loan, repay yourself when enough money builds up in the account that you can do so. As this account grows, you will reinvest profits into more real estate, not go out and buy new cars or boats.

3. Buying Upscale Properties

You make money consistently with bread and butter properties. These attract tenants who are good people, many of whom will always be renters, not owners. Upscale properties, those in the upper third of the market, don't attract stable renters. The people who rent higher-end properties usually fall into one of three groups. They are either new to the area and want to rent temporarily while they decide on the area in which they want to buy; they are between homes because they have sold one and are waiting on a new one to be finished; or they have the ability to earn a high income, but a financial setback has damaged their credit to the point that they cannot buy at the time. None of these three groups makes for stable tenants, and when a property does go vacant, finding another tenant is difficult and time consuming. Although you may not want to live in any of your rental houses, stick with ones that attract tenants who are proud to live there and will take good care of your property.

4. Buying Property Just Because It Is Cheap

Don't buy properties in bad neighborhoods just because they are cheap. Those properties seem like bargains, but they are loaded with problems. An easy test is to ask yourself if you would feel comfortable walking the neighborhood alone and chatting with the people who live there (we're talking about during the day, of course. These days it's not smart to wander any neighborhood at night). Unless you plan to buy the whole neighborhood and rehab it to attract better tenants, you're better off looking elsewhere than you are to buy properties in neighborhoods where you don't feel comfortable.

In fact, use extra caution when looking at any properties that look like super bargains. There is usually something, often something hidden, that makes the deals so good. Some of the worst buys we've ever made have looked like bargains up front; while some of the best investments were when we paid the maximum we could justify. Just keep in mind that there's probably a reason why bargain properties are such bargains. Unless you can find the problems and have plans to deal with them, you'd be wise to pass on the properties just as other potential buyers have done.

5. Inflating Your Net Worth

We hope this doesn't shock you, but real estate investors tend to inflate their net worth. At the cocktail party, they'll brag that they own $5 million dollars worth of property and only owe $3 million, which gives them a net worth of $2 million. Well, maybe so, but if they were forced to liquidate the property in the next 90 days, would it sell for that much? Maybe—maybe not! Inflated net worth seems to inflate egos; maybe that's why they do it. When preparing a financial statement, the value you place on your properties should come from certified appraisals, tax appraisals, or actual purchase prices. If time has lapsed since the establishment of one of these values, keep your inflation adjustments at or below actual inflation rates. Lenders will appreciate you more when you do this.

Bragging in a bar about how much property you own is fine, but we would much prefer to see you focus on your monthly income stream. Having a steady income stream of $10,000 a month says more about your wealth than the value of what you own. We have seen people who own hundreds of millions of dollars worth of assets file bankruptcy because they didn't have any cash flow.

6. Not Understanding That Wealth Is an Income Stream

Understand that it's not how much property you own, it's the income it generates that makes you wealthy. People who live in big homes, drive fine cars, and take fabulous vacations are not necessarily wealthy. Wealth is not the standard of living you enjoy; it's your ability to sustain that standard of living if you suddenly can't earn income. That $25 a month you make from your first rental property may sound like a drop in the bucket, but as it grows to $50, $100, $200, and more, the drop turns into a trickle. As you add more and more properties, the trickle gradually turns into a stream, and the stream becomes a river of wealth that will allow you to enjoy and sustain a lifestyle of which you never even dreamed. Don't ever make the mistake of thinking wealth is what you own. Wealth is an income stream.

7. Trying to Do Everything Yourself

Probably the top reason why investors quit buying real estate is that they become overwhelmed with the work involved. They tie up every spare minute fixing properties, mowing lawns, washing windows, checking out tenants, and collecting rents. Property management is a job, a profession, so why not leave it to the professionals. If you are going to be an investor, be an investor; don't take on a second job. We teach you to use professional management from the very first property you buy. That will free up your time to find and buy more properties.

You'll hear some good arguments from property owners who do the work themselves. Here's one that we heard recently: "Why should I pay an electrician $100 to change a breaker, when I can pick one up at Home Depot and change it myself for $20?" Not a bad argument, is it? You save $80, and it only takes you two hours. That's $40 an hour; not bad, but what if instead you spent those two hours making an offer on a property that might make you $10,000? Wouldn't that make more sense? Weekend Millionaires always focus on the highest and best use of their time, which is researching and making offers on properties. Don't spend $100-an-hour time doing $10-an-hour work.

8. Fear of Bad Experience

Almost everyone has heard horror stories about renters damaging properties. We have had numerous people tell us they wouldn't think of renting properties because of a bad experience someone they know has had with a tenant. Yes, there are problem tenants. Some do damage, some don't pay their rent, some are obnoxious, and some do just about any other bad thing you can name. If you're in the business long enough, you will run into a few of these bad tenants, but don't let a few bad apples prevent you from building your future.

The reserves that we teach you to set aside take into consideration the fact that occasionally you will have to pay for tenant damage. We recommend that you use professional management because it insulates you from the undesirable tasks of evicting tenants and dealing with disorderly and obnoxious people. The money you pay for management is not just for showing properties and collecting rents. It's for handling the undesirable aspects of being a landlord.

Tenant problems are as much a part of the cost of doing business for real estate investors as shoplifters, vandals, accidents, and other unusual costs are for other businesses. Allowing occasional bad experiences with tenants to stop you from building wealth and securing your retirement would be like other businesses closing their doors because of a few problems. Even banks are robbed occasionally. Accept the fact that there will be an occasional problem and move on.

9. Buying Out of Area

Focus your efforts on properties within 10 miles of where you live. Even though you'll be using a property manager to handle the day-to-day activities, it is much easier to farm neighborhoods that are nearby. If you're going to allocate four hours per week to real estate investing, you don't want to spend most of your time driving back and forth instead of locating properties. When you stick close to home, you live in the center of the area you are farming. That means you can be looking for investments almost from the time you pull out of your driveway. In addition, it's comforting to be able to drive by your properties on your way home from your real job. Be very wary of acquiring properties that are a considerable distance from where you live and regularly travel. As the old saying goes, "The grass always seems greener on the other side of the fence." Just remember that you have to mow it too.

10. Buying Other Than Basic Rental Property

Once you've built a portfolio of basic rental properties, you'll be tempted to reach out and buy some more exotic properties, such as ranches, hotels, motels, or condominiums in Hawaii. It's a lot like the board game Monopoly. After you've been playing the game for a while, you get bored with the little green houses and you want to buy some big red hotels. That thinking will usually get you into trouble until you become wealthy enough to withstand the risk. Stick with the bread and butter rental properties until you establish a solid cash flow before moving to larger properties. For security, each new purchase should not exceed 15 percent of what you own at the time of the purchase, which means if you own 40 units it's probably safe to buy a 6-unit property. If you move to larger properties too quickly, you risk putting yourself in a position where the tail can wag the dog.

11. Gambling on Prices Going Up

Throughout this book, we have taught you to buy based on values calculated using the current NOI. Knowing how property values and rents have increased over the years, you will be tempted to pay too much, hoping values and rents will increase. That can be deadly. Many investors have gone broke buying real estate by betting on future growth. Don't do it!

During the Carter administration of the late 1970s, inflation was driving prices and rents up rapidly. Houses in some areas were going up in value $5,000 a week! Investors were piling into the market. Lines were forming at new tract sales offices. Some developers even ran lotteries to select the lucky buyers. To cap it off, when Ronald Reagan became President and announced that he would cut taxes while raising military expenditure, every economist in the country saw that as a recipe for hyperinflation. More investors piled into the market because real estate is such a good hedge against inflation.

What nobody predicted was that President Reagan would be willing to take extreme measures to stop inflation. The prime interest rate went to 21.5 percent in December 1980. Unemployment reached 15 percent. Inflation came to a screeching halt; the price of real estate started to drop, and investors who bought because they were counting on inflation to make them rich went broke.

To become a Weekend Millionaire, don't buy real estate because you think it will go up in value because of scarcity or inflation. Buy it right so that it makes sense at the time of purchase. That will make it a good investment even if it never goes up in value.

12. Blanket Encumbrances

Many investors have gotten into trouble because their lenders talked them into giving blanket encumbrances on most or all of their properties. Blanket encumbrances are ones in which two or more properties secure a single loan. If you are buying like we have taught you, each transaction should stand on its own. Only in rare instances is it sensible to give lenders a blanket mortgage. If a lender says, "You don't have enough equity in this property for me to make you the loan, but I'll do it if you'll secure it with more property," take a second look at the deal. Often the property they want for additional security is your home. Never do that! This is different from loaning your investment account money from a home equity loan that you will pay back in a year or two. See mistake number 2. Since real estate is for your retirement, don't put your present in jeopardy trying to secure your future.

Blanket mortgages also limit your options, even when you are only offering other investment properties as security. Roger made this mistake once when he bought five 20-acre parcels of land. He paid 20 percent down, and the seller carried back the financing on a 15-year loan. A buyer contacted him wanting to buy one of the parcels at a high price, but the original seller wouldn't release the title until Roger had paid off the entire underlying loan. Fortunately, using his negotiating skills, he was able to obtain a release of the parcel he wanted to sell, but he had to give the note holder the entire proceeds of the sale in order to do so. Eventually, he profited quite well from the property, but until the note was paid, the holder of the note had all the power.

If you ever agree to a blanket encumbrance, be sure that you include release clauses in the initial loan documents. A typical release clause says that you must pay off the portion of the loan that applies to the property you want to release, plus a percentage of that amount. It's much simpler just to stay away from blanket encumbrances, period.

13. Buying Properties Controlled by a Homeowners Association

You should approach the purchase of condominiums and houses in planned unit developments with extreme caution. Although homeowners associations do a good job of maintaining a building or a development, you give up a lot of control. The board of directors of a homeowners association consists of a group of residents who may have completely different objectives than you.

Roger once bought a home in a huge development in Palm Springs. He bought it new from the developer and paid $145,000. The homeowner's dues were $240 a month. A little high but it was a terrific property with a 27-hole golf course in a gated and guarded community. The association maintained the community beautifully. Once the developer was out of the picture, the homeowner's dues started to creep up. The board of directors voted more and more improvements, and they eventually voted to purchase and operate the golf course.

When Roger finally sold the property 12 years later, the monthly dues were over $500. Almost every potential buyer thought that was outrageous. The high dues depressed the value of the property, and Roger finally sold it for $100,000 and took a loss of 12 years and $45,000.

Be wary of investments that put control of your property into the hands of a committee of strangers. That's why they call them homeowners associations and not renters associations or investors associations.

14. Procrastination

Procrastination is the biggest enemy of success. If you stall out in the planning stage, you'll never get ahead. You can study real estate investing for a lifetime and never know everything you need to know, but you have to get out there and be willing to risk making a few mistakes. Remember the old adage, "Getting started is half done." Do something! Do it now! Get some business cards printed, start passing them out, go look at some properties, and start making offers! Don't procrastinate; do it now!

Happy Investing!

You now have the basic information you need to become a Weekend Millionaire. Much of what we have taught you will feel awkward in the beginning, like anything else new. The more you keep at it, the more comfortable you will become. Each time you inspect a property, make an offer, secure a loan, or do any of the other things that seem so unnatural to you now, you will learn and become more confident. If you invest four hours a week for the next year, you will not only own one, two, or three investment properties, but you will feel 10 times more confident and be well on your way to becoming a Weekend Millionaire.

Appendix A

INSPECTION FORM

Property Address _____

Inspection Date: _____

EXTERIOR

Item Inspected	N/A	No.	Excellent	Average	Poor	Est. Repair Cost
Roof						
Gutters						
Walls						
Foundation						
Porchs & decks						
Outside electrical fixtures						
Exterior doors & locks						
Windows & screens						
Shutters						
Outside storage						
Septic system						
Lawn						
Landscaping						
Drainage						
Driveway						
Walks & steps						
Fence						
Mailbox						
Other						

INTERIOR

General

Item Inspected	N/A	No.	Excel- lent	Aver- age	Poor	Est. Repair Cost
Smoke detectors						
Doorbell						
Intercom						
Water heater						
Water softener/filter system						
Sump pump						
Heat system						
Cooling system						
Security system						
Washer/dryer connections						
General cleanliness & odor						
Other						

Living Room

Item Inspected	N/A	No.	Excel- lent	Aver- age	Poor	Est. Repair Cost
Walls & ceiling						
Floor covering						
Light fixtures/ceiling fans						
Windows & screens						
Window treatments						
Fireplace						
Doors & locks						
Closet						
Other						

Page 2 of 8

Dining Room/Area

Item Inspected	N/A	No.	Excel- lent	Aver- age	Poor	Est. Repair Cost
Walls & ceiling						
Floor covering						
Light fixtures/ceiling fans						
Windows & screens						
Window treatments						
Doors & locks						

Den

Item Inspected	N/A	No.	Excel- lent	Aver- age	Poor	Est. Repair Cost
Walls & ceiling						
Floor covering						
Light fixtures/ceiling fans						
Windows & screens						
Window treatments						
Fireplace						
Doors & locks						

Kitchen

Item Inspected	N/A	No.	Excel- lent	Aver- age	Poor	Est. Repair Cost
Walls & ceiling						
Floor covering						
Light fixtures/ceiling fans						
Windows & screens						
Window treatments						
Doors & locks						

Page 3 of 8

Appendix A

Item Inspected	N/A	No.	Excel-lent	Aver-age	Poor	Est. Repair Cost
Sink & faucets						
Cabinets						
Range & oven						
Exhaust fan						
Refrigerator						
Dishwasher						
Garbage disposal						

Master Bedroom

Item Inspected	N/A	No.	Excel-lent	Aver-age	Poor	Est. Repair Cost
Walls & ceiling						
Floor covering						
Light fixtures/ceiling fans						
Windows & screens						
Window treatments						
Doors & locks						
Closets						

Bedroom 2

Item Inspected	N/A	No.	Excel-lent	Aver-age	Poor	Est. Repair Cost
Walls & ceiling						
Floor covering						
Light fixtures/ceiling fans						
Windows & screens						
Window treatments						
Doors & locks						
Closets						

Bedroom 3

Item Inspected	N/A	No.	Excel-lent	Aver-age	Poor	Est. Repair Cost
Walls & ceiling						
Floor covering						
Light fixtures/ceiling fans						
Windows & screens						
Window treatments						
Doors & locks						
Closets						

Bedroom 4

Item Inspected	N/A	No.	Excel-lent	Aver-age	Poor	Est. Repair Cost
Walls & ceiling						
Floor covering						
Light fixtures/ceiling fans						
Windows & screens						
Window treatments						
Doors & locks						
Closets						

Bathroom 1

Item Inspected	N/A	No.	Excel-lent	Aver-age	Poor	Est. Repair Cost
Walls & ceiling						
Floor covering						
Window & treatments						
Doors & locks						
Light fixtures						
Sink & faucets						

Item Inspected	N/A	No.	Excel-lent	Aver-age	Poor	Est. Repair Cost
Toilet						
Tub & shower						
Tissue holder & towel racks						
Exhaust fan						
Vanity						
Medicine cabinet						

Bathroom 2

Item Inspected	N/A	No.	Excel-lent	Aver-age	Poor	Est. Repair Cost
Walls & ceiling						
Floor covering						
Window & treatments						
Doors & locks						
Light fixtures						
Sink & faucets						
Toilet						
Tub & shower						
Tissue holder & towel racks						
Exhaust fan						
Vanity						
Medicine cabinet						

Bathroom 3

Item Inspected	N/A	No.	Excel-lent	Aver-age	Poor	Est. Repair Cost
Walls & ceiling						
Floor covering						
Window & treatments						

Appendix A

Item Inspected	N/A	No.	Excellent	Average	Poor	Est. Repair Cost
Doors & locks						
Light fixtures						
Sink & faucets						
Toilet						
Tub & shower						
Tissue holder & towel racks						
Exhaust fan						
Vanity						
Medicine cabinet						

Garage

Item Inspected	N/A	No.	Excellent	Average	Poor	Est. Repair Cost
Walls & ceiling						
Windows & doors						
Light fixtures						
Door opener & remote units						
General cleanliness						
Other						

Unfinished Basement

Item Inspected	N/A	No.	Excellent	Average	Poor	Est. Repair Cost
Foundation walls						
Insulation						
Drainage						
Moisture						
Windows & doors						
Light fixtures						
General cleanliness						
Other						

Appendix A

Miscellaneous Items

Item Inspected	N/A	No.	Excel-lent	Aver-age	Poor	Est. Repair Cost
Hallways						
Exterior handrails						
Interior handrails						

OTHER ITEMS OR COMMENTS NOT LISTED ABOVE:

Appendix B

NET OPERATING INCOME CALCULATION FORM

Property Address _____

	Monthly	Annually
Income		
Gross rent		
Vacancy factor		
Net rent		
Expenses		
Management fee		
Maintenance reserve		
Utilities		
Taxes		
Insurance		
Other expenses		
Net operating income (NOI)		

Real Estate Investment Glossary

A

Abstract The notes made by a title examiner based on his or her examination of the land records. These notes are a concise summary of the transactions affecting the property.

Abstract of Title Tells what the title professional found about the title to the property. Shows any title defects that could prevent you from getting clear, marketable, and insurable title.

Abutting Adjacent parcels of land having a common boundary; for example, Nevada abuts California.

Acceleration Clause Present in most loan documents these days, this clause gives a lender the power to call for payment in full of a loan if the property is sold or if the loan becomes delinquent.

Accretion When natural causes such as tides or river motion increase the size of your property, it's called accretion.

Real Estate Investment Glossary

Acknowledgment   The oath you give to a notary public confirming that the signature upon a document is in fact yours and was placed there of your own free will.

Acre   A parcel of land containing 43,560 square feet.

Adjustable Rate Mortgage (ARM)   A mortgage in which the rate of interest may be periodically adjusted by the lender based upon some constant such as the rate of interest paid on 30-year treasury notes. ARMs usually carry a lower interest rate than fixed-rate mortgages, but you are taking a risk because rates can rise well above what you could have gotten with a fixed rate mortgage.

Administrator   If you die without a will, the court may appoint an administrator to administer your estate.

Agency   The authority, which is created when one person authorizes another to act on his or her behalf. When sellers list property with brokers, they create an agency.

Agreement of Sale   A contract in which sellers agree to sell and buyers agree to buy, under certain specific terms and conditions spelled out in writing and signed by both parties. In some states, it is known as a purchase agreement, land contract, or earnest money contract. Real estate contracts must be in writing to be valid.

Alligator.   A property that costs money each month to own because the rental income doesn't cover the expenses. This won't happen if you buy right with the Weekend Millionaire program.

Amortization The paying of a loan with regular payments. Amortization periods for real estate loans usually range from 15 to 30 years. Some loans may be amortized with payments based on a 15 to 30-year amortization, with the full principal balance becoming due and payable after 3 to 10 years. (See *Balloon Payment*.)

Application   The information provided to a lender when applying for a loan. This includes personal and financial information the lender may require to approve a loan.

Real Estate Investment Glossary

Application Fee   The fee charged by a lender, at the time of application for a loan. This fee includes the cost of obtaining credit reports and processing other information in connection with a new loan.

Appraisal   The expert opinion of a licensed appraiser regarding the fair market value of a property. The estimate of the value of real estate, made by an appraiser, as of a given date. Most states require appraisers to be licensed. An appraisal is an opinion as to the price that a willing buyer will pay and a willing seller will accept when both are informed and neither is under pressure.

Appraisal fee   The fee charged by the appraiser for a written opinion of value.

Appreciation   The increase in value or worth of a property due to inflation, demand, or other external factors.

Appurtenance   Anything permanently attached to the land that will pass with it to a new owner. Deeds generally do not distinguish between raw land and land containing a mansion on the property. It is assumed that appurtenances permanently attached to the land transfer with the property, but it is wise to clarify specific items that could be in doubt in the purchase contract.

Arrears   Payment made after the time for which it accrues has lapsed. Interest, which is due and payable on the first of the month following the month in which it accrues, is said to be interest in arrears.

Assessed Valuation   The value placed on real estate by governmental authorities as the basis for levying property taxes. This is not necessarily the same as appraised or market value.

Assessment   The tax levied against property by a local taxing authority such as a county, city, or fire or school district. Also, the fee levied against property by homeowners or condominium associations.

Asset   Any possession that has value.

Assign   To transfer interest.

Assignee   One who receives an assignment or transfer of rights. An assignment of a contract transfers the right to buy property.

Real Estate Investment Glossary

Assignment   Transfer of one's rights to another.

Assignor   The one who assigns to another person.

Assumable Mortgage   An existing mortgage that a new buyer can assume under the same terms given to the original borrower.

Attached Homes   A home that has one or more common walls shared with another home. Condominiums, town houses, and row houses are attached homes.

Attorney in Fact   A person who has been given a written power of attorney to act on behalf of the grantor.

Attorney's Opinion of Title   An instrument written and signed by an attorney at law who has examined the abstract of title for a property, giving an opinion as to whether a seller may convey good title.

Auction   A sale of property to the highest bidder.

B

Balloon Payment   A payment that is larger than the regular payment of a specific amortization schedule. Many real estate loans are written with an amortization schedule based on 15 to 30 years with a balloon payment for the remaining principal due at the end of 3 to 10 years. A balloon payment can be for all or a portion of the remaining principal balance.

Basis   The original cost of a property, plus the value of any improvements, minus any depreciation taken. In the event of a sale, capital gains taxes are computed on the difference between the sales price and the seller's basis.

Beneficiary   The legal term used to describe anyone receiving a benefit. In the case of a real estate loan, the lender is the beneficiary of the note.

Bill of Sale   A written statement certifying that the ownership of something has been transferred by a sale. In real estate transactions, a bill of sale is used to transfer ownership of personal property.

Blanket Mortgage   A single mortgage secured by more than one parcel of real property.

Bridge Financing   An interim loan, given by a lender to fund construction prior to making a permanent mortgage or to fund a gap between the purchase of one property and the sale of another.

British Thermal Unit (BTU)   Unit of heat required to raise 1 pound of water 1 degree Fahrenheit at sea level.

Building Code   A body of government regulations specifying standards that construction must meet. These can be city, county, or state regulations, and if they differ, the stricter rule usually applies.

Building Line (Setback)   A distance measured from property lines within which structures may not be built. These setback distances usually apply to the front and sides of a lot, but can apply to rear lot lines as well.

Buyer's Broker   A real estate broker who represents only the buyer in a transaction. A buyer's broker may charge a flat fee or a percentage of the purchase price, which is paid by the buyer.

C

Cap   The maximum rate of interest or monthly payment increase allowable under the terms of an adjustable rate mortgage (ARM).

Capital Gain   Taxable profit on the sale of an appreciated asset. It is usually taxed at a lower rate than income tax.

Capitalization Rate (CAP Rate)   The rate of return on investment an income-producing property yields, assuming a cash purchase. The CAP rate is calculated by dividing the annual net income by the purchase price.

Caveat Emptor   A legal term meaning "let the buyer beware."

Ceiling   The maximum interest permitted under the terms of an adjustable rate mortgage.

Certificate of Eligibility   A certificate obtained from a Veterans Administration (VA) office that states that a veteran is eligible for a VA insured loan.

Certificate of Occupancy   A certificate issued by a local governmental agency that states a property meets the local standards for occupancy.

Certificate of Reasonable Value (CRV) An appraisal of property for the purpose of insurance by the Veterans Administration.

Chain of Title A history of conveyances and encumbrances of a property from some starting point that chronicles how the present owner derived title.

Chattel Movable items of personal property such as appliances, furniture, and automobiles.

Clear Title A land title with no liens (such as mortgages or tax liens) against it.

Client A person (or other entity such as a company) for whom an agent is acting. Typically, a seller is a client of a listing agent and a buyer is a client of a buyer's agent. A fiduciary relationship generally exists between agents and their clients.

Closing The act of consummating the transfer of title to property from a seller to a buyer. The conclusion of a sales transaction when the seller transfers title to the buyer in exchange for consideration.

Closing Costs Expenses associated with the transfer of real estate that are usually in addition to the purchase price specified in the contract. These expenses may include legal fees, mortgage fees, surveys, inspections, deed preparation, recording fees, and other miscellaneous fees that are paid at the closing.

Closing Statement A detailed written summary of the financial settlement of a real estate transaction, showing all charges and credits for both buyer and seller and all cash received and paid out.

Cloud on Title A lien or encumbrance that may affect title to land.

Collateral Something of value pledged to a lender to secure repayment of a loan.

Commingling The practice of depositing a client's funds into the same account with an agent's funds. This practice is illegal in most jurisdictions.

Real Estate Investment Glossary

Comparables   Properties similar to a specific property that are used by appraisers to compare and establish the value of a property.

Compound Interest.   Interest that is computed on both the principal balance and any interest which has accrued but not been paid.

Condemnation.   The procedure under which a government agency takes possession of property with its powers of eminent domain. Commonly used to acquire land for roads, utilities, and other uses by the public. Also the declaration that a property is unsafe or unfit for use or service.

Condominium   A building containing individual units owned by multiple owners that is governed by declarations, which specify how maintenance costs are to be shared and how common areas may be used. The declarations establishing a condominium are typically administered by an association made up of the owners.

Consideration   What a buyer puts into a transaction. This can be cash, notes, personal property, or even an exchange of services.

Construction Loan   The short-term financing of real estate construction. Construction loans are generally paid upon the sale of properties or by long-term financing called *take out* loans.

Contingency   An act or event that must occur for a contract to be binding. For example, a contract is contingent upon buyers selling their present home within 60 days or a contract is contingent upon the seller installing new roof shingles.

Contract for Deed   A contract for the sale of real estate where the deed (title) of the property is transferred only after all payments have been made. Also known as a land contract, conditional sales contract, or installment contract.

Contract Sales Price   The full purchase price as stated in the contract.

Conventional Loan   A real estate loan not insured by the FHA or guaranteed by the VA.

Convertible ARMs   Adjustable rate mortgages that have a provision allowing the borrower to convert the mortgage to a fixed-rate term under specified conditions.

Conveyance   A written instrument, such as a deed or lease, evidencing the transfer of all or part of the ownership in real property from one person to another.

Cost Approach to Value   An estimate of value based on current construction costs, less depreciation, plus land value.

Cost Basis   Accounting figure that includes the original cost of property plus money spent on permanent improvements and other costs, minus any depreciation claimed on tax returns over the years.

Covenant   A written restriction on the use of the property. Homeowners associations often enforce restrictive covenants governing architectural controls and maintenance responsibilities. Also, any former owner could have included a covenant when he or she sold the property. Some are ridiculous, such as "No dogs or liquor on the property." It's one of the reasons why you should get an abstract of title and purchase title insurance. To remove covenants, one must go into court and petition for a quiet title.

Cul-de-Sac   A dead-end street; one that usually widens sufficiently at the end to permit an automobile to make a U-turn.

Customer   A person who buys. A buyer is the customer of a real estate agent who lists a property for sale.

D

DBA   Doing business as. Business names or aliases filed with the county.

Debt-Service Ratio   The measurement of debt payments to gross household income.

Dedication   The voluntary giving of private property to some public use by the owner, as the dedication of land for streets, schools, etc., in a development.

Deed   A formal written instrument by which title to real property is transferred from one owner to another. There are two parties to a deed: the grantor (seller) and the grantee (buyer).

Deed of Trust   A deed given to a trustee to hold in trust as security for the repayment of a loan on real estate. If the loan is not paid, the holder of the loan can foreclose on the deed of trust and take title to the property.

Deed Restriction   Restrictions placed on use of real property that are included in the deed transferring ownership of the property. These restrictions survive the transfer of ownership and limit the property's use by future owners.

Default   The failure to make payments as agreed or to comply with other covenants contained in leases, mortgages, and other legal documents. In general, the failure to perform as agreed.

Defective Title.   A title to real property that lacks some of the elements necessary to transfer good marketable title.

Deficiency Judgment   A judgment in favor of a mortgagee for the remainder of a debt not completely paid off by foreclosure and sale of the mortgaged property.

Depreciation   A decrease in value of property through wear, deterioration, obsolescence, or other factors. Also, a deduction you take on your tax return to allow for depreciation of the building (not the land) whether or not depreciation is actually taking place.

Discount Points (or Points)   A fee charged by lenders in exchange for a lower interest rate. Each point is equal to 1 percent of the loan amount, but the amount each discount point will reduce the interest rate on the loan varies.

Documentary Tax Stamps   Stamps, affixed to a deed, based on the amount of consideration in a property transfer. A transfer tax by another name.

Due on Sale   A clause in a mortgage that grants the lender the right to call the full outstanding balance due in the event of a sale of the property.

Duress   The use of force or threat to cause a person to take an action or inaction against his or her will.

E

Earnest Money   A deposit made as part payment and as a pledge to bind an offer to purchase. It is held in escrow until acceptance of the offer, and then it remains in escrow until the closing when it is applied to the purchase. It may be forfeited if the buyer fails to close on the sale.

Easement   The right to use the land of another for a specific purpose. It could be on the ground such as a driveway that crosses another property, under the ground such as a sewer or water line, or in the air above your property for power, phone, or cable lines.

Eminent Domain   The right of government to take private property for public use, provided just compensation is paid to the owner of the property.

Encroachment   A fixture, or structure, which encroaches upon the property of another.

Encumbrance   A cloud against free and clear title to a property which does not prevent conveyance, such as unpaid taxes, easements, deed restrictions, or mortgage loans.

Equity   The difference between the market value of a property and the debt upon it.

Escrow   Something of value put in the hands of a third party that is not to be delivered until certain conditions are met.

Estimated Closing Costs Statement   A statement that estimates the costs for both the buyer and seller in a real estate transaction.

Exclusive Agency   The practice of representing either a buyer or a seller in a transaction. An agent's fiduciary relationship is to the party being represented.

Exclusive Buyer Agency   An agent who represents only buyers and never sellers in a transaction.

Exclusive Right to Sell An agreement a broker wants sellers to sign when listing their property for sale. This is essentially an employment contract. Exclusive means that the broker gets paid regardless of who sells the property, including the seller.

F

Federal Home Loan Bank Provides liquidity to supervised financial service companies, such as savings and loans and credit unions. The bank system has several districts.

Federal Home Loan Board The board that charters and regulates federal savings and loan associations, as well as controlling the system of Federal Home Loan Banks.

Federal Home Loan Mortgage Corporation (FHLMC) Known as Freddie Mac. A federal agency purchasing first mortgages, both conventional and federally insured, from members of the Federal Reserve System, and the Federal Home Loan Bank System.

Federal Housing Administration (FHA) A federal agency that insures first mortgages, enabling lenders to loan a very high percentage of the sale price.

Federal National Mortgage Association (FNMA) Popularly known as Fannie Mae, FNMA was established for the purpose of purchasing loans from primary lenders (mortgage companies). FNMA is a private corporation, and its stock is traded on the New York Stock Exchange.

Federal Reserve Bank The regulatory agency that oversees commercial banks and bank holding companies, sets monetary policy for the country, and provides liquidity for supervised financial institutions.

Fee Simple Estate Indicates absolute ownership of a property.

FHA See *Federal Housing Administration*.

First Mortgage A mortgage that is in first lien position, taking priority over all other financial encumbrances.

Fixer-Uppers Properties that need major repairs to make them marketable.

Real Estate Investment Glossary

Fixture Personal property that has been attached to real estate so that it becomes part of the real property. A fixture must meet at least one of three conditions: (1) It must be attached in a permanent manner; (2) It must be specially adapted to the property; (3) It must be intentionally made part of the real property. If there's any question about whether a fixture goes with a property, it should be addressed in the offer to purchase.

Foreclosure The process through which a lender takes possession of a property when the debtor defaults on the mortgage. The property is sold on the courthouse steps, and anyone can bid on it. The first lien holder will typically bid the amount of their loan, and then if someone else wants to outbid them, they can.

FSBO For sale by owner.

G

General Warranty Deed A deed in which sellers warrant that they are the owners in fee simple of the property, that they have the right to convey the property in fee simple, that the title is marketable and free of all encumbrances except as stated in the deed, and that they will warrant and defend the title against the lawful claims of all persons.

H

HUD Homes Homes acquired by FHA through foreclosure. HUD (The Federal Department of Housing and Urban Development) ends up owning these properties. They usually fix them up a little and resell them through HUD authorized real estate brokers. The website: www.hud.gov can provide information on properties available in specific neighborhoods. These are one- to four-unit buildings, and the prices are often below market.

I

Impound Account An account held by a lender for payment of taxes, insurance, or other expenses.

Inspection Clause A stipulation in an offer to purchase that makes the sale contingent upon the findings of an inspector. This could be a termite, mold, home, or other inspector.

Intestate   Having made no will. A person who has died without leaving a will.

J

Joint Tenancy   A type of ownership in which two or more people have an undivided interest in an entire property, with the right of survivorship. Upon the death of one owner, his or her interest passes to the remaining owners rather than the persons named in their will.

Judgment   A debt or other obligation resulting from a court order. If you lose a case in court, the judge will create a judgment against you that may be collected through a forced sale of assets.

L

Laches   The negligent failure to do the required thing at the proper time. An inexcusable delay in enforcing a claim.

Lease with Option to Purchase   A lease under which a tenant has the right to purchase the property, usually at a predetermined price. Often all or a portion of the rent is applied to the purchase when the option is exercised.

Legal Description   The description of a specific parcel of real estate as it appears on a deed. It could be described by lot and block number from a recorded plat; metes and bounds describing in feet and compass direction the boundaries of the property; or by reference to a government survey (e.g., the southern half of section 32).

Lender   An individual or institution that lends money.

Lessee   A tenant who is leasing a property.

Lessor   An owner who leases property to a tenant.

Leverage   The use of borrowed funds to finance an investment and to magnify the rate of return.

Lien   A claim against property as security for the payment of a just debt.

Life Estate   An interest in real property for the life of a living person. The interest that is created in a property when it is sold and the sellers retain the right to use it for the rest of their lives.

Limited Warranty Deed   A deed similar to a general warranty deed except it contains specified limitations of warranty by the seller.

Loan to Value Ratio (Loan Ratio)   The percent of the purchase price or appraised value that a mortgage loan represents.

Lis Pendens   A legal notice attached to a property that tells you there is a lawsuit pending.

Listing Agreement   The legal agreement with owners of property that engages the services of an agent or broker to assist with the sale or rental of the property.

M

Market Approach to Value   An estimate of value based on the actual sales prices of comparable properties.

Market Value   The price at which a willing buyer will purchase and a willing seller will sell when both are fully informed and neither are under pressure to act.

Marketable Title   A title that can be readily marketed to a reasonably prudent buyer that is aware of the facts regarding any liens or encumbrances.

Mechanic's Lien   A lien filed by a worker to secure the payment of services rendered on a property. This type of lien may be filed by a subcontractor who is not paid by a general contractor.

Misrepresentation   A false statement, or concealment, of material fact with the intention of inducing action of another.

Mortgagee   The lender of money or the receiver of the mortgage document.

Mortgage Guaranty Insurance Corporation (MGIC)   A private corporation which, for a fee, insures mortgage loans similar to FHA and VA insurance.

Mortgage Insurance   Insurance on the repayment of a mortgage loan.

Mortgage Loan   A loan, the repayment of which is secured or collateralized with real estate. The mortgage is your agreement to pledge your home or other real estate as security.

Mortgage Note   A written agreement to repay a mortgage loan. An agreement secured by a mortgage, which serves as proof of indebtedness and states the manner in which it shall be paid. The note states the actual amount of the debt that the mortgage secures and includes all information regarding interest rate and repayment terms.

Mortgagor   The borrower of money or the giver of the mortgage document.

Multiple Listing Service (MLS)   A service of the Board of Realtors that lists properties for sale by member brokers.

N

Net Lease   A lease in which the tenant pays all expenses such as taxes, insurance, repairs, and utilities.

Net Listing   A contract to sell property in which the broker receives, as commission, the excess over and above the net listing price agreed upon with the seller.

No Money Down or Nothing Down   The term used to describe the purchase of real estate with 100 percent financing. (Our friend Robert Allen didn't invent the concept, but he sure marketed the heck out of it and became known as the father of no-money-down purchases. His book *Nothing Down* is a classic and well worth reading.)

Nonconforming Use   A property that does not conform to the zoning laws of an area.

O

OPM Stands for other people's money. Often pronounced "opium" by real estate investors. It refers to the use of financing or shared equity to purchase real estate without using your own money.

Open Listing An agreement under which sellers offer to pay a commission to any broker that secures an acceptable buyer.

Option The right to purchase property within a definite time at a specified price. There is no obligation to purchase, but the seller is obligated to sell if the option holder exercises the right to purchase. For the option to be valid, it must include consideration.

Origination Fee A fee charged for the work involved in evaluating, preparing, and making a mortgage loan. Usually a percentage of the loan amount.

Owners Title Policy Insurance to protect the owner from encumbrances against the title to property. The title insurance company will require that legal records be researched for existing liens or encumbrances and may require that the property be surveyed prior to issuing a policy.

P

Parish In Louisiana, a division encompassing one or more cities or towns. In other states, this division is known as a county.

Partial Release The release of a portion of property covered by a mortgage.

Percentage Lease A lease in which all or part of the rental is a specified percentage of gross income from total sales made upon the premises.

Permanent Mortgage Typically a long-term mortgage that replaces temporary financing following the completion of construction.

Personal Property Tangible property that is movable and not affixed to the land. Property that remains with the seller unless it is included in the purchase contract.

PITI Stands for *principal, interest, taxes, and insurance*. This acronym is used to describe a mortgage payment that includes an impound or escrow for taxes and insurance in addition to the regular principal and interest amount.

Plat Book   A book in which subdivisions of land are recorded.

PMI   See *Private Mortgage Insurance*.

Pocket Listing   Colloquialism used by real estate agents. A listing agent may not want to put a listing on the MLS for a few days while he or she tries to find a buyer and earn both ends of the commission, known as a *double whammy*.

Points   See *Discount Points*.

Police Power   The principle of law that allows the government to use or seize property to promote public health, safety, and welfare or for other uses deemed to be in the public interest.

Power of Attorney   A written document legally authorizing a person to act on behalf of another person. The person receiving this authority does not have to be an attorney at law.

Prepayment Clause in a Mortgage   A provision in a loan document giving the borrower the right to pay principal prior to the due date. Some loans specify a penalty fee if the loan is paid early.

Primary Mortgage Market   Institutional lenders who originate loans and make funds available directly to borrowers.

Prime Rate   The interest, or discount rate, charged by commercial banks to their largest and financially strongest customers.

Private Mortgage Insurance (PMI)   Insurance similar to FHA or VA insurance, insuring payment of a mortgage or deed of trust. Often required by lenders when making conventional loans that are a high percentage of a property's value.

Prorate   To divide or distribute proportionally. At real estate closings, various expenses such as taxes, insurance, interest, and rents are divided between the seller and buyer based on the number of days each owns the property.

Real Estate Investment Glossary

Puffing   An exaggerated claim made by a salesperson that falls short of misrepresentation, such as "this is the best maintained home in town."

Purchase Money Mortgage   A mortgage given to the sellers of property that fully or partially finances its purchase.

Q

Qualifying Ratios   Compares a borrower's debts and gross monthly income.

Quit Claim Deed   A deed that makes no warranties as to the title, but simply transfers to the buyer whatever interest the grantor has.

R

Ready, Willing, and Able   A buyer who is prepared to buy on the agreed upon terms and has the financial capability to do so.

Real Estate Board   A nonprofit organization representing local real estate agents and brokers and salespeople, which provides services to its members and maintains, and usually operates, the Multiple Listing Service in the community.

Receiver   A court-appointed administrator who holds in trust property in bankruptcy or litigation.

Recorded Plat   A subdivision map filed with the county recorder's office that shows the location and boundaries (lot and block number) of individual parcels of land.

Recording   The act of entering in the public records, documents of public interest such as deeds, plats, leases, marriages, divorces, births, deaths, and judgments, thereby giving constructive notice to the public.

Recourse   The right of the holder of a note secured by a mortgage or deed of trust to look beyond the collateral to the borrower personally for payment of the debt.

Refinancing   The establishing of a new loan in order to pay off an existing indebtedness. Generally done to gain better terms, a lower interest rate, or a different amortization.

REIT (Real Estate Investment Trust)   A trust created to purchase real estate that provides certain tax advantages to those who invest in the trust. REITs are designed to do for investors in real estate what mutual funds do for investors in securities.

REOs (Real Estate Owned)   The term by which properties owned by a bank as the result of foreclosure are known. These are liabilities for banks.

Rescission of Contract Annulling a contract and placing the parties to it in a position as if there had not been a contract.

Restrictions   Limitations on the use or occupancy of real estate contained in local ordinances pertaining to land use.

Restrictive Covenants   Private restrictions limiting the use of real property. Restrictive covenants are created by deed and may "run with the land," binding all subsequent purchasers of the land.

S

Second Mortgage   A mortgage loan that is in a second or junior position behind only one other mortgage.

Secondary Financing   A loan secured by a mortgage or trust deed, which is subordinate to another mortgage or trust deed.

Secondary Mortgage Market   The buying and selling of existing mortgage loans. The largest secondary mortgage market is the Federal National Mortgage Association (FNMA).

Security   Real or personal property pledged by a borrower to secure the protection of a lender's interest.

Senior encumbrance.   Any encumbrance on the title that comes before or takes precedence over another encumbrance. For example, property taxes are senior to mortgage loans; and first mortgages are senior to second mortgages.

Septic System   A sewage system that collects waste in an underground fermentation tank and the excess water is filtered into the ground through an underground drain field. Common in rural areas.

Servicing a Loan   The ongoing process of collecting monthly payments, maintaining escrow accounts, paying taxes and insurance premiums, and any other record keeping associated with a mortgage loan.

Setback   The distance a building must be set back from the property lines in accordance with local zoning ordinances or deed restrictions.

Settlement Statement   See *Closing Statement*.

Sheets, Carleton   Creator of *How To Buy Your First Home or Investment Property with No Down Payment* and numerous other real estate related programs. Also the star of the longest running infomercial in television history where he is seen interviewing some of his most successful students.

Sheriff's Deed   A deed given at a sheriff's sale in foreclosure of a mortgage.

Square Footage   The area in square feet of a structure calculated by multiplying the length times the width of each area.

Subordinated Loan.   Any loan in which the holders of the note agree in writing to allow a senior encumbrance to be placed ahead of their interest and this agreement is recorded.

Sweat Equity   The equity generated in property through personal labor. A property manager may be given an equity interest in a property in exchange for managing it.

T

Tax Lien   A lien against property for nonpayment of taxes.

Tax Sale   Public sale of property at auction by a governmental authority to recover unpaid property taxes.

Tenancy in Common   A type of ownership in which two or more people have an undivided interest in property, without the right of survivorship. Upon the death of one of the owners, the interest passes to that person's heirs.

Timeshare   The sale of specific time periods in which a purchaser may use a property. The purchaser receives an interest in the real property only for the specified period purchased. Used primarily for selling vacation properties.

Title Insurance   An insurance policy that protects the insured (purchaser and/or lender) against loss arising from defects in title.

Title Search   A search of the public records relating to a property to determine if there are liens or other encumbrances that affect the title.

TLC (Tender, Loving Care)   A property advertised, as "Needs TLC" probably needs a lot of fixing up.

Townhouse   A dwelling unit usually containing two or three floors and having shared walls. It can be a condominium, a cooperative, or rental property.

Triple Net Lease   A common form of lease for commercial property in which the tenant pays the three major expenses of maintenance, insurance, and property taxes in addition to the agreed upon lease payment.

Trustee   In a trust deed state (as opposed to mortgage state), this is the agent who holds the trust deed for the beneficiary (lender).

U

Underwriting   The process of confirming and evaluating data, analyzing risk, and quantifying the feasibility of approving a loan.

Usury   The act or practice of lending money at an interest rate that is excessive or unlawfully high.

V

VA Loans.   Loans to qualified military veterans that are guaranteed by the Veterans Administration.

Index

Abstract, 257
Abstract of title, 257
Abutting (term), 257
Acceleration clause, 257
Accountants, 139, 199–200
Accounts:
   commingling, 239
   impound, 268
Accretion, 257
Acknowledgment, 258
Acre (term), 258
Adjustable interest rates, 10–11
Adjustable rate mortgage (ARM), 258,
   264
Adjustment rental clause, 197–198
Administrator, 258
Agency, 258
Agreement(s):
   listing, 270
   property management, 33
   of Sale, 258

Allen, Robert, 142, 180, 271
Alligators, 148, 162, 258
Amortization, 258
Annual gross multipliers, 15–16
Apartment buildings, 22, 189–193
   advantages/disadvantages of,
      192–193
   expenses for, 191–192
   resident managers in, 191–192
Application, 258
Application fee, 259
Apportionment of purchase price, 167
Appraisal, 259
Appraisal fee, 259
Appraised value, 22, 44–45
Appreciation, 259
Appurtenance, 259
ARM (*see* Adjustable rate mortgage)
Arrears, 259
Asking for more than you expect to get,
   67, 107–108

Index

Asking price:
  bracketing the seller's, 110–111
  selling price vs., 44, 46–47
Assessed valuation, 259
Assessment, 259
Asset, 259
Assign (term), 259
Assignee, 259
Assignment, 167, 260
Assignor, 260
Assumable mortgage, 260
Attached homes, 260
Attorney in fact, 260
Attorney(s), 199–200
  in fact, 260
  negotiating with, 139
  opinion of title, 260
  power of, 273
Attorney's opinion of title, 260
Auctions, 82–83, 260

Bad tenants, 242
Balloon payment, 260
Bankers, 202–206
Bank-owned properties, 81–89
Basis, 260
Beginning negotiating gambit(s), 107–117
  asking for more than you expect to get
    as, 67, 107–110
  bracketing the seller's asking price as,
    110–111
  expansion of negotiating range as,
    108–109
  flinching at price as, 112–114
  reluctant buyer as, 114
  saying no to first proposal as, 111–112
  vise as, 115–117
Beneficiary, 260
Benefits, tax, 6–7, 181–185
"Bigger fool" theory, 8, 93
Bill of Sale, 260
Binding effect, 166
Blanket encumbrances, 124, 244–245
Blanket mortgage, 260
Board of Realtors, 213, 271
Bread and butter properties, 37–39
Bridge financing, 261

British Thermal Unit (BTU), 261
Broker(s):
  buyer's, 261
  negotiating with, 139
BTU (British Thermal Unit), 261
Building code, 261
Building line (setback), 261
Build-to-suit commercial properties, 198
Business cards, 43, 49–50, 51–52, 57, 233
Buyer's broker, 261
Buy/sell investors, 14–15
Buy/sell speculators, 15–16

Calculator, using a, 149
Cap, 261
Capital gains, 261
  long-term, 7, 185
  tax on, 185
Capitalization rate (CAP rate), 261
Car dealerships, negotiating with, 139
Carleton Sheets Real Estate Toolkit, 163,
  223
Carnegie, Andrew, 1
Cash down payment, 152
Cash flow, 9
Cash reserves, building, 203–204
Caveat emptor, 261
Ceiling, 261
Certificate of eligibility, 261
Certificate of occupancy, 261
Certificate of reasonable value (CRV), 262
Chain of title, 262
Chattel, 262
Cheap properties, 237–238
Clauses:
  acceleration, 257
  adjustment rental, 197–198
  due-on-sale, 75
  inspection, 268–269
  prepayment, 273
Clear title, 262
Client, 262
Closed-ended questions, 100
Closing, 262
Closing costs, 165, 262
Closing date, 164
Closing statement, 262

Index

Cloud on title, 262
Collateral, 262
Commercial property(-ies):
  and adjustment rental clause, 197–198
  build-to-suit, 198
  customizing, 196–197
  generic, 195–196
  no-money-down purchase of, 176–180
  types of, 189
  valuing, 194–198
Commingling (accounts), 239, 262
Commitment, getting, 122–123
Comparables, 263
Compound interest, 263
Condemnation, 263
Condition of property, 164
Condominiums, 168, 189, 245, 263
Consideration, 263
Construction loan, 263
Contingency, 263
Contract sales price, 263
Contractors, negotiating with, 139
Contract(s):
  for deed, 263
  recission of, 275
Conventional loan, 263
Convertible ARMs, 264
Conveyance, 264
Cost approach to value, 264
Cost basis, 264
Costs:
  closing, 165, 262
  management, 191–192
  repair, 220
  utility, 191
  (*See also* Expenses)
Counter gambit(s):
  to good guy/bad guy gambit, 132–133
  to higher authority gambit, 121–123
  to nibble gambit, 134–135
  to vise gambit, 115
Covenants, 264, 275
Crime, 39
CRV (certificate of reasonable value), 262
Cul-de-sac, 264
Customer (term), 264

Dawson, Roger, 119–120, 130–131
DBA, 264
Deadlocks, 110
Debt reduction, 9
Debt-service ratio, 264
Dedication, 264
Deductions, tax:
  for depreciation, 7, 183–184
  for interest paid, 7, 182–183
  for passive losses, 7, 182
Deed restriction, 265
Deed(s), 164, 265
  contract for, 263
  general warranty, 268
  limited warranty, 270
  quit claim, 274
  restriction, 265
  sheriff's, 276
  of trust, 265
Default, 166, 265
Defective title, 265
Deferrals, tax, 7, 184
Deficiency judgment, 265
Depreciation, 7, 183–184, 265
Description, property, 164
Desperate people, dealing with, 41–42
Details, tying up, 98
Developments, planned unit, 245
Difference, splitting the, 124–126
Direct principal reduction (zero-interest loans), 72, 73
Discount points, 265
Divorce, 58–65
Documentary tax stamps, 265
Down payment, cash, 152
Due on sale, 265
Due-on-sale clauses, 75, 172
Duress, 266

Earnest money, 266
Easement, 266
Ego, appealing to seller's, 122
Elderly sellers, 71–75
Eminent domain, 266
Encroachment, 266
Encumbrance, 266

Index

Ending negotiating gambit(s), 128–137
 good guy/bad guy as, 128–133
 nibble as, 133–135
 positioning for easy acceptance as,
  136–137
 walking away as, 135–136
Entire agreement, 166
Equity:
 definition of, 266
 financing purchases with, 176
 rapid buildup of, 8
 retirement income from conversion of,
  71–75
 sellers with high, 66–70
 sweat, 276
Escrow, 266
Estimated closing costs statement, 266
Exclusive agency, 266
Exclusive buyer agency, 266
Exclusive right to sell, 267
Exotic properties, 243
Expenses:
 for apartment buildings, 191–192
 on Net Operating Income Calculation
  Form, 27, 145–147
 and structuring an offer, 154–155
 (See also Costs)

Failed business, buying from owners of,
  76–77
Fair, being, 41–42, 204–205
Fair play, 124
Farm, 29
 close to home, 242–243
 exploring your, 210
 viewing your target area as, 41
FDIC (Federal Deposit Insurance
  Corporation), 203
Fear, 242
Federal Deposit Insurance Corporation
  (FDIC), 203
Federal home loan bank, 267
Federal home loan board, 267
Federal Home Loan Mortgage
  Corporation (FHLMC), 267
Federal Housing Administration (FHA),
  210, 267

Federal National Mortgage Association
  (FNMA), 267
Federal Reserve Bank, 267
Federal Reserve Board, 94
Fee simple estate, 267
Fees:
 application, 259
 appraisal, 259
 origination, 272
FHA (see Federal Housing
  Administration)
Field, Marshall, 238
Financial trouble, sellers in, 76–80
Financing:
 conventional bank, 155
 and price, 148–149
 seller-carried, 155–156, 168
 terms and conditions of, 168
 third-party, 168
 using home equity for, 176
First deal, structuring your, 154–162
 and determination of income/expenses,
  154–155
 and price vs. terms, 156–161
 and running the numbers, 155–156
 and writing up the offer, 161–162
First mortgage, 267
First proposals, 111–112
First-year profit, 24–25
Fixer-uppers, 267–268
Fixture, 268
Flexibility, 109
Flinching (at selling price), 112–114
FNMA (Federal National Mortgage
  Association), 267
For sale by owner (FSBO), 217, 268
Foreclosures, 81–89, 268
Form(s):
 inspection, 219–220
 net operating income calculation,
  255
 Offer to Purchase and Contract, 161,
  162, 228
Free-and-clear ownership, 172–173
 sellers with, 172–173
 value of, 175–176
FSBO (see For sale by owner)

Index

Gambit(s):
  beginning, 107–117
  counter, 115, 121–123, 132–133,
    134–135
  ending, 128–137
  good guy/bad guy, 128–133
  higher authority, 118–120
  middle, 118–127
  nibble, 133–135
  positioning for easy acceptance,
    136–137
  reluctant buyer, 114
  trade-off, 126–127
  vise, 115–117
  walk-away, 135–136
Gambling (on real estate market),
  243–244
Garn–St. Germain Federal Depository
  Institutions Act (1992), 172
General warranty deed, 268
Getting rich slowly, 3–9
Getting started, 207–246
  first weekend, 209–211
  second weekend, 212–215
  third weekend, 216–218
  fourth weekend, 219–221
  fifth weekend, 222–225
  sixth weekend, 226–227
  seventh weekend, 228–230
  eighth weekend, 232–234
  and avoiding mistakes, 237–246
Gone with the Wind (film), 103
Good buys, finding, 23–28
Good guy/bad guy gambit, 128–133
Governing law, 166
Gross multipliers:
  annual, 15–16
  and apartment buildings, 190–191
  fallacy of, 16–17
  monthly, 16

Higher authority gambit, 118–123
Home equity (*see* Equity)
Homeowners association, 168, 245
Honesty, 202
Housing and Urban Development (HUD)
  homes, 268

*How I Turned $1000 into 5 Million
  Investing in Real Estate in my Spare
  Time* (William Nickerson), 16
*How to Buy Your First Home or
  Investment Property with No Down
  Payment* (Carleton Sheets), 142,
  180, 238, 276
HUD (Housing and Urban Development)
  homes, 268

Impound account, 268
Income, separating investment and
  earned, 239
Income stream, developing an, 10–13, 241
Income tax, 7, 182
Income to value ratios, 14–17
Indifference, 103
Inflating your net worth, 240
Inflation, 8, 94–95
Information:
  collecting, 99–100
  in offers, 163–169
Inspecting properties, 25–26, 168
Inspection clause, 268–269
Inspection form, 219–220, 247–254
Insurance, 27, 147
  mortgage, 271, 273
  title, 167–168, 277
Interest:
  adjustable, rates, 10–11
  compound, 263
  deduction for, 7, 182–183
Interest rates, 72
  adjustable, 10–11
  and due-on-sale clauses, 172
Internal Revenue Service (IRS), 182
Internet, researching properties via,
  213–214
Intestate (term), 269
Investing, principles of (*see* Principle[s] of
  investing)
Investments, real estate vs. other, 20–21
Investors:
  buy/sell, 14–15
  reluctant, 21
  speculators vs., 15, 95
IRS (Internal Revenue Service), 182

Index

Joint tenancy, 269
Judgment, 269

Kipling, Rudyard, 100
Kissinger, Henry, 108

Laches, 269
Larger properties, 187–188 (*See also* Commercial property[-ies]; Multifamily properties)
Learning your market, 40–43
Lease(s):
  net, 271
  with option to purchase, 269
  percentage, 272
  triple-net, 195, 277
Legal description, 269
Lender, 269
Lessee, 269
Lessor, 269
Letter of intent, 229–230
Leverage, 4–6, 269
Liens, 270
Life estate, 270
Limited warranty deed, 270
Liquidity, 39
Lis pendens, 270
Listing:
  net, 271
  open, 272
Listing agreements, 270
Loan to value ratio (loan ratio), 270
Loan(s):
  construction, 263
  conventional, 263
  direct principal reduction, 72, 73
  FHA, 210
  length of, 150–152
  mortgage, 271
  Veterans Administration, 210, 277
  zero-interest, 72, 73
Local governments, negotiating with, 139

Maintenance, 204
  reserve, 27, 146
  yard, 191

Maintenance workers, negotiating with, 139
Management costs, 27, 146, 191–192
Management fee, 146
Mapping your area, 41
Market approach to value, 270
Market value, 270
Marketable title, 270
Markets:
  primary mortgage, 273
  secondary mortgage, 275
  (*See also* Real estate market[s])
Marshall Field & Company, 238
Mechanic's lien, 270
MGIC (mortgage guaranty insurance corporation), 271
Middle negotiating gambit(s), 118–127
  higher authority as, 118–123
  trade-off as, 126–127
Minimum plausible position (MPP), 108–109
Misrepresentation, 270
Mistakes, investment, 237–246
MLS (*see* Multiple Listing Service)
Mortgage guaranty insurance corporation (MGIC), 271
Mortgage insurance, 271, 273
Mortgage loans, 271
Mortgage market:
  primary, 273
  secondary, 275
Mortgage note, 271
Mortgagee (term), 270
Mortgages:
  adjustable rate, 258
  assumable, 260
  first, 267
  permanent, 272
  prepayment clause in, 273
  purchase money, 274
  second, 275
Mortgagor, 271
Moved, seller, 51–57
MPP (*see* Minimum plausible position)
Multifamily properties, 189–193
  advantages/disadvantages of buying, 192–193

Index

Multifamily properties (*Cont.*):
  expenses for, 191–192
  and gross multipliers, 190–191
  pricing, 190
Multiple Listing Service (MLS), 213, 271

National Association of Realtors, 214
National Automobile Dealers Association, 159
Negotiating/negotiation, 91–139
  expanding range of, 108–109
  importance of, 91–95
  "no" as opening position in, 111
  with other than sellers, 138–139
  pressure points of, 96–101
  room for, 110
  and splitting the difference, 124–126
  win-win, 102–106
  (*See also* Gambit[s])
Neighbors, talking with, 42–43, 60
Net lease, 271
Net listing, 271
Net operating income (NOI), 144–147, 144–153
  form for calculating, 26–27, 145, 255
  and insurance, 147
  and maintenance reserve, 146
  and management fee, 146
  and ROI, 147–153
  and taxes, 147
  and utilities, 146–147
  and vacancy factor, 145–146
Net return on investment, 17
Net worth, 18, 238
Nibble gambit, 133–135
Nickerson, William, 16
"No," as opening negotiating position, 111
NOI (*see* net operating income)
No-money-down (nothing-down) deals, 170–180, 271
  commercial purchases, 176–180
  and due-on-sale clauses, 172
  and sellers with no mortgage, 172–173
  steps in, 174–175
  and structuring of NOI, 173–174
Nonconforming use, 271

Nothing Down for the '90s (Robert Allen), 142, 180
Nothing Down (Robert Allen), 142, 180, 271
Notices, 166

Occupancy, 164
Offer to Purchase and Contract forms, 161, 162, 228
Offer(s), 141–180
  information included in, 163–169
  and no-money-down deals, 170–180
  and valuation of single-family properties, 144–153
  writing the, 161–169
  in your first deal, 154–162
Open listing, 272
Open-ended questions, 100
OPM (*see* Other people's money)
Option, 272
Origination fee, 272
Other people's money (OPM), 173, 182, 272
Overextended sellers, buying from, 77–80
Owners title policy, 272

Parish, 272
Partial release, 272
Passive loss deductions, 7, 182
Patience, 11, 162, 236
Payment of purchase price, 164
Peer groups, 99–100
Percentage lease, 272
Permanent mortgage, 272
Personal property, 168, 272
PIN (property identification number), 164
PITI (*see* Principal, interest, taxes, and insurance)
Planned unit developments, 245
Plat, recorded, 274
Plat book, 273
Plausibility, 108–109
PMI (private mortgage insurance), 273
Pocket listing, 273
Points, 265, 273
Police power, 273
Positioning for easy acceptance gambit, 136–137

Index

Power of attorney, 273
Prepayment clauses, 273
Price:
    asking, 44, 46–47, 110–111
    contract sales, 263
    definition of, 15
    and financing, 148–149
    purchase, 164, 167
    and rental rates, 23–24
    selling, 44, 46–47
    value vs., 17, 142
    wholesale, 142
    "wish," 114
Primary mortgage market, 273
Prime rate, 273
Principal, interest, taxes, and insurance
        (PITI), 272–273
Principle(s) of investing, 1–28
    finding good buys as, 23–28
    generating an income stream as, 10–13
    getting rich slowly as, 3–9
    income to value ratios as, 14–17
    rent increases as, 18–22
Private mortgage insurance (PMI), 273
Procrastination, 245–246
Profit, first-year, 24–25
Property identification number (PIN),
        164
Property management, 241
    importance of, 19, 241
    licensing of, 33
Property management agreement, 33
Property management firms, 32
Property managers, 26, 29, 31–34
    building relationship with, 34
    negotiating with, 138
    researching properties with, 217
Property values, calculating, 25, 45
Property(-ies):
    bank-owned, 81–89
    bread and butter, 37–39
    cheap, 237–238
    commercial (see Commercial
        property[-ies])
    condition of, 164
    controlled by homeowners associations,
        243

Property(-ies) (Cont.):
    description, 164
    exotic, 241
    expensive, 38
    foreclosed, 81–89
    inexpensive, 38–39
    inspecting, 25–26, 168, 219–220,
        247–254
    on the Internet, 213–214
    larger, 187–188
    multifamily, 189–193
    personal, 168, 272
    single-family, 144–153
    "slumlord," 39
    upscale, 237
    valuating, 190
Proposals, first, 111–112
Prorate (term), 273
Public records, 59–60
Puffing, 274
Purchase money mortgage, 274
Purchase price, 164, 167

Qualifying ratios, 274
Questions:
    asking the tough, 99
    open-ended vs. closed-ended, 100
    for sellers, 98
Quit claim deed, 274

Ratio(s):
    debt-service, 264
    income to value, 14–17
    loan to value, 270
    qualifying, 274
Ready, willing, and able, 274
Reagan, Ronald, 241–242
Real estate agents, negotiating with, 139
Real Estate Board, 274
Real Estate Investment Trust (REIT),
        275
Real estate market(s), 23–24, 29–48
    and asking prices, 44–47
    bread and butter properties in your,
        37–39
    finding a property manager in your,
        31–34

Index

Real estate market(s) (*Cont.*):
  learning your, 40–43
  and threshold theory, 35–36
Real estate owned (REO), 81–89, 275
Receiver, 274
Recission of contract, 275
Recorded plat, 274
Recording, 274
Recourse, 274
Refinancing, 275
REIT (Real Estate Investment Trust), 275
Reluctant buyer gambit, 114
Reluctant investors, 21
Rental rates:
  increases in, 18–22
  and neighborhood conditions, 39
  and purchase price, 23–24
REO (*see* Real estate owned)
Repairs, cost of, 152–153, 220
Resident managers, 191–192
Restrictions:
  definition of, 275
  use, 168
Restrictive covenants, 275
Retail stores, negotiating with, 139
Retirement income, converting home
    equity to, 71–75
Return on investment (ROI):
  on cash down payment, 152
  and financing, 148–149
  and length of loan, 150–152
  net, 17
  and repair costs, 152–153
  and valuation, 149–150
Rhett Butler (fictional character), 103
Riding around, 40–41, 204
Risk of loss, 166
Rogers, Will, 7
ROI (*see* Return on investment)
Running the numbers, 155–156

Scarcity, 94
Second mortgage, 275
Secondary financing, 275
Secondary mortgage market, 275
Secrets of Power Negotiating (Roger
    Dawson), 119–120, 130–131

Security, 275
Seller(s):
  banks as, 81–89
  dissatisfied, 45–46
  divorced, 58–65
  elderly, 71–75
  in financial trouble, 76–80
  finding, 49–50
  as free and clear owners, 172–173
  with high equity, 66–70
  moving, 51–57
  retiring, 71–75
Selling price, asking price vs., 44, 46–47
Senior encumbrance, 275–276
Septic system, 276
Servicing a loan, 276
Setback (building line), 261, 276
Settlement statement (closing statement),
    262
Sheets, Carleton, 142, 180, 236, 276
Sheriff's deed, 276
Single-family properties, valuation of,
    144–153
"Slumlord properties," 39
Speculation, 15–16, 94–95
Splitting the difference, 124–126
Square footage, 276
Starting out (*see* Getting started)
Statements:
  closing, 262
  estimated closing costs, 266
  settlement, 262
Structuring the offer (*see* Offer[s])
"Subject to" close, 123
Subordinated loan, 276
Support team, 199–206
  bankers as part of, 202–206
  benefits of having a, 200
  members of your, 188
  rewarding your, 201
Survey, 167
Survival clause, 166
Sweat equity, 276

Talking with neighborhood residents,
    42–43, 60
Tax liens, 276

Index

Tax sales, 276
Tax(-es), 27, 147
  and benefits of real estate ownership,
    6–7, 181–185
  capital gains, 185
  and deductions, 182–184
  documentary tax stamps, 265
  exchanges, tax deferral on, 7, 184
  on income, 7, 182
Tax-free sale potential, 7, 184–185
Team, support (*see* Support team)
1031 Exchanges, 184
Tenancy in common, 277
Tenants:
  bad, 242
  negotiating with, 138–139
Tender loving care (TLC), 277
Termination clause, 166
Threshold theory, 29, 35–36
Time pressure, 96–99
Timeshare, 277
Title insurance, 167–168, 277
Title review period, 165
Title search, 277
Title(s):
  abstract of, 257
  attorney's opinion of, 260
  chain of, 262
  clear, 262
  cloud on, 262
  defective, 265
  marketable, 270
  owners, policy, 272
TLC (tender loving care), 277
Townhouse, 277
Trade-off gambit, 126–127
Triple-net leases, 195, 277
Trump, Donald, 95
Trustee, 277

Underwriting, 277
Upscale properties, 239
Use restrictions, 168
Usury, 277

Utilities, 146–147
  cost of, 191

VA loans (*see* Veterans Administration
  loans)
Vacancy factor, 145–146
Valuation:
  of apartment buildings, 190
  assessed, 259
  of commercial properties, 194–198
  of single-family properties, 144–153
Value:
  appraised, 44–45
  calculating, 25, 149–150
  as combination of price and terms, 142,
    156–161
  cost approach to, 264
  definition of, 15
  and liquidity, 39
  market, 270
  market approach to, 270
  price vs., 17, 142
  real estate as solid, 7–8
Veterans Administration (VA) loans, 210,
  277
Vise technique (vise gambit), 115–117
Vulnerability of sellers, 41–42

Walk away:
  being prepared to, 100–101
  as gambit, 135–136
Warranties, 164
Wealth, 239
Win-win negotiating, 102–106
"Wish price," 114
Writing the offer:
  for first offer, 161–162
  optional items, 167–168
  required items, 163–167

Yard maintenance, 191

Zero-interest loans (direct principal
  reduction), 72, 73